HM
20
KNI

FHSW

Small-Scale Research

Small-Scale Research

Pragmatic Inquiry in Social Science and the Caring Professions

Peter T. Knight

SAGE Publications
London • Thousand Oaks • New Delhi

SAGE Publications Ltd
6 Bonhill Street
London EC2A 4PU

SAGE Publications Inc
2455 Teller Road
Thousand Oaks, California 91320

SAGE Publications India Pvt Ltd
32, M-Block Market
Greater Kailash - I
New Delhi 110 048

British Library Cataloguing in Publication data

A catalogue record for this book is available from
the British Library

ISBN 0 7619 6861 X
ISBN 0 7619 6862 8 (pbk)

Library of Congress control number available

Typeset by SIVA Math Setters, Chennai, India
Printed in Great Britain by Biddles Ltd, Guildford, Surrey

Contents

Boxes

Figures

Tables

Preface

In the twentieth century the amount of research into social thought and action grew relentlessly and rapidly. Scientific management and rational decision-making depended upon it, as did cost–benefit analyses, environmental and social audits, and evaluations. Social policies were supposedly informed by research, which also 'benchmarked' the best practices that then became the goals for all to pursue; and who could disagree with the common-sense idea that social problems could best be tackled once they had been understood thanks to penetrating inquiries? Sociologists, psychologists and historians obviously had a research interest in the social but so too did those interested in marketing, management and organizations, and others concerned with fields such as health, deviance and welfare. And new questions – about gender, everyday cultures, sexualities, discourses and the media, for example – joined older ones.

Not surprisingly the number of researchers grew, helped by the massive expansion in post-war higher education. So too did the number of research-literate practitioners because many occupations were caught up in a conspicuous consumption of credentials which led to a first degree becoming an entry qualification and a master's degree a passport to promotion. In order to establish their academic credentials these bachelor's and master's degrees in education, management, criminology and public health (for example) exposed students to research findings, as you would expect, and increasingly expected students themselves to do research.

As social research spread across the English-speaking nations, collecting more and more initiates in the process, so too it changed. Earlier in the century it was mainly seen as a pursuit of truth (or, according to some, of *truths*) that would succeed as long as the right methods were rigorously applied in many large studies. Social research was an elite activity at the beginning of the century and an open one by the end. Beliefs in the triumph of the method were supplanted by beliefs that anyone could inquire into social thought and practices and that anything that could be used as a method of inquiry could be used as a method of inquiry. Nor were massive attacks on problems seen as the only, the best, or even useful ways of trying to understand social practices that were increasingly understood to be distinctively marked by particular circumstances, people, beliefs and thoughts. At the same time microelectronics made it possible for one person with a computer, a Walkman and a photocopier to do alone what once needed a team.

Small-scale research became legitimate and possible. By 'small-scale research' I mainly mean systematic inquiries that involve one person, little or no funding and a fairly short period of time to complete the inquiry and the report, but I also include as small-scale researchers two hard-pressed students with a bit of money for travel and coffee and a project to get done in almost no time at all. Small-scale researchers like them make up the majority – probably the great majority – of the people who at any one time are doing research projects. Nevertheless, small-scale inquiry can still be seen as the runt, a puny form of the real thing – probably harmless but hardly something to be taken seriously. This book says otherwise, claiming that it is of value to the inquirer herself or himself (and that is not a trivial matter); that it may be of value to the research participants; and that it can be presented as a valuable contribution to the wider worlds of practice, policy and theory.

The big problem with small-scale research is not that it is small scale: it is the naïve belief that good research depends on finding the 'killer' method and then making more effort to get more information to be analysed more thoroughly. If small-scale research has a problem it is because method and effort routinely displace thinking, sensemaking and claimsmaking.

Books are organized by authors, although skilled readers use the index to stamp out their own pathways, as you are advised to. But the author still organizes the book by putting one thing before another, forcing a linear pattern onto things that might be very different. Despite my best efforts this book still suggests that researchers do this, then that, then that, then 'abracadabra', it's finished. But social research is not like building a house: foundations, walls, roof. It is more like a nest of snakes with separate bodies looping back on themselves and tangled one around another, all moving and alive. As Chapter 6 argues, it is complex.

A recurrent theme is that doing social research is about making pragmatic judgements about what look to be the best ways of getting a grip on your research questions in specific settings. What seems to make sense in one research setting might be less attractive in another; research methods that work for one investigator may not satisfy others or may disappoint that investigator when used in a different inquiry or on a different site; and different investigators may reasonably differ about the questions to ask in the same setting or agree on the questions but differ about the understandings they construct through their research.

Despite the emphasis on sensemaking, claimsmaking and complexity, this book is full of advice on methods, designs and analytical techniques. For people who need to get straight into that material, the extended Contents is a good place to start, quickly followed by reference to the Index. Tables and figures, such as Tables 5.1 and 7.1 and Figures 2.3 and 8.1, are intended to be useful summaries of much of the information about research methods, and although the boxes mainly contain illustrative material, some, such as Boxes 7.1 and 9.1, are also intended as convenient reference points. The two lists in the final, brief chapter can be read as a recapitulation of the book's main themes.

Three people I write with have commented on parts of drafts of this book. I am grateful to Lee Harvey (University of Central England), Jo Tait (The Open University) and Paul Trowler (Lancaster University) for what I have gained by working with them and for their comments on what I have tried to do here.

1

Starting with Writing

As you would expect, in this book there are chapters on research methods – what they are and how to use them – and on data analysis. Chapters 3, 4 and 8 deal with those topics. However, you might not expect the headline message to be that these chapters do not contain the key to doing good research. Thinking and writing matter more: ideally, they are part of the same process. What matters is how you adopt and adapt evaluation and inquiry methods so that you can offer some answers to worthwhile research questions. This means that the methods and the overall research design (Chapter 5) need to be fit for the purpose of trying to make the claim that the understandings you develop should be seen as a plausible and careful set of answers to those research questions. That, in turn, means that methods should be mindfully chosen, because otherwise it would be pure chance should they turn out to be fit for your research purpose. This chapter pursues those ideas by exploring the interplay of writing and thinking *from the beginning* of the small-scale inquiry. This is really a chapter about writing as a part of that research process, about private writing, which is treated very much as a form of thinking about what the research is *for* and about the ways in which research questions are identified and discarded or developed. Chapter 9 is about the public writing involved in reporting the responses you construct to the research questions that emerge from this early thinking and writing.

Private Writing

Although reading and writing need some technical knowledge, such as knowledge of phonics, letters and spelling, experts agree that both are, first and foremost, thinking processes. Researchers should start writing from the moment that they see a glimmer of an inquiry because it helps them to think and to capture their thinking. In both cases this written thinking is intended as a private act but researchers who are relaxed about others seeing their raw, naked writing benefit a lot by sharing their private writing with critical friends.

It is easiest to see the value of private writing as a record of the inquiry process. Even small-scale projects can be quite complex and develop in unexpected ways. When researchers come to produce a public account of their inquiry and claims it can be surprisingly hard to remember what happened and why. This is why so many of them keep research journals, diaries or logs, sometimes handwritten in a notebook, often as a file of papers and increasingly as a folder in a word-processing program. Journals, *which are started as early as possible, when the study is being planned,* will usually include:

1   Messages to yourself about why you are doing what you are doing.
2   Jottings about ideas that you may be able to use as you try and make sense of what your inquiry is showing. These insights will be valuable when you analyse your data (Chapter 8).
3   Jottings about claims you might be able to make – for example, a note that what you see in an HIV education programme shows perfectly how policies are always changed when they are implemented.
4   Notes of what you did (which ought to have an explanation of why you did them firmly attached).
5   Copies of draft instruments (such as questionnaires, Likert scales, tests, q-sorts) and friends' comments on your proposed designs and instruments. Other documents and images will be filed with the main set of research information.
6   Reflections about how you, the researcher, are influencing the research findings and on the significance of that influence.
7   Lists of things to do.
8   Lists of things to avoid ('I must stop getting involved in helping out and stand aside and be a non-participant researcher because when I'm a participant I stop researching').
9   Neat sentences, draft paragraphs, notes of headings or themes that you might use in your public presentation of your inquiry.

These nine categories do overlap a lot and most investigators only use some of them. Nor is a research diary something that has to be completed every day, although ethnographic researchers, who participate in a social setting and immerse themselves in its cultures, are fanatical journal keepers because their fieldnotes usually *are* their research evidence. What is indisputable is that researchers who do not keep some form of journal create two nasty problems for themselves: at any point when they are thinking about the inquiry (and thinking ought to saturate the whole project) they are cut off from their earlier reasoning and insights; and when writing a public account of the project they find that they cannot properly explain why the inquiry was designed the way it was, why Likert scales were preferred to a q-sort and what was wrong with the first draft interview schedule (which has been lost in any case).

Private writing is important as a way of creating a research memory but its other use is no less significant. This can be best explained by extending the idea that research is primarily about thinking and saying that it pivots on sensemaking and claimsmaking. By sensemaking (a term taken from Weick, 1995) I mean creating understandings of the research topic, situation and questions. Claimsmaking is about connecting those understandings to ideas that are discussed in academic communities, amongst practitioners or in policy-making circles. It entails arguing that your inquiry is significant because it is reasonable to believe that it can contribute to thought or practice in the ways that you indicate. Chapter 2 has more to say about claimsmaking and Chapter 8 treats data analysis as acts of sensemaking. Chapter 6 sets out some further ideas on the ways in which sense and claims can be constructed. As far as this chapter is concerned the point is that researchers ought to be continually pondering how they are to go about making sense, about the sorts of claims they might make and how those claims might be sustained. Writing helps many people in at least two ways. It requires concentrated attention that may be missing from other, more fragile, ways of thinking. The other contribution is writing's challenge to say things precisely and to make connections between ideas. It is a challenge which ought to sharpen thinking and make it possible to develop the more complex understandings that come from spinning webs of ideas.

The great advantage of writing-to-think that is proper, joined-up and grammatical is that it can be edited at a later date and dropped directly into public reports and research papers. Private writing alternatives can be just as valuable. Three that I use are:

- Jotting ideas on Post-its or scraps of paper and putting them in folders organized by theme. Newspaper cuttings and references to publications that I ought to read go in there too. This book started with 13 folders (one for each chapter I expected to write) whose contents were rearranged several times as I reconsidered how to organize it.
- Mind mapping™ key ideas and themes. This is more an organizing than a writing tool. Having read through a folder, I jot the main ideas that I want to use on a blank page and rearrange them in successive versions so that similar ideas are put next to each other, boundaries are drawn (and redrawn) around them to show that these are coherent sets of ideas, and lines are added to link clusters and show how they relate to each other. See Chapter 4 and Buzan (1974) for examples and a complete explanation.
- Summary notes. Piles of the notes I have made on books and articles need to be compressed, which involves trying to get the main ideas, the best examples and apposite quotations on to, say, three sides of paper. Different coloured marker pens are then used to highlight things on these three pages that are on similar themes. A fresh set of notes is then made with care taken to ensure that I make it clear to myself what ideas and arguments I am using to organize each section and to connect sections to each other. I depend upon these 'connected plans' (see Chapter 9) when writing my first full drafts.

This writing does not have to be formal and polished because it is being treated as a way of supporting thinking and it is the quality of thinking that is important. This is writing as a way of working out what you want to say. Many people do small-scale research and tell interesting stories but it's often not at all clear what they want readers to learn or understand from it. It's not clear how the research findings fit with what they're trying to say and that seems to be because they are not really very clear what they really do want to say. So, it would be very harmful if a writing block, which many people have, obstructed this private writing. That means learning to have an informal view of writing so that there is much less chance that fear of writing will inhibit thought. Following Boice's (1992) finding that the new lecturers who published the most were those who wrote at least a little most days, my advice to small-scale researchers is to write something – formal writing, mind maps^{TM}, summary notes or jottings – often. He also found that those who deferred writing until they had good, clear stretches of time were the least productive.

Box 1.1 Alternatives to traditional research reports

Visual representations, including posters, photography, collage, video, exhibits of work
Novels, dramatic works and other creative writing
Fiction
Biography and autobiography
Presentations by researchers (sometimes including informants)
Artefacts
Innovative practices, programmes and products

In emphasizing the value of informal writing I am not minimizing the importance of good public writing. It is the main way of making claims about the significance of investigations, although alternative ways of representing research findings find favour in some research communities. Box 1.1 lists some of them. It will become clearer in Chapter 9 that plentiful private writing is a part of good public writing. Briefly, the point is that for most people polished writing is the product of several drafts and that redrafting is best if critical friends advise on improvement. In other words, the first three (or five, or n) versions will get junked. Seen like this, anyone who invests a lot of time in getting a first draft as perfect as they can make it is wasting a lot of time because nothing is more certain than that friends will see ways of improving it that had eluded the writer. Efficient writers understand that the sooner they can get an intelligible but unfinished draft to friends the better. It means they have few hang-ups about sharing incomplete and imperfect work because they recognize that no matter how long they spend alone trying to get it right, others will see ways in which it could be better. They share their private writing as part of the process of making it into public writing, which means they are not precious about their writing and that they have learned to trust friends to be critical to their drafts.

Creating Research Questions

If writing is a way of sensemaking and claimsmaking, and if they are at the heart of social research, then it is important early in an inquiry to be clear about the inquiry's purposes – about the research questions. They define the types of understandings to be sought and the sorts of claims that might be made. When investigators have a topic of interest but do not themselves know what their research questions are then, unless their purpose really is just to see how things are, their private writing and thinking will be difficult because they lack focus.

Imagine a case study of a hospital ward. It would certainly be possible to go into the ward, watch, listen and ask. There are circumstances when this sort of unfocused inquiry is useful, especially when inquirers are venturing into new worlds, in the early stages of a goal-free evaluation or as pilot work for a larger study. As the inquiry progresses, researchers begin to identify key questions amongst the welter of commonplace observations, such as that nurses are busy, the food is awful and humour is important. This approach, sometimes called 'progressive focusing', is one way for investigators to identify organizing questions that direct their research gaze and which help to identify the sorts of claims they might make about the significance of their inquiries.

Suppose that a researcher had been visiting a relative in hospital and thought that a hospital ward must be a good site for a small-scale study for an undergraduate dissertation. In my experience it is quite common for students to say that they want to study an area such as this because it has caught their interest, or because they are doing a course on, say, racism and would like to find out more. Of course students should choose research themes that interest them but unless someone, such as a supervisor, can compel them to identify some feasible research questions within the theme of life on the wards or racism, then they are headed for a lot of grief. Worse, they may be blasé and not realize that an inquiry, whether it is large scale or small, is not done by collecting information willy-nilly. Quite simply, there is too much going on for it to be possible for anyone to capture everything from every possible perspective, let alone to make sense of it and represent it to an audience. Research questions are needed to select, specify and connect, as Table 1.1 indicates:

- In order to make a study manageable, it is necessary to narrow it down by selecting an aspect or two for study. Novice researchers – some experienced ones as well – always choose studies that are too

Table 1.1 *Selecting, Specifying and Connecting*

'My research is going to be about...'	Supervisor's response
A study of old people's living environments	Topic too big. Focus unclear. No indication of what the value of the study might be, or of who might be interested by it. See also Box 4.8
An action research project to reduce drug taking in prisons	Too general – what is going to be the research side of the project? Why? What action is going to be taken? And with action research, it is important to know that you can make changes, see them through and evaluate them. Box 4.5 shows some of the things to consider
How effective is this teaching department?	More focused than the other questions but the notion of 'effectiveness' is a minefield: it is really too big to tackle in one undergraduate study
How effective do clients of Social Work Team PR5 believe it to be?	Much better. With the right literature review this could be good, because work on effectiveness has been more producer-centred than client-centred. This could question the validity of that tendency
A study of attitudes to crime	Crime is too broad a topic. And there is a problem of significance: is the study likely to tell us anything new?
An interview study with homeless people to see how fairly they are treated by the police	Defining 'fairly' is going to be tricky. Remember that interviews do not give information about practice: *they tell us what people believe happens*. So, how might you claim that this work is significant?
What is the best way of teaching the science concept of 'fair testing' to six-year-olds?	A well-formed question that will not yield to interview methods. A long-term, quasi-experimental design will give the most secure results. In practice, that puts it outside the range of most small-scale researchers
Do people who are learning to read rely more on sounds than on images (more on phonemes than on graphemes)?	An experimental study is called for and should be quite feasible for most small-scale researchers with a suitable training in this form of inquiry. Box 3.9 shows how more tightly specified hypotheses were devised and also, to my mind, raises doubts about the value of conclusions drawn from such artificial investigations

(Continued)

Table 1.1 *(Continued)*

'My research is going to be about...'	Supervisor's response
How did the Australian tabloid and quality papers report child abuse cases in 1995?	Good to see a focus on contrasting newspapers and on a manageable sample. The summary in Box 4.12 suggests that this was assumed to be a significant inquiry, although a counter-view is that all this hard work told us nothing remotely surprising
A survey of the needs of recently bereaved unemployed men below retirement age	In many ways a well-defined study. However, is a survey the right way to proceed? Yes, if there has been a good reading of other research and some unstructured or semi-structured pilot work leading to sharp and worthwhile questions. Otherwise...

ambitious, which are like trying to find the meaning of life through 20 questionnaires and an interview with Nellie. In the case of the hospital ward selection might lead to a decision to concentrate on some people; typical incidents; critical incidents; people's beliefs and attitudes; and so on. Obviously a researcher with an interest in social psychology will tend to select different phenomena from one interested in nursing practice or organizational behaviour.

- Specifying is like selecting but is more about defining exactly what the research questions are, what could count as information to be used in answering them and how that information is to be amassed. It involves identifying the questions to be addressed, and deciding on sampling and on the methods to be used.
- Connecting involves facing the 'So what?' question. All research needs to have an answer to the sceptic who reads the report, agrees that it has told her a great deal about how people feel about hospital food on Ward M3 in Bognor Regis, and says, 'So what? Who cares? Why bother?' Connecting, which is dealt with more fully in the next section, is about knowing the literature well enough to be able to make the claim that this stuff on hospital food is important because...

A skilled supervisor who was faced with a student interested in hospital wards would insist that some selection took place. For example, within the same maternity ward it would be reasonable to explore any of these three questions and another 50 besides:

1   Are structural changes in the health service sapping morale *and* harming patient care? A case study could contribute to this debate by producing confirmatory or disconfirmatory evidence.

Table 1.2 *Small-scale inquiries into the assessment of nurse competence*

Research question	Focus and significance
1 In what respects does ward-based assessment of nursing competence conform to notions of good assessment practice?	A study of the match between the research literature and practice: is competence assessed in ways that research says it should be? Significant for those who claim that competence must be and can be assessed in the workplace; for those responsible for assessments of competence; for theories of competence and assessment
2 Are all aspects of competence equally well judged by ward-based assessments?	Previous research has raised doubts about whether workplace assessments of job performance give good estimates of people's knowledge of theories, facts etc., so this could be a worthwhile study. It might be best to concentrate on the assessment of knowledge alone and it would be easiest to explore whether people *think* that this is a good way of measuring this sort of knowledge. Notice that this focusing has produced a manageable research question that is less ambitious and more limited than the original
3 How can the reliability of ward-based assessments of nursing competence be improved?	More focused than study 1. This could be a study of sources of unreliability and/or an action research attempt to do something about them. Action research (see Chapter 2) would be significant for those involved and it, as well as the other lines of inquiry, could have similar significance to study 1

2   How good is the quality of patient care? A study of the literature provides a model of good patient care against which practice in this ward could be judged.
3   Can maternal postpartum urinary incontinence be reduced through an antenatal education programme? This could be an action research study.

These questions need to become more specified and connected. Suppose a fourth general question had been identified which was about the ways in which nurses' competence was assessed on the ward. Table 1.2 sets out three research questions that could be derived from it. Notice that we are told why each question is worth asking. Any of the three would be quite enough for a small-scale study and, in practice, it is likely that an investigator would further restrict the inquiry by sampling and concentrating on the easier-to-get information.

   Creating research questions about a topic involves first deciding whether
to investigate actions or beliefs (which include people's reports of actions).
The research questions will then tend to fall into one of these categories:

1 Descriptive. Key words are what, who, where and when. Descriptive
   research has been regarded as aimless, low-level information collection, especially by those influenced by the methods of natural science
   which centre upon the development and testing of explanatory
   hypotheses. However, a view that is gaining strength is that descriptions and narratives necessarily contain theories: what they include
   represents a theory of significance and what they exclude does the
   same. The language and form of the description are also theory-rich
   and in need, according to some post-structuralists, of deconstruction
   (see Box 4.9 for an example). If description and narrative can be taken
   as acts of theorizing, then it can be important to know, for example,
   whether beliefs or actions really are as people say and whether they
   vary according to time, place and the people involved. Descriptive
   research questions are powerful ones if the person asking the questions can explain why the resulting descriptions might be significant
   for practitioners, other researchers or theory. This implies that descriptions and narratives may make us revise the account that dominates
   the research literature by bringing to view differences between a
   researcher's representation of what is and widely held beliefs about it.
   Note the implication that writing descriptions and narratives should
   be a mindful act involving close attention to what is being said and
   how, as well as to what is being left out. That, in turn, implies that the
   writer should be reflexive, which means thoughtful about the way his
   or her experiences, thoughts, feelings and positionings are shaping the
   writing. It is usual to put some evidence of this reflexivity alongside
   the description or narrative (Polkinghorne, 1988; Witherell and
   Noddings, 1991).
2 Evaluative. The key phrase is 'How good?' but evaluative research
   questions cannot avoid asking from whose point of view, at what
   price, when, where and according to what criteria of judgement. When
   a small-scale evaluation study asks questions about one site that relate
   to issues of interest in the research literature it can do a lot more than
   offer a judgement about that site alone.
3 Narrative. These are research questions about what happens and how it
   happens. They are about dynamics and, unless simplified social phenomena are being treated as if they operated like systems in physics,
   the findings will tend to take the form of a narrative description. As
   with descriptive research questions, these can lead to some deeply
   uninteresting slabs of information unless they are connected, from the
   beginning, to the literature.
4 Causal. The key word is why. 'Why?' questions are powerful and
   attractive but asking them does not mean that an answer can be

found. Some social scientists say that only experiments provide secure answers to 'Why?' questions. Those who are less scrupulous are still likely to be sceptical of claims that a study has answered the 'Why?' question rather than made tentative claims about what an answer might look like. Again, the person asking the question needs to say why anyone should be interested by claims about an answer to the 'Why?' question in this specific case.

5   Effects. This concern with the effects of a change or intervention could be seen as a hybrid of types 1 and 2 but it is also distinctive of action research, which is discussed in Chapter 2. It is very attractive to ask about the effects of a new policy or practice, especially because there are sure to be some. The sceptic would also say that (the generally positive) effects will tend to be mis-measured, exaggerated by the investigator and short-lived. She or he would add that it is unlikely to be clear what caused the effect and quite possible that almost any injection of money, interest or novelty would have produced the same sorts of difference.

When creating these or other types of research questions it is advisable to:

1   Ask one thing per question, which means that questions are often one sentence long and do not contain the word 'and'.
2   Be clear about why each question is significant. Who cares about the answer? Why does it *matter*?
3   Be precise and say who or what will be studied – category C male prisoners in one jail, domiciliary nursing provision in a rural area, etc.
4   Stick to a few pointed questions.
5   Be confident that you will be able to collect information that will allow you to make claims in response to the questions.

These research questions have three main functions. They say what we will be especially sensitive to when we are looking for information, although there is a real danger that they will induce selective vision which hinders us from seeing other important things. Secondly, they should get us thinking about the claims we are likely to make about the significance of whatever it is that we find, which involves connecting to the academic literature and with the concerns of our likely audiences. Thirdly, they start us on the task of specifying our methods of inquiry. But where do research questions come from? It has been suggested that interest in a topic may be a starting point, although it has also been insisted that interest can be a treacherous guide unless there is someone around to bring it within manageable and worthwhile bounds. Exploratory work has also been noticed as a source of questions. The student interested in hospital wards might become a participant by helping and use his or her own insights to get a question or ask people to say what questions they would most like to see answered. Professional researchers often get questions by identifying 'holes' in the literature. Holes in the literature take several forms, especially:

- Someone has made claims based on one sort of study with a certain sort of sample. A good research question explores whether the claims stand up with different samples or a variant of the original methods.
- It is possible to claim that a key concept has been defined too narrowly or too broadly, and/or that it has been measured inappropriately. Your research question uses a different definition or operationalization.
- The literature contains claims that seem to be justified but no-one has established whether consequences that should follow really do follow. That could provide your research questions.

The writing – and the thinking – that you can do are limited until you have constructed some specific research questions which should connect with the wider academic literature. This implies that reading around the topic is going to be important in the early stages of a small-scale project, when it also makes sense to write about the reading.

Writing a Literature Review

Your small-scale inquiry needs to be connected to the relevant literature even if your main aim is to study a situation, intervene and monitor the outcomes so that you could make further improvements (which is called 'action research'). A knowledge of the literature gives you ideas about what you could be alert for; the changes that other people have had success with; the ways in which those changes might best be introduced; and methods for evaluating the outcomes. If you are going to report the work to other practitioners or academics you will want to make claims about its significance, which again means connecting it to the debates in the professional or academic literatures. Lastly, as was said in the previous section, it is a good way of identifying research questions and methods. Reading goes hand-in-hand with forming research questions. When questions are formed without sustained reference to the literature, then the resulting study is likely to be a bland exercise in collecting information marked by (1) naïve research instruments that lack any obvious conceptual or theoretical underpinning, (2) problems with sensemaking (because the inquirer is not alert to themes that are likely to be identifiable), and (3) problems with claimsmaking (because the inquirer lacks the knowledge that is needed in order to link the study to the concerns of the academic or practitioner communities). In sum, reviewing the literature helps you to avoid mistakes and gives you ideas; helps you to devise inquiries that have not already been done; and, consequently, makes you clearer about ways of claiming that your small-scale study will have significance for practitioners or academics.

Two difficulties are identifying relevant publications and obtaining them. An introduction to academic databases and search techniques can be found on the Research Training Initiative website

<http://www.biad.uce.ac.uk/research/guides/index.html>, which also contains advice and learning activities, as well as discussion group facilities. Although electronic searches are fast and convenient it is still possible to miss important papers because the key words they use and the ones you have searched for are different. You are also likely to get far more 'hits' than you can cope with. A good coping strategy is to restrict searches to the past four or five years only and to restrict your search to papers published in your country. The reason for the geographical restriction is that important articles will have been published elsewhere but academic libraries tend not to have extensive holdings of foreign journals. There is little point in identifying a paper if you cannot get it. This coping strategy is a robust way of reducing a hit list to a size big enough to scroll through and identify papers that look promising and are available in your library. When deciding on the 20 or so that you will examine (and you might only read half of them properly), then you are likely to prefer papers that are billed as reviews of the research, ones by authors who you know to be recognized authorities, longer papers, and ones in the more prestigious journals in the area in which you are interested. Beware of the temptation to try and read everything you can get on a topic. The most likely consequences are guilt (because there is always more to read) and panic (because all other work will be blocked).

A third problem is being critical. Part of the problem comes from the term 'critical thinking' itself. Doing a literature review does not mean that you have to do a hatchet job on the existing literature, not least because criticism is about appraising and judging, which can be positive and appreciative, as well as negative. It can also involve looking at taken-for-granteds and considering alternative angles on matters, so that researchers working within a critical theory approach will be asking whose interests are served and in what ways by policies, practices, customs or discourses. (There is more about critical theory in Chapter 2.) So, being critical can mean looking for faults but it can also mean appreciating, as well as asking what lies underneath appearances. Intelligent literature searches will usually identify summaries of the main views and concise accounts of the problems with them, and some review articles ask sharp questions about who benefits from social practices and mainstream ways of thinking about them. Novice small-scale researchers seem to find it harder to be positive in their critical appraisals, especially where official policies or practices are concerned. And there is a sense in which students doing small-scale studies are as likely to be looking for gaps in the literature as for problems with any one interpretation; for opportunities to take established studies and rework them in different settings or with different people. In such cases what matters is not so much whether you are an acid critic as whether you have a point of view and can make claims about why your projected study is worth doing. To use Eisner's words, 'Criticism ... does not impose an obligation to make derogatory comments. Criticism can be laudatory. Its aim is to illuminate a situation or object so that it can be appreciated. We appreciate virtues as well as vices' (1991: 7). Again: 'Criticism is the art of saying useful things about complex and subtle objects and events so that others less sophisticated, or sophisticated in different ways, can see and understand what they did not see and understand before' (1991: 3). Ludema and colleagues (2001) recommend 'appreciative inquiry', which means being sensitive to what works well and is praiseworthy, going on to look then at areas for improvement.

After your first bite at the literature, write. Some of what you write will be used in the literature review of your final report and the rest is necessary as a way of helping you to make sense of it and to help think yourself into some research questions and ideas of the claims you will later make about the significance of your study. Table 1.3 shows one way of organizing this writing. The writing should be revised several times before appearing in a research report. Some revision is needed because you read a new paper and need to add its conclusions to the review and, as your work progresses, you will often identify papers that were missed by your early searches because they weren't tagged with the key words you used then. You should get copies of them or good summaries and work them into the literature review. As the study develops something also needs to be done about the parochialism of the coping strategy I recommended for the initial search. Five strategies are:

1   Browse through recent copies of overseas journals that your library does take. The book reviews can be extremely useful summaries of research and thinking.
2   Visit another library which has a better range of journals (university library catalogues can be checked on the web before you make a visit).
3   Do another search but of the American (or British, Australian, French) literature and give the abstracts serious attention. They should alert you to any ideas or findings that you really ought to heed.
4   Search for relevant websites and on-line papers. There are plenty of them but some, perhaps a lot, will be junk. Look for evidence that some authoritative-sounding organization has refereed them. (Mind you, some journals publish junk, so refereeing cannot be taken as a guarantee of quality.)
5   Ask your supervisor for suggestions.

Writing drafts of a literature review tightens research questions, helps you to see what sense you might make of the findings you might get, and indicates ways of making claims about the possible significance. It is private writing, although the more you can share your emerging review with others, the better for your writing, thinking and inquiry. Whatever was drafted in the early days of the study will need to be revised for the final report to ensure that it is integral to it. Check that the final literature review

1   is clearly connected to the research questions
2   is connected to the choice of methods and research design (Chapters 2–5)

3   is acknowledged as a source of ideas used in data analysis (Chapter 8)
4   is fundamental to the conclusions you draw and the claims you make
    about the research; in your final report weave together data, discus-
    sion, what others have said or found and your conclusions (Chapter 9).

Table 1.3   *Elements of a literature review*

Literature review theme	Comment
What's the area of concern?	Introduce readers to the topic and consider explaining how you have come to be engaged with it. Take care not to clutter it up with background information, especially historical narratives. Keep it short
Why is it important and to whom?	Tackle the 'Who cares?' question early. Identify your audience by saying who the problem matters to and why. Say how a small-scale study could illuminate, test, complicate or resolve it
Summarize the points of agreement in the literature	It's important for you and your readers to appreciate what is not in dispute. Keep this concise
What are the main areas of disagreement and uncertainty?	If possible begin this section by saying that there are many disputed areas (which you list) and that you are concentrating on the three or four most important. Present them so that the one you are going to study – the target issue – comes last
Accounting for disagreements	You need to offer a story to explain why people have come to different conclusions about the target issue. For example, is it a matter of metaphysics, sampling, research instruments, conceptualization, data analysis? You may be able to make the strong claim that your inquiry is particularly important because you think that the other disagreements have the same source as disagreement on the target issue. Your conclusions will then have wider implications
Set out your research questions. Three or four may be manageable but one can be enough and half-a-dozen is usually too many to manage	Write them in the most specific terms that you can. You may need to explain how they arise from the works you have been reviewing, although it may be obvious. It should also be clear why these questions are worth asking and who is likely to be interested in them
(Positivist researchers may set out the hypotheses that they will test. By convention they test the null hypothesis that there is not a difference between phenomena in different places or times, or under different conditions)	
What methods have been used in other studies? Are they suitable for yours? Would other methods be better? Why?	Reading other research should give you lots of ideas about methods to use and designs to adopt (and to avoid). It is quite proper to use other people's methods, instruments and designs as long as you acknowledge them and explain what will be fresh about your use of them

Students often treat the literature review as a chore that prevents them
from getting on with the research. That is absurd. If research is about

sensemaking, claimsmaking and thinking in general, then the literature review is absolutely fundamental. The ideas it sets out should seep through the study and flow through the report. More substantial advice is provided by Cooper (1998) and Locke et al. (1998). The reference to meta-analysis in Chapter 4 is also relevant.

This chapter has argued that small-scale studies need to begin with good thinking and it has recommended that writing be a natural part of that thinking. In addition to thinking about the research questions it is also important to think about the nature of research itself in order to get a clear view of the sorts of claims that different research approaches can sustain. That is the theme of the next chapter.

2

Research as Claimsmaking

The view of research that pervaded Chapter 1 leads to two propositions:

1   Research is more thinking than doing, so research is not what you thought it was. Research is what you think.
2   There are many research methods and a range of views about what good research could look like. Good practice involves having some match between views and methods you choose and the sorts of claims you hope to offer as responses to your research questions.

By 'research' I mean systematic inquiry. 'Systematic' echoes proposition 1 by indicating that the work should be purposeful and implies that it should be thorough as well. 'Inquiry' has many meanings, which is why it has been chosen. My view is that library-based work, experiments, reanalysis of data collected by others and interviewing can all be counted as research activities. The point is that research is not about using some methods rather than others; it is about using any methods you know or imagine that are fit for your inquiring purpose and about using any information that can be used to address research questions. This echoes proposition 2. One implication is that there is no hard-and-fast divide between 'research' and other inquiries. Journalists, for example (should) do research, which means that the distinction between research and journalism becomes one of degree. Seale says that,

> Journalism shares similarities with qualitative research writing genres, but there are important dilemmas, and these are generally based on a commitment to greater depth of thought, more sustained periods of investigation, and a more rigorously self-critical approach in the service of higher ideals than scandal mongering, entertainment or immediate emotional and dramatic gratification. (1999: 15–16)

The difference between a novelist and a 'researcher' can also be slimmer than you might assume, the main difference being that serious novelists sometimes make substantial inquiries before presenting their conclusions in a creative and entertaining form. Few researchers have the ability to write that way and fewer are prepared to risk representing their findings through fiction, although it is not unknown.

What would count as *small-scale* research? My starting point is that it involves (1) one person, not a team, (2) no funding or little more than some contribution to the costs of printing and travel, and (3) a fairly short period of time to complete the inquiry and the report. Then I recognize that it is still small scale if there are two or three people working on it who are trying to do other things as well, rather like undergraduates doing a no-budget group project as part of their programme of study; even if there is some money to pay for tape transcription, I would still call it small scale; and a research student might have three years from start to finish but still work on a small scale. Plainly, my definition of 'small scale' is a fuzzy one whose centre is people working alone, under pressure and without funds. This book offers research guidance that has their stretched-to-the-limit situation in mind. Advice needs to be pragmatic, which means it needs to give guidance on mindfully choosing from the possibilities described in this and many other books in order to customize an inquiry for a particular audience and context. The emphasis must be on intelligent action rather than on following research recipes and, in so doing, restates proposition 1.

Research is more Thinking than Doing

Stacey has observed that,

> people [tend] to believe that the open-endedness they face is the result of their ignorance: they have not done enough research into the laws of causations and have not gathered enough data to work out the future consequences of their actions. Or the data and analogies are available but others are either too incompetent or too badly behaved to use them properly. The immediate conclusion drawn is that ignorance can be overcome by greater investment in gathering information, funneling it to some central point where it can be analyzed, and then taking it back to the actors. The dominant schema there-fore leads people to believe that ignorance can be overcome by research ... incompetence can be overcome by training ... and systems can be used to prevent bad behavior. (1996: 268)

The opposite view, that the difference between good and indifferent pro-jects, inquiries, evaluations and case studies is not so much a difference in the methods used as in the quality of thinking behind them, pervades this book. Indifferent reports are pervaded by data and descriptions. Better reports are pervaded by discussion of what the data and descriptions mean and could mean. The one is about specifics. The other brings mind-fulness to the specifics and uses the specifics to develop claims that enhance our understanding of the general.

People often find it hard to carry out small-scale inquiries for projects, term papers, dissertations and other academic or professional purposes. One reason is because their available energies, both mental and physical, get applied to the wrong things. Novices, such as those who are told to 'do some research' and then to write it up in an academic report, dissertation, term paper, coursework or suchlike, are the most likely to mis-channel their energies and worry about the wrong things. That is a sign of someone following a naïve 'doing research' schema which tells them that the thing to concentrate on is getting the methods right and then using them correctly. The host of research methods books on the market is a sign that people do get fixated by technique. Consider the case of a friend, Judith, who said that her master's dissertation would have been 'better if only I'd talked to [interviewed] more people'. She was wrong. She'd talked to enough people and it didn't seem likely that she'd get much by doing another slew of talking, taping and transcribing. The limitations to her perfectly acceptable dissertation did not lie in the methods but someplace else. People with the naïve 'doing research' schema often have the sort of sample size envy that Judith showed and, like Judith, they also fret in search of *the* killer, elusive technique – video recording, role playing, computer-based monitoring of website usage – that will bring truth much closer and inspire the magic insight that finally explains what it is all about. One purpose of this book is to indicate that this 'doing research' schema may be prevalent but, like many of the concepts, scripts or schemata we use in our daily life, it is faulty. And like other faulty concepts – that fat people are gluttons, that people's appearances are reliable guides to their character or intelligence – this one can have serious consequences, at least for people doing small-scale inquiries.

Yet the choice of methods is important, because it does take skill to use them and because an investigation can be pointless when inappropriate methods are used. And there are deeper reasons why people fixate on inquiry-as-methods. You can be taught methods. It is fairly easy to alight upon promising methods, such as experiments or focus group work, and then to take a course or read up on how to do them. From then onwards it is possible to cling for far too long to the belief that you are being a good researcher in proportion to the amount of dedication with which you apply these respectable methods. Two slippery beliefs sustain this cookbook approach, this painting-by-numbers view of social inquiry. The first is the idea that somehow these methods deliver understanding. They don't.

The second is the work ethic, with its stories that good results come through hard labour, better results come with harder labour – and even if bad luck means that those two stories don't work, then hard work will stave off complete failure. Research becomes hoarding, with the inquirer collecting data like a miser grabbing gold. Yet progress and achievement are not proportional to the fatness of the data archive. Lots of data can give the researcher false confidence, much as alcohol can provide 'Dutch courage', but people who have problems getting their doctoral theses accepted usually have problems convincing examiners that what they have found is significant, worthwhile and contributes to understanding of the phenomenon. Inadequate data collection is not the main reason for rejecting articles submitted to journals or referring a thesis back to the author for revision. Good research certainly involves hard work and often creates large amounts of data but effort and data do not guarantee good research because, by themselves, they provide no answer to the sceptic who asks, 'So what? Who cares? What does it *mean*?' The lack of any answer to those questions was the problem with the diligent study described in Box 2.1. The last section of Chapter 4 goes further and argues that valuable claims can be made by analysing data that others have collected and by suggesting better ways of understanding phenomena.

Box 2.1 Pattie's study

Pattie was doing the taught part of a part-time doctoral programme. She had to do an empirical study illuminating issues about the assessment of competence and produce an academic report of the inquiry. The stipulated length was 6000 words (25 pages) and the course tutors would read the reports as if they were articles submitted for publication in a refereed journal. Doctoral students were encouraged to choose topics that could be investigated in their workplaces. Three months were available for designing, doing and drafting a paper.

   Her case study was based upon interview and questionnaire inquiries. It clearly had these strengths:

- The seriousness and commitment of the inquirer were evident from the fact that an eight-page questionnaire had been devised and given to all 14 people in her 'community of practice' or workgroup. Nine had been returned and seven of those people had also been interviewed at length. Interviews had been tape-recorded, transcribed and analysed in detail.
- Transcripts (77 single-spaced pages) and tables based on the questionnaires were appended to the paper.
- The paper was somewhat over 8000 words long, excluding appendices.
- References in the paper showed that she had read a lot on how to do questionnaires and interviews.
- Quotations were included in the paper and supported a complex and nuanced description of the assessment of competence in that setting.
- The presentation was immaculate and the references had been perfectly given, right down to the last comma.

The tutor read the paper as if she were a referee for a professional journal and had no hesitation in recommending rejection. Fortunately, the stakes for this reading were relatively low, since the immediate outcome was intended to be a discussion between the student and the tutor about ways of improving upon the draft. The student was distraught: 'But damn it, I gave this my best. I stayed up nights, I interviewed people through mealtimes, I sweated [a standard research methods book]. Do you know, I hardly got to see my partner and when I did I was so tired, you know, he said he'd be better off in a monastery. And you say it's not good enough? I don't think so.' The tutor replied that the case study did seem to be a good description of the situation in one workplace – and it'd be a lot easier to accept that if people in the workplace had also commented on the draft report. The problem wasn't down to any moral failing, lack of work, or even lack of ability. The problem was that anyone seeing this full description of what people said in one workgroup would likely say, 'So what? Who cares? What does it *mean*?'

The point can be developed a little by referring to a distinction that can be made between knowledge, information and data that I have derived from research into knowledge management in organizations (Cleveland, 1985: Davenport and Prusak, 1998). These are not interchangeable concepts. Data surround us. Data are raw calls on our attention, bits and pieces that are all around; there but often outside our threshold of consciousness. Information, on the other hand, has relevance, purpose and consequently meaning. Information comes from questions and purposes, from centring attention. Information is data that are noticed and organized, perhaps very loosely, for a reason. A crude way of explaining the distinction is to think of a supermarket. It's full of food but for shoppers who want to create meals that suit their needs and tastes, the food is just raw material, much as data are. Now, once there is a purpose, a viewpoint, some of the data are tagged as information. To resume the analogy, with a meal in mind some of the foodstuffs become ingredients to be gathered and put together. In practice we are seldom conscious of processing of data into information. The meal itself comes from cleaning, chopping, cooking and combining the ingredients to serve a purpose, which might be to delight in one case, to build muscle in another, and to control weight in a third. In this way it is like the understandings that research reports contain, under-standings created for different purposes and audiences by working upon the research information.

Knowledge is a creation of minds at work and, I suggest, is best described as 'understanding'. Although there are philosophical and psychological uncertainties about what understanding is, I am using it (1) to include explanation and interpretation and (2) to identify a mental process that uses information but which is more than just amassing information. To put it another way, understanding comes from making sense of information which involves connecting the information with existing understandings, either by assimilating the new understandings to the old ones (in which case the old understandings are enriched) or by accommodating the old understandings to the new information (in which case the old understand-ings are changed). Put simply, data are everywhere, raw and inchoate; information is organized data, which presumes an underlying purpose; understanding (knowledge) is integrated information.

This twofold distinction has two important implications. First, assuming that personal understanding is the main goal of inquiry and that contribut-ing to public understanding is the second, then no amount of information gathering can be sufficient. Understanding comes from the quality of think-ing; from mindfulness (having a view of what you are doing and why), sensemaking (integrating the information with existing understandings) and claimsmaking (saying why your understanding is significant and should be of interest to others). Secondly, it ought to be impossible for inquirers to collect data because they ought to have a clarity of purpose that means they only collect information. However, there is an approach that I call 'hunter-gatherer' research in which data are captured indiscriminately in the belief that an extensive sweep of the right environment must produce information and knowledge. Not so. Purposefulness is a precondition of information, sensemaking a precondition of personal understanding and claimsmaking a precondition of contributing to public understanding.

The distinction between data, information and understanding has implied that industrious data collection does not lead to good research. It is necessary but it is not sufficient because good research also needs good information to be constructed from the data and it needs understandings to be created that are fit for the audience and research purposes. In everyday practice people are more likely to make a simpler distinction between understanding and the data/information on which it is based. To avoid confusion, from here onwards I shall use 'data' and 'information' interchangeably.

Inquiry and Claimsmaking

Of course scrupulousness about research methods is important. It is good to make sure that enough information has been collected to offer a good chance that good understandings can be constructed and defended. It is desirable that a range of methods has been used because when different methods yield similar data, then it is easier to be confident about the understandings that follow (and, as Chapter 6 explains, it is also significant when a mix of methods yields apparently conflicting data). It is publicly expected that methods will be used properly and punctiliously and it is hard to see who would praise a narrow and slapdash approach that collected few data in a faulty way. So, people who do small-scale research projects, evaluations, action research and the like, whether it is as a necessary part of their job or as evidence of suitability for an academic award, do need to be proficient and versatile users of research methods. They also need to be serious about their inquiries, not least in terms of taking the pains that are needed to get data that are fit for the purpose.

Box 2.2 Advice to Pattie on rescuing her study

1 Pattie, what I'm saying here is not too helpful for you today but it's powerful for the future. Don't do anything whilst your intention is 'to find out about ...'. Plan your study once your aim is to explore a theme, controversy, hypothesis or concept of *some general significance* through a small-scale investigation.

2 Most inquiries can be connected with several literatures. Where the topic is the assessment of competence in the workplace, a study might lock on to one or more of the controversies about:

- Specifying competence. This is a major, tricky issue because it arises from some long-standing and deep questions that lie in philosophy and psychology. One interesting line is that competence is such an

continued

embedded, context-specific notion that it cannot be specified – it is always negotiated. A small empirical study could help to address these deeper matters.

- Assessing competence. This invokes a raft of standard problems in assessment, compounded by the different requirements of assessment for the purposes of certification as opposed to assessment as a guide to further learning.
- Workplace assessment. This is really a variant of the general assessment theme. The big interest is that workplace assessment is rather in vogue, so evidence about its cost, trustworthiness and robustness could be a useful contribution to policy and practice.
- Power and equity. Power is often unevenly distributed in organizations so that some groups tend to be more or less privileged. This study might illuminate a particular theory or story about power and equity in organizational subunits.
- Change. If workplace assessments of competence are new, then theories of change, of which there are plenty, can be instantiated.
- Best practice. Evaluations often check how something measures up to 'best practice' (and that's always an idea worth picking away at: who says it's 'best practice'?). There's a lot to be had by exploring why there are mismatches between 'best' and 'ordinary' practice. Often it looks as if 'ordinary' practice serves all sorts of important but non-obvious purposes that 'best' practice would jeopardize. A good area for theorizing with many practical implications.

Can you think back to your reading on these general issues of importance and then reflect on all the data you've collected and see how your study might be reframed to illuminate issues of general concern? When I'm refereeing for a journal I often ask myself whether it would say anything to a professor in Harrisonburg, Virginia or Leuven, Belgium. In other words, does the specific illuminate matters of widespread concern? Can you retune your description so as to get a purchase on one or two issues like those?

3 Rewrite the introductory section to highlight the issues. Say that you've done small-scale work that illuminates them and say, precisely, what you conclude and what your argument is. Once you've got these issues or questions up front you'll see ways of making your description substantially more concise. However, do add 'bridges' between the sections: summarize what you've said in each section, explain why it's significant for your argument and say how it fits with the next section. By all means sum up in the Conclusion but keep that crisp. Try to assess the implications of what you've argued for policy and/or practice and/or theorizing and conceptualizing and/or future research.
4 In a nutshell: *think* about how the specifics of your case study might be connected or generalized to public understanding of an aspect of the assessment of competence.

Personal understanding is valuable but it is unusual to do a study for personal interest alone. Normally there is an audience – one's colleagues in an action research project, a policy team in an evaluation study, or developmental psychologists in a study of young children's understanding of rules. Good small-scale studies contain clear claims about the possible significance for others of the personal understandings that the researcher has constructed. In this sense research involves claimsmaking. That means indicating how the specifics of a small-scale inquiry, which might legitimately only have examined one person, site or incident, could affect public thinking or action. Box 2.2 returns to Pattie's study to illustrate the ways in which personal understandings of one case can be connected or generalized to public discourses. While it may be personally satisfying to get an understanding of a case, as did Pattie, it is unlikely to get high academic rewards because they usually go to reports which use the particular case, site or incident to suggest improvements to the public understanding of such instances. However, it ought not to be supposed that any serious claims can be based on any methods. Claimsmaking and research methods are intertwined and making sense of their association means having an overview of the sorts of claims that social research can make and of their relation to methods of inquiry.

Claims that Research may Make

Some of the ideas sketched in this section are further developed in Chapter 7. The main aim is to show that there is a range of views about what exists (ontology) and how we may know about it (epistemology). Two consequences are considered. One is that different views imply that researchers may be able to sustain very different claims, and the second is that some inquiry methods are more congenial to some epistemological and ontological views than to others. It is not appropriate to explore these views with a philosopher's zeal: Searle (2000) provides a clear and concise opinion on metaphysical matters, Sayer (1992) gives more systematic attention to philosophical issues in the social sciences, and Smith (1998) offers a full and sometimes difficult view of the relationship between social research and different metaphysical beliefs. My concern is the more limited one of encouraging small-scale researchers to be alert to the significance of different ontologies and epistemologies for the claims they might wish to make.

Searle (2000: 10) argues that by default we make five background assumptions:

1   There is a real world existing independent of us.
2   We have direct perceptual access to it.
3   Words have reasonably clear meanings and can refer to real objects in the world.
4   True statements correspond to how things are, to the facts of the world.
5   Causes really do produce effects.

This can be described as a realist position. It has been attacked. The strong anti-realist position *denies* each of the following four realist claims:

1   There exists a real world independent of us and our interests...
2   There is an objective way that things are in the world...
3   We ought to be able to say how they are.
4   If we can say how they are, then what we say is objectively true or
    false depending on the extent to which we succeed or fail in saying
    how they are. (2000: 15)

Some anti-realists have the view that reality is essentially constructed, a
social artefact, a product of mind and language. For Rorty 'all our thought
is simply "marks and noises" which we are "caused" to produce by a
blind material world to which we cannot so much as *refer*', and for Derrida
'there is nothing outside the text' (both quotations from Putnam, 1995: 75).
Views like these imply that there are no certainties, but only social constructs, so research becomes inquiry into the ways in which social constructs are formed, operate and are sustained, and for whose benefit and
to whose detriment. There are those, such as Scott and Usher (2000), who
are enthusiastic about the potential that such thinking has for educational
research and, by implication, for social research in general, giving it the
role of questioning, deconstructing and transgressing taken-for-granted
thinking and practices – of being unruly. Others believe it favours feminist projects and puts the whole notion of patriarchy 'under erasure'
(Smith, 1998: 318; Coffey and Delamont, 2000).
   Most critics of realism would confine their serious reservations to the
fourth of Searle's realist claims and say either that truth is an illusion, or
that it is always contexted and conditional, or that it is elusive in other
ways (see Audi, 1998 for a philosopher's substantial summary). Even so,
they would be likely to accept that all five of Searle's background assumptions hold good for the physical world (to the world of energy and matter
that is independent of the observer), but would be far more problematic
if inquiry moves away from the world of brute matter. Although there are
features of human communication and action that could fit the background assumptions, there are many that do not. A social researcher
might establish that most drivers break the speed limits when (1) they
think it is safe and (2) they do not expect to be caught. There is no need to
question the five background assumptions in this case but it would be different if the researcher were interested in *why* people break speed limits.
Inquiries about people's feelings – the meanings they attach to an event
such as the millennium celebrations, their views on how to reduce urban
crime, or their opinion of a painting by Paul Klee – will seldom be exploring phenomena that can be treated like those of the physical world. Many
of the things in which social researchers are interested are not independent of the subject but are, quite literally, subjective (to a greater or lesser
degree). Searle's five assumptions are far more vulnerable to criticism
when applied to human thought and action and the four anti-realist
doubts have more force in those cases. Conversely, doubts are lessened
and the assumptions are more secure when we are only interested in

recording behaviours, not meanings, beliefs, feelings, attributions or self-theories.

However, critiques of realism are not attractive to all, even in modified and temperate forms. Some feminist researchers fear that post-structuralism's position that no discourse or interpretation is inherently superior to another threatens their view that women's perspectives should be privileged. Others are critical of the language of post-structuralism, saying that 'much of what is written is impenetrable, self-referential, confusing and exclusive' (Schratz and Walker, 1995: 168), while some feel that constructionist perspectives and tinges of post-structuralism seem to exaggerate a perfectly good idea and damage it in the process. Hacking (1999) argues that 'reality' need not be seen as a single thing, so that some things, especially objects, can be treated as 'real' while others, especially ideas, can be treated as constructions. Furthermore, many constructs can be and are reasonably treated as 'real': paying rent is epistemologically real, even though it is ontologically a social construct. Hacking also points out that it is one thing to identify an idea as a construct and another to take a moral position about that construct. He identifies four propositions about any social construct: (1999: 12, 6, rearranged):

1   In the present state of affairs, X (something that is socially constructed) is taken for granted; X appears to be inevitable.
2   X need not have existed, or need not be as it is. X, or X as it is at present, is not determined by the nature of things; it is not inevitable.
3   X is quite bad as it is.
4   We would be much better off if X were done away with, or at least radically transformed.

Neither proposition [3] nor proposition [4] inevitably follows from [2], although Hacking argues that some constructionists assume that either or both of them do. Nor does accepting proposition [2] necessarily have any great implications because it is obvious that many aspects of human life and thought are historically shaped, which means that proposition [2] will very often be a truism and we learn nothing by showing that is the case. For example, American citizens' right to bear arms is a consequence of the constitution-makers' drafting of a response to a specific practical problem. In that sense, the right is very much a construct. It is hard to see what is gained by identifying it as such: who would try to claim other-wise? Likewise, the research questions which attract funding in natural science are a selection of all the questions that could be explored, a selec-tion that is partly made on historical, social and contingent grounds. That does not mean that the questions are scientifically trivial, it just means that choosing amongst important questions brings to the surface social assumptions about what matters most – quantum mechanics, the human genome or the life-cycle of tropical parasites.

What I have been trying to show is that there are two extreme answers to questions about what exists and how we may know. I have labelled them

	Commonplace, communal phenomenon (high generalizability)	Unusual but communal phenomenon (medium generalizability)	Commonplace, individual phenomenon (medium contingency)	Unusual, individual phenomenon (high contingency)
Scientific understanding, especially of the natural and observer-independent world, logic and mathematics	Clock time Probability Microelectronics	Global warming Genetic engineering Necrotizing fasciitis	Young children's concepts – of time, for example	Terminal illness
Ethics (study of goodness and of right action)	Leading organizations effectively Living happily	Murder Same sex marriage To build a new bypass or not?	Religious experience and/or belief	How can I do the best for a specific person in this situation now?
Aesthetics (taste, beauty, imagination, creativity, representation, expression, style etc. with regard to art and the natural environment)	Autumn scenery in New England The Gap brand The Beatles' music	Total solar eclipse	Orgasm	Hallucinations, out-of-body experiences

Figure 2.1   *Convergence and divergence in human experience*[1,2]
1 The more lightly shaded areas in the Figure identify aspects of human experience that are more congenial to anti-realist thinking.
2 The examples in the 12 cells represent one way of seeing the world. People living in different cultures would give different examples and might prefer to rename the rows and columns, or to represent their humanity in quite different ways.

realist and anti-realist and suggested that the realist position is more congenial to some areas of experience than others. Likewise, I have used Hacking's work to show that there is a variety of positions that are not realist and I have summarized some characteristics of out-and-out anti-realism. Figure 2.1 implies that the realist position is weaker in aesthetics and ethics (two areas characterized by very human judgements) than in natural science, where judgement has often been turned into the rigorous application of approved procedures. It also indicates that social phenomena which are unusual and individual are not as controlled by the repeated deployment of a shared language to describe them as are commonplace and communal phenomena. This means that a greater diversity of discourse and feeling can be expected and it becomes harder to sustain realist beliefs in the possibility of objectivity and certainty. A pragmatic position holds that realism is a fair description of some aspects of the world and says that the rest is observer relative. Indeed, social phenomena that are often seen as objective or observer independent – customary behaviours are a good example – may also be reappraised to reveal subjective or observer-dependent elements, which are especially likely to be associated with meanings, explanations, feelings and judgements. So, the crime of breaking speed limits might be investigated from a realist standpoint, when researchers might be interested in capturing data about 'surface' features, such as who breaks which limits where, when and by how much, and from a non-realist position with an emphasis on subject-relative features, such as understanding *why* people break speed limits. These mid-range positions could be grouped together under the heading of pragmatism or of 'critical realism'. (Critical realism holds that reality exists *and* that our understanding of it is a social construct that is continually tested against the real: Bhaskar, 1986). These mid-range positions say that much can be taken at face value, although the more we move towards the bottom right corner of Figure 2.1 the less this is so and everything could be opened to scrutiny and re-interpretation. Yet, even if it is legitimate to appreciate ideas, feelings and behaviours in a constructionist or post-structural way, Lloyd (2000) reminds us that many people ask the 'What is the point?' question about the constructs and deconstructions of playful post-structuralists. They expect, for example, that researchers into cervical smear programmes should be able to advise a woman on whether to have a smear test or not. This suggests that an epistemology that might be appropriate when a researcher is trying to satisfy herself by better understanding a social system would be inappropriate if the audience and purpose were different.

Some of the ramifications of this distinction between realism and anti-realism and of the identification of pragmatic and critical stances in between them are captured in Table 2.1. With this table I want to suggest that research is not a straightforward activity because the assumptions that we make about what exists and how we might know about it affect the sorts of claims we are likely to make and can make, as well as the ways we are likely to try and represent what we have learned from the research. Of course, it would be possible to identify more than 16 sets of differences, or to collapse categories, or to rename the column headings, or to prefer five, nine or *n* columns. The table is important as an illustration of the ways in which different ontological and epistemological positions imply different research methods and favour different claimsmaking in different styles.

Row 15 needs more careful treatment. It suggests that realism commonly means using positivist or 'scientific' research methods, while researchers more interested in explanations, understanding meanings or exploring feelings will use far less structured methods which are variously referred to as qualitative, interpretive, *verstehen* (to do with understanding, especially empathic understanding), illuminative, ethnographic or hermeneutic (hermeneutic means to do with interpretation). The suggestion is repeated in Table 5.1. I do want to maintain that researchers with certain ontological and epistemological positions congregate around certain research methods, which is what Tables 2.1 and 5.1 indicate. *And* I want to insist that methods are not bonded to ontologies and

Table 2.1 *Three tendencies in research thinking and practice*

	Realism and positivism	Critical realism and pragmatism	Anti-realism and post-structuralism
1 Most commonly applied to	Nowadays dominant in natural science and in studies of 'objective' social phenomena. Formerly, all-pervasive	Studies of natural phenomena and the conventional ranges of human action and thought – for example, applied sciences, professions, social science, history and politics	Evident in much modern work on aesthetics and ethics, and all fields celebrating the subjectivity of human being, thought and experience
2 Ontology: what exists?	Strong form: there is a physical and social reality with corresponding scientific knowledge, aesthetic and ethical truths. Weaker form does not insist on aesthetic and/or moral truths	The physical world and social facts exist independently of the observer but they may be understood and experienced differently. Aesthetics and ethics are socially shaped, so it is hard to claim that there are any transcendent standards or truths	Strong form: what we take to exist is what our minds create. Weaker form: Our experience of even the physical world is so wrapped in socially shaped language that it is misleading to talk of 'reality'.
3 What may we know?	A correspondence view of knowledge: true knowledge corresponds to reality and reality can be known in the form of facts Facts and values are different and the search for fact must be value-free	Although truth may correspond to reality it is not possible to verify that: there are different perspectives on truth An alternative is the coherence view: a thing is true if it is consistent with other evidence – that from practice, for example	Sceptics doubt whether 'reality' exists. Knowledge is seen as something that is locally negotiated, reflecting perspectives, times and contexts. It cannot be value-free. In this sense knowledge is created in discourse – in language and action
4 How do we know?	Truth may be known through diligent inquiry using established methods. The more subtle realists are cautious about entirely endorsing this position for all types of knowledge. Peirce's pragmatism is close to this view of knowledge and truth; other forms of pragmatism are reluctant to see truth as a useful concept in *all* areas of knowledge	Truth is seen to be situated, changing and, for some, an illusion. Critical realists may incline to this position on aesthetic and moral issues. James' pragmatism saw truth as subjective to a greater or lesser degree. Dewey's pragmatism held that understanding comes from consideration of actions and their effects	

(Continued)

Table 2.1 (Continued)

	Realism and positivism	Critical realism and pragmatism	Anti-realism and post-structuralism
5 How secure is knowledge?	All knowledge is, in principle, open to being refuted, although it is *highly* improbable that established theories will be ...→	→ ... especially in the natural sciences. In other areas, such as history, the taken-for-granted is much more liable to displacement	With the grudging exception of much natural science knowledge, the position is that knowledge is a temporary, contexted, somewhat personal construct
6 To what degree do samples represent the whole? (see also Chapter 5)	Reality is homogeneous: samples of matter in one place will be identical to samples taken in the same way from another. Pragmatists and others taking a middle way incline to this position when dealing with natural science and with social sciences on a large scale	Realities are created by their participants and are, to a greater or lesser extent, local, complex, shifting and uneven. No two samples can be the same. Pragmatists, especially James, and others of a middling tendency incline to these positions in small-scale social science inquiries in the fields of aesthetics and ethics	
7 Is it possible to understand complex systems by studying their parts, one by one?	Through studies of parts in isolation a picture can be constructed of the operation of whole systems (reductionism and the control of variables)	When the aim is to understand social practices, then parts cannot be treated like atoms (but individual differences can be disregarded in large surveys). Small-scale researchers often recognize this by their preference for naturalistic inquiries of thinking and acting in real-life social contexts	Inquiry should not be about causes but should be a search for meaning and understanding. Reductionism and control of variables are inappropriate because systems have 'emergent properties' so that the whole is greater than the sum of its parts. Consequently, the whole can never be understood by a study of its parts
8 Causation	Physical causes and effects can be identified and the ways in which causes produce effects may be known. As far as human affairs are concerned, critical realist and pragmatist positions are more common. They tend to the view that some causes and effects may be identified through experimental methods (notably in psychology) and others may be more tentatively identified by correlational studies or by rational analysis (as in historical explanation)	Either causes and effects are in complex and dynamic relations that can only be approximately and tentatively described or classical notions of cause and effect are mistaken. The first position means that complex, near chaotic situations have unpredictable outcomes; the second that causes are created in narratives that are temporary after-the-event rationalizations of what has happened. Both views, especially the second, imply that knowing involves making webs of understanding and meaning, not about isolating 'causes'	

(Continued)

Table 2.1 (Continued)

	Realism and positivism	Critical realism and pragmatism	Anti-realism and post-structuralism
9 Generalization	Expectation that the researcher will generalize about the population from a study of samples	Methodological rigour is valued, although it is recognized that the ideals of positivist methodology cannot necessarily be achieved. The distinctive feature is that when researchers try to generalize or predict they are dependent on making the case that their view	Generalizing is a fundamental part of perception and sensemaking and is consolidated by language and shared social practices. Readers are inveterate generalizers. Researchers may offer generalizations for them to consider
10 Prediction	Generalizations, in the form of laws, for example, allow predictions to be made	is right because they cannot use the positivist manoeuvre of saying that they must be right because they rigorously used the right methods	Prediction is at variance with a complex, dynamic, uneven, subjective etc. world of free will, contingency and uncertainty
11 Reliability of inquiry methods (see also Chapter 5)	Reliable methods are a fundamental necessity The inquirer must be objective and not a participant	See above As far as possible, researchers and the methods they use should be unbiased but (1) humans can never be objective in the same way that a thermometer is objective; (2) such objectivity that can be attained is always objectivity *within* a culture, for it is almost impossible for researchers to shed their identities as people who have biographies and are in a time and a place	Quests for reliability and objectivity obstruct attempts to explore meanings and create understandings. The idea that researchers can be objective is ludicrous but descriptions should be honestly based on serious and reflexive inquiries. The notion of accuracy is misconceived in that it assumes a fundamental truth, which this position denies
12 Measurement accuracy or reliability (see also Chapter 5)	Importance of accurate description in the form of measurement		
13 Is knowledge cumulative?	Knowledge grows in a cumulative fashion. Pragmatists and critical realists would have no problem with this position in the natural sciences	In practice, post-structuralists would accept the cumulative achievements of natural science. Elsewhere, the idea of cumulative knowledge would generally be rejected because it assumes a growth towards one truth or reality	

(Continued)

Table 2.1 (Continued)

	Realism and positivism	Critical realism and pragmatism	Anti-realism and post-structuralism
14	Relationship of knowledge to action or practice (see also Chapter 9)	Knowledge is the goal. Practice is another matter. Opinion differs on how far knowledge ought to be useful and on the extent to which inquiry should be designed to have practical value		One position is Dewey's view that knowledge and action combine in praxis, that inquiry should involve action and action, inquiry. An alternative is that in so far as it is possible to separate action and inquiry, acting is more important than inquiring
15	Conventional data sources and inquiry methods (see also Chapters 3, 4 and 5)	Methods intended to capture verifiable regularities. Low-inference observation, using detailed schedules; survey interviews, including CATI (See Chapter 3) and web or e-mail surveys; highly structured questionnaires; experiments and field, natural or quasi-experiments; rating scales, tests and measures; Likert 'scales'; repertory grid technique, Nominal group Technique, concept mapping, q-sort and Thurstone scales; sociograms and distance scaling; IQ tests and other psychometric tests; physiological measurements. Social data frequently come from (paid) volunteers and captive groups (undergraduates). Also 'cold calling', as with intercept interviewing and mailshots.	Methods more sensitive to the individual and personal – meanings, beliefs, feelings etc. Small samples, even $n=1$, often acceptable. Tend to go for looser, higher-inference versions of positivist methods – natural and quasi-experiments, semi-structured or lightly structured questionnaires, interviews and observations. Positivist data sources widely copied but with less concern that data and interpretation are clear-cut and 'objective'. Other data sources include life stories and other narratives; role play and simulations; focus groups; action interviews and analysis of critical incidents; diaries, journals and portfolios; photos, pictures, and video; documents in general, including novels and journalism; analysis of secondary data; memory work; unobtrusive measures, 'post-empirical' approaches	Full participation in research situation and absorption of informants' perspectives and beliefs (as in some ethnographic work) is acceptable, even desirable. Emphasis on in-depth, naturalistic inquiries of specific cases, persons etc. Anything that can be imagined as a method is a method. Anything that can be imagined as data is data. Anything that can be inferred is an interpretation. Everything is contexted and changing. Everything can be deconstructed

(Continued)

Table 2.1 (Continued)

	Realism and positivism	Critical realism and pragmatism	Anti-realism and post-structuralism
16 Representations of knowledge (see also Chapter 9)	Results of inquiries presented in formal scientific terms to scientific community. Established formats should be followed. Obsession with dehumanized prose, passive voice and technical language. Statistics and charts valued	More flexibility of format – for example, research reports may be presented in lay language with executive summaries and action points. Human language may be permissible and writers are not bound to one reporting format	A crisis of representation that comes from the need to find ways of representing overlapping, interwoven, fragmentary and contradictory experiences. Although no medium (print, image or sound) or style is obviously better than any other, collage is intended to represent exactly this sort of complexity

epistemologies, or to any of the research forms described in the next section. For example, Machado et al. (2000) show that psychologists tend to define the discipline in positivist terms centring on the collection and manipulation of quantitative data. That does not mean that others are illegitimate, although the apparent incongruity of positivism and unconventional inquiry methods would have to be fully justified by a researcher using methods that lay outside the canon.

In other words, the claims researchers can most readily sustain are related to the epistemologies and ontologies on which their inquiries are based. Since the same phenomena can be studied from different ontological or epistemological positions, it follows that researchers should explain their choice of positions and explain how their positions lend themselves to making certain sorts of claims. Skilled researchers check that the claims they hope to make are fit for the purpose and audience, which means that they are mindful in their epistemological and ontological positionings. They also make sure that their choice of methods is conventional or carefully defended.

Six implications for small-scale research practice are:

1   Different ontologies and epistemologies imply a preference for different methods.
2   Different concerns – with the physical world, observing behaviour, understanding mental states, ethics, aesthetics – imply a preference for different methods.
3   Different methods imply being able to make different sorts of claims. Researchers can generalize from 'methodologically proper' surveys, while those doing case studies may invite readers to generalize (see below).
4   Different claims, concerns and methods will be differently received by different communities of practice. Psychologists would tend to sniff at deconstructive discourse analysis (see Box 4.9) and experimentation is widely seen as weird stuff by social work, probation, health and education practitioners (see Box 3.10).
5   Methods are not all easily compatible with each other. This is suggested by Table 2.1 and developed in Chapter 5.
6   Most researchers have mid-range, pragmatist views. Since they cannot operate, as natural scientists do, by saying that their claims are justified because they have followed approved methods, they are forced, as Searle said of philosophers, 'to fall back to even greater degrees of clarity, rigor and precision' combined with 'original, imaginative sensibility' (2000: 159).

Research Standpoints

Positivism, as Table 2.1 records, values objective inquiry but other positions take different standpoints. There are five basic possibilities here.

1   Objectivity is valued and should be sought.
2   It is valued but hard to achieve because of the complexity of the social
    world and because anything to do with observer-dependent pheno-
    mena, like feelings, meanings or judgements, is invariably tinged with
    subjectivity.
3   It is impossible to achieve either for the same practical reasons or, for
    some post-structuralists, because there is nothing but subjectivity.
4   Attempts to achieve it are damaging either because if investigators are
    really to learn about the world as it is to their informants then they need
    to build rapport with them as individuals, or because investigators and
    informants together create understandings of social phenomena.
5   The aim is to change the world through research – by deconstructing
    it or by trying to make it fairer. Objectivity is incompatible with this
    mission.

This section identifies two versions of this fifth standpoint, concentrating
on one in order to illustrate the distinctiveness of research that takes this
standpoint that research is not neutral but should change the world.
    The first version, critical theory,

> is critical in the sense that it stands apart from the prevailing order of the
> world and asks how that order came about … [It] does not take institutions
> and social and power relations for granted but calls them into question … It
> is directed towards the very framework for action … to the social and politi-
> cal complex as a whole rather than to the separate parts. (Cox, 1980: 130)

Researchers operating within critical theory tend to hold that the social
order in all its aspects perpetuates inequalities and that research should
identify and try to erode them. Although it is often associated with
Marxian analyses of economic inequalities and the way that capitalist
power relations are perpetuated at the expense of the labouring classes, it
can be extended to others, including those based upon gender, race and
sexual orientation. Robinson says that, 'The starting point of a critical project is the frustration or unhappiness of a group of people' (1996: 1071).
This leads to an analysis of their sufferings in terms of the conditions,
including self-understandings, that maintain it. A small-scale research
project might explore the conditions and ideologies that seem to sustain
this state. The researcher should anticipate 'debate about the accuracy of
the critical theorist's analysis' (1996: 1071) and recognize that 'the audience' is better understood as co-participants in the collective exploration
of a situation and its underpinnings. This 'is followed by a social action
phase, in which participants collaborate to redress the problem … action
and ideas are interdependent in the process of understanding and changing the world' (1996: 1071). The researcher is not alone and not neutral;
the research is not an event but a process in which a variety of understandings will be generated and survive; the outcomes are enlightenment
and action. And, according to Ozga, 'Working within a critical frame

places requirements on the researcher to pursue ethical research principles and to assess research activity in relation to what might broadly be termed social justice concerns' (2000: 46).

In some ways the second standpoint considered here, feminist research approaches, could be seen as a subset of critical theory but that would not do justice to what feminist researchers have achieved. The women who have documented inequalities and sustained attempts on many fronts to reduce them have made an enormous impact on the way social research is seen. This is often trivialized by talk of 'feminist research methods' as though there was one sort of feminism (there isn't: *feminisms* is more accurate) and as though feminists invented some magic inquiry method, which they didn't. Smith puts it like this: 'for postmodern feminists ... [there is] an emphasis on pluralism, complexity, difference and diversity. There is no one feminist account which can accommodate all the experiences of women. Attention should be directed towards the relationship between the sexist, racist, ethnocentric, classist and hetero-sexist discourses which are involved in the formation of gender identities' (1998: 318). My story is that feminist researchers have done something far more important than developing 'feminist research methods' by showing that it could be legitimate – even necessary – to take established methods of inquiry, such as interviews and observation, and use them subjectively for a higher moral purpose; to alleviate and ultimately eradicate the 'otherness' of woman by exposing the workings of patriarchy and the part that 'malestream' social science plays in perpetuating it.

Before describing feminisms in more depth I want to anticipate the objection that this makes it acceptable for any other group, fascists for example, to do research designed to further their own interests. Research then becomes propaganda. There seem to be three ways of responding to that. One is to say that researchers who take up the fifth standpoint need to sustain the claim that they are serving a *moral* purpose. The second follows from that, namely that the standpoint must be set clearly before the audience who should understand that it has informed the whole project. Thirdly, having a moral purpose does not excuse investigators from doing honest work, a theme that is taken up in Chapter 5.

The first feminist social scientists described and attacked the marginalization of women in social practice and the indifference of most psycho-sociological theorizing to important elements of women's lives. They wanted to make sure women's voices were heard, believing that articulating the experiences of women was central to bringing about social change and emancipating women from their condition of subordination. In this way research would contribute to psycho-social knowledge and theory building but share with critical theory and action research the aim of making a difference. Obviously, realist research assumptions were incompatible with these projects and were harassed with such vigour that in many communities of practice there is a subliminal belief that positivism has *no* place in social research. For example, Oakley (1981) argued that attempts to achieve 'objective' interviews controlled by the investigator dehumanized the interview situation, and unethically disempowered exploited informants. Her alternative was interviewing characterized by notions of collaboration, egalitarianism, commitment and even friendship between researchers and informants. Not all feminist researchers see the relevance of such principles to all research purposes, nor is there unanimity on how to implement them where they are considered desirable. And feminist researchers do not have a monopoly on them. However, it would be hard to deny that this research standpoint has become far more widely adopted as a result of the efforts of feminist researchers.

When applied to research based upon in-depth, lightly structured interviews, Arksey and Knight (1999: 12) considered that this standpoint implied some or all of:

- high levels of trust and confidence
- continual attention to ethical issues
- reciprocity: sharing knowledge and experiences, responding to questions, giving support
- equity: the researcher not attempting to exert control
- greater personal involvement on the part of the researcher, including self-disclosure so that the interviewee is familiar with her background and interests
- a more active role by the interviewee
- inviting feedback on interview transcripts and the subsequent data analysis
- that interviewers should be women of similar standing in a culture to the informants (Riessman, 1987).

In a widely cited book, Lather said that, 'Very simply, to do feminist research is to put the social construction of gender at the centre of our inquiry ... [to acknowledge] the centrality of gender in the shaping of our consciousness, skills and interactions as well as in the distribution of power and privilege' (1991: 75). So, 'women's studies are counter-hegemonic work' (1991: 71). For her the implication was that feminists should be committed to action for change and be committed to inquiry – to praxis (inquiry-and-action). Not all feminists would subscribe to that account and others might be happier with it with respect to some inquiries than others. That said, the appeal of feminist research approaches clearly indicates that subjective stances in social research are acceptable in some communities of practice when the investigators are open about their standpoint and can argue that their work has been honestly done. In other communities, the idea of objective social inquiries is plain laughable and in others still it is a shibboleth.

Research Forms

The argument so far has been that the claims to significance are related to the metaphysical position that is appropriate to the study, with all that means for methods of inquiry. Secondly, claims are also affected by any research standpoint, such as a commitment to critical theory. Thirdly, and the subject of this section, the form the research takes affects the sorts of claims it is easiest to sustain.

By research form I mean an established approach to inquiry that does not dictate that any particular methods will be used, or presume a standpoint, but does nevertheless influence what gets done and how. For example, a longitudinal study involves keeping an investigation going long enough to identify changes and continuities. Large-scale examples are the studies that most nations sponsor to follow through a cohort of citizens born in, say, 1950 or 2000 and see how their health and social lives develop. Any research methods fit for the purpose can be used within this form. Small-scale longitudinal studies are not common because (1) with the possible exception of PhD students, especially part-time ones, people doing studies as part of degree courses are operating within timescales that are too short; (2) researchers have tended to use longitudinal studies to make generalizations to the population, which implies larger sample sizes than small-scale researchers can afford; and (3) the cost of repeated observation, interviewing or whatever also puts them beyond the reach of small-scale researchers. Yet, ethnographers working on a fairly small scale do manage to be immersed in a research site for over a year (note that their repeated observations are to help them understand a setting better, where longitudinal research looks for change). That is long enough for a short longitudinal study, and I was able to run a small two-year study as part of my doctoral research. Bryant (1986) makes a case for longitudinal studies as more naturalistic and authentic ways of looking at change than the cross-sectional methods that researchers have relied upon, identifying changes by comparing the results from separate samples of, say, children aged 6, 8, 10, 12 and so on.

The three forms mentioned here – action research, evaluations and case studies – are commonly used by small-scale researchers. Any of them could be a part of a larger inquiry or could stand alone. Table 2.2 lists some key features.

Action Research

Action research which is often participant (see also Chapter 7), is usually small scale and is always geared to making a difference. It can hardly be called 'objective' and it is often a passionate matter for the researcher, who may bring to it considerable commitment, energy and spikiness. It has considerable promise as a way of making a contribution to social science knowledge because it is rooted in deep involvement with real problem situations and 'is likely to produce insights which cannot be gleaned in

Table 2.2 *Some characteristics of three research forms*

	Action research	Case study research	Evaluation research
Audience concerns often play a large part in study's design	Aim is to affect practice, so fellow practitioners' voices important	Depends. No reason why they should – or should not	Audience dictates what is done. Researcher must be independent in all other ways
Sampling issues are important – the research can be seriously compromised by sampling deficiencies	Samples must, of course, be fit for the purpose. The choice of method (focus groups, telephone interviewing, observations) will largely determine how sampling should be done (see Chapter 5) Note: the choice of method will itself have to be justified and shown to be fit for the purpose		
Main aim is to make a difference to practice in the research site	√	?	?
Positivist epistemology not likely to be prominent – multiple perspectives likely to emerge	√	√	√
Quantitative data likely to be collected	Each of these three approaches is enriched by counting and numerical data. The difference lies in the claims that are made about the meaning of the figures (see Chapter 8)		
Often involves participant researchers	√	√	?
Researchers are likely to indicate points for readers to consider and less likely to make generalizations	√	√	?

any other way' (Eden and Huxham, 1996: 536). Partly to ensure that researchers are as deeply involved as possible and partly on ethical grounds, Heron (1996) argues that if the researchers are outsiders, then it should be co-operative inquiry, an equal partnership between researchers and practitioners (who he calls co-researchers). While many feminist researchers would agree, others would say that researchers have expertise and priorities that make true, equal collaboration elusive.

Action research (AR) is usually described as a cycle through stages such as those shown in Figure 2.2, although it would be better to speak of an action research *spiral*.

Levin and Greenwood say that

> AR is not applied research. AR explicitly rejects the separation between thought and action that underlies the pure–applied distinction … valid social knowledge is derived from practical reasoning engaged in through action. As action researchers, we believe that action is the only sensible way to promote and test new knowledge. (1998: 6)

This implies that AR can be seen as praxis, the inseparable interplay of practice and theory. However, the praxis often becomes unbalanced

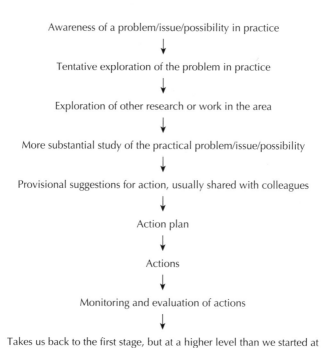

Awareness of a problem/issue/possibility in practice

↓

Tentative exploration of the problem in practice

↓

Exploration of other research or work in the area

↓

More substantial study of the practical problem/issue/possibility

↓

Provisional suggestions for action, usually shared with colleagues

↓

Action plan

↓

Actions

↓

Monitoring and evaluation of actions

↓

Takes us back to the first stage, but at a higher level than we started at

Figure 2.2   *Typical stages in action research inquiries*

because there can be so much emphasis on the 'here-and-now' of the problem/issue/possibility that insights from the general literature and other research get missed at the design stage. As a result action researchers may needlessly reinvent the wheel and end up with too much action and not enough research, although some, such as Elliott, think that 'the fundamental aim of action research is to improve practice rather than to produce theory' (1991: 49). One result is that action researchers frequently have difficulty publishing in academic journals because general audiences are likely to be indifferent to a report of the impact of an awareness-raising collective on glue-sniffing in Byker, Newcastle. What seems to happen is that the special, contexted nature of trying to make a difference to practice overshadows thinking about how generalizations might come from it. Sometimes this is almost inevitable if researchers move from project to project, contract to contract, and get little time to write a report to their sponsors and none to consider how to connect the specifics to the general. But, Checkland and Holwell (1998) suggest that action researchers are not always sufficiently thoughtful, before acting, about their framework of ideas and the research themes associated with it. Failing to 'think general' from the start, they compromise not only the practical impact of their work (because their actions are dimly illuminated by relevant theories, findings and suggestions) but also its potential contribution to valid understandings of social phenomena. Checkland's soft systems methodology (SSM), on the other hand, works by comparing a model of how systems might operate with evidence about how given systems do operate. The aim is to learn from comparison, not to presume that either practice or theory is superior. Notice, though, that SSM researchers have, from the start, to bring the general (theories, concepts, literature reviews) into their work on the specific.

There is also a fear that action researchers, like evaluation and case study researchers, can be captured by the specifics of what they are analysing and fail to appraise the ideologies and taken-for-granteds that saturate the situation. The fear is that AR, evaluations and case study too can be rather conservative and concerned with improving situations which would be better exposed to critical appraisal and opened out for fundamental change. The concern is worth noting and it is important to say that Levin and Greenwood are not the only action researchers who would protest that it is appropriate to use AR within critical theory and to intend to make deep, not cosmetic changes.

Books on action research tend to be keen to justify AR generally and the authors' versions in particular. I prefer Checkland and Scholes' (1990) account of SSM in action-focused inquiries because it presents a powerful and flexible model that integrates thinking, inquiring and acting and which has been extensively used to improve the way that messy human systems and complex organizations operate.

Evaluations

Evaluation studies are concerned with the quality of something, which means that they usually have a definite audience that wants to know how good an innovation, practice or organization is. In practice the audience has a great effect on how the inquiry is done by identifying the main question, setting the budget and timescale, and explaining whether they want a quick-and-dirty judgement to feed into decision-making or a fine-grained and 'objective' assessment that can be used to compare one place or practice with others. If these sponsors say that there are factors at work that are outside their control then it makes sense to concentrate the inquiries on variables that they can influence.

Evaluations tend to be designed to help decision-making, which means that there is a sense in which good evaluations are ones that make it more likely that good decisions will get made. There is an obvious danger here that evaluators can become partisans, too ready to see things through the eyes of the decision-makers who commissioned the research. Informants can be few and reticent because they fear that the evaluators are management spies or in some other ways prejudicial to their best interests (Scott and Usher, 2000). Evaluators who are aware of this danger are more able to resist the pressures to compromise their neutrality and it helps if there is a set of evaluation principles that have been agreed with the sponsors and which can be shown to everyone who the evaluators speak to. An extract from an evaluation agreement is in Box 2.3.

Box 2.3 Extract from an evaluation agreement: principles guiding the Townside High School evaluation

1   Everything about Townside High School that the evaluator sees, hears or reads is treated as confidential in that it will not be attributed to any person without prior permission and reasonable attempts will be made to prevent the identity being deduced of any informant who wishes to remain anonymous.
2   The evaluator will not identify Townside High School or any member of it in any reference to this evaluation in any of his other professional activities.
3   Drafts of the evaluation report will be made available to stakeholders and the evaluator will correct any errors of fact that are identified at that point.
4   The report will be the property of Learning Support Centre (LSC) staff and school managers to do with as they wish. The evaluator may refer to this work in his other professional activities, subject to points 1 and 2 above.

Like action research there is the problem of praxis, which is when evaluators fail to identify in advance the general themes that can be explored by the evaluation and, for whatever reasons, pay insufficient attention to generalizing their findings. I admire Patton's (1997) book, which is a good introduction to qualitative inquiries.

Case Study

This is a study of one of something – an event, an organizational unit, a person, a site or whatever. A common difficulty is defining the boundaries of the case. This is seldom simple. Indeed, soft systems thinking (Checkland and Scholes, 1990) says that the boundaries we choose to draw round a problem – the way we conceptualize and define it – are fundamental to the findings we create. Change the bounds of the case and you are likely to be changing the research findings. There are, then, no real rules for setting the limits to a case study. The best advice is to follow the principles for doing persuasive research and explain to readers why the boundaries you set make good sense.

Advantages of case studies are that they:

1   do tend to be small-scale works
2   are not artificial like experiments and surveys
3   encourage investigators to work in depth, to really go beyond superficial research approaches
4   compel researchers to look for meaning and try to construct understandings, to learn what is really going on

5   should remind inquirers of the complexity and variability of the social
     world
6   can therefore be powerful antidotes to determinism and over-
     generalization
7   tend to be very *human* – very person centred.

Ethnographers, who closely and empathically study cultures and sub-
cultures to understand, for example, prison life, the police canteens and
working-class adolescent experiences, are great users of case studies,
although Schratz and Walker observe that, 'Ethnography ... may appear
as a one word justification for copious atheoretical description' (1995: 75).
They extend their criticisms to case study research in general, saying
that they often yield 'Slabs of lightly-edited transcript which are
organized into ad hoc categories ... [with] little questioning or demon-
strated understanding of the problem of making it mean something ...
all ground and no theory' (1995: 168). Their intention was not to
attack either ethnography or case studies but to warn that there is more
to each of them than collecting lots of data: what matters is how
information is used.
   The power of case study can be illustrated by an example, in this
instance Boyle and Woods' (1996) study of one primary headteacher.
Most researchers into schoolteachers' work and schools as organizations
had suggested that increasing and increasingly complex workloads, the
growth of managerialism and an emphasis on bureaucratic tasks had
transformed primary headteachers' roles and marginalized the caring
and educational priorities that used to characterize the job. The study of
a single headteacher, Chris, showed that these generalizations were too
sweeping. This is an example of generalizing from one case to others.
Boyle and Woods extended it to criticize theories that say that changes
to social structures determine people's behaviour. They invoked social
interactionist theory to argue that people have choices in the ways in
which they respond to structural changes. Here the case study was
being generalized to overarching social theories about the structure–
agency relationship. It is also possible to do several case studies on a
topic and then use the process of analytical generalization (Firestone,
1993) to test theories more strenuously. For example, the study of educational markets in three areas, which centred on case studies of 12 schools,
provided a very powerful test of existing theories about the effects of
what the authors called 'public markets' on educational practices and
has generated new theories (Woods et al., 1998). Smyth and colleagues
(2000) are working towards a view of school effectiveness by analytical generalization from linked case studies, each done by a PhD
student. Stake (1995) has produced an accessible guide to case study
inquiries and Gillham (2000a) has written a shorter, simpler one for
complete beginners.

Generalizing and Learning from Research

It is often assumed that rigorous use of proven research methods on substantial samples provides knowledge that is representative of the population at large. If research meets these technical requirements, then rational readers should conclude that it really has identified something about the wider world. No thought is needed: the positivist researcher can claim that the findings are generalizable from the sample to the population and readers should accept it unless methodological flaws can be identified. It is sometimes said that the work has high external validity, although I prefer to talk about generalizability.

This positivist approach has dominated research in the natural sciences and has been very effective. It is still a powerful approach where certain assumptions can be made about the things under investigation. One is that subjects of inquiry are homogeneous, much as one atom of iridium is the same as another, so it does not matter that *these* iridium atoms are being studied rather than *those*. Social science researchers cannot assume that people are identical on any dimension, whether it is height, religious beliefs, extroversion or whatever. However, positivist social research projects assume that a sufficiently large sample, which has been appropriately selected (see Chapter 5), will be a good representation of the range of diversity in the population, and that for their purposes it does not matter whether Theodora Ahmed, Wayne Grits, Jane Doe or Jean-Luc Poirot appear in the sample or not. The assumption is that good sampling methods cover the range in the population and that, from that point of view, one person is substitutable for another. No-one's individuality matters and one person's free will actions cancel out another's.

The second assumption is that what is studied is either stable or changes in predictable ways. The substance H_2O has known and predictable chemical and physical characteristics, which means that researchers can know the range of circumstances to which findings can be generalized. Although much social research makes assumptions that phenomena are stable or predictable, this is not necessarily true. Take attitudes, for example. The attitudes that people report tend to be context- and topic-specific and to change over time. I may be a generous person but not to this beggar today, or not to beggars in general, although I may contribute to charities that work with homeless people. Ten years ago, when beggars were fewer, my attitudes might have been different.

Thirdly, there is the problem of artificiality. Positivist researchers try to isolate variables by manipulating and controlling the research situation. This control of variables is characteristic of experiments in which one thing only is varied and the effects are observed. But in social research this can require some rather artificial situations and it always means looking at some aspects of people, their thinking and acting, in isolation. Researchers may then generalize findings and say that they are confident that what they have found does describe the population. One problem is that the population is not normally placed in artificial and experimental situations, so there are difficulties about generalizing to normal circumstances. The difficulty of applying generalizations from positivist social science are still more complex. Suppose that a substantial study has found that most of those in public service professions (midwifery, social work, policing etc.) are mainly motivated by the psychic rewards of the work – by the enjoyment of successful interpersonal work. It may be likely that any one public service professional will be motivated by these intrinsic, psychic rewards than by extrinsic ones, such as pay, but we cannot be certain. Again, a medicine may have side effects in only 1% of the adult male population, but how to know whether this man will be one of them? Put this way, the problem is not so much generalizing from well-designed studies to populations as 'un-generalizing' from the studies to individuals and cases. Secure research methods may allow secure claims that the findings are true for the population but they are of little help in knowing whether the findings are true, in any sense, for an individual in a context.

So, it is quite reasonable to accept that positivist research can produce inductive generalizations about some aspects of human life that have authority derived from the methodological rigour of the investigations. Notice, though, that readers or consumers of the research are still left with substantial problems in knowing how to use it, how to apply the generalized claims to any situation. They have to make inferences about what the findings mean, to make their own sense of the general claims. In other words, there is generalization to the population (which positivist researchers do) and then inference from the generalization (which is the sensemaking that readers do). Both generalizations are about attributing meanings to the findings. In positivist research the investigators indicate what the findings mean about the social world in general and readers deduce implications for their own understandings and practices.

Table 2.1 summarized alternatives to positivism: for example the view that reality is created in language (Rorty), that meanings are elusive and ever-changeable (Derrida), and that understandings are created with the capillary action of power (Foucault). Theirs is a universe of contingency (things are the product of specific chains of circumstances which may – or may not – recur), complexity (see Chapter 6), subjectivity and simultaneous multiple meanings. Truth is created locally, negotiated and shared (to a greater or lesser degree), and the search for causes is answered by narratives that tell stories about what happened. History, with its emphasis on the particular, displaces science, with its emphasis on the general. But where do these metaphysics leave the idea of generalization? In the mind of readers who make their own sense of the researcher's narrative. The process is much the same as making inferences from statements about a population to an individual, although here it is inference from the researcher's story to the reader's existing understandings. This sensemaking is an act of generalizing: the reader gives the text meaning by connecting it to existing understandings (which is necessary even if the researcher's story is rejected because it will be rejected on the grounds that it is a bad fit with what the reader already knows, believes or feels). This connecting is an evaluative process, not a passive one and, as such, it includes making some appraisal of the significance of the new information and ideas in the text.

It might be objected that this does not really say much about how readers judge whether a narrative which they take to be true should be regarded as true for some, many or all similar cases. This is a real issue for qualitative small-scale research where intense study frequently creates understandings of one site or event, or of a few informants' world views. One answer is to say that this is no concern of the researcher because, regardless of assumptions that are often made about the authority of the text, it is really the reader who creates meaning and significance and so it is pointless – and perhaps duplicitous – for the researcher to have anything to do with how readers generalize from research narratives. An alternative response that lays two duties on researchers may be more palatable. Researchers can help readers to judge how applicable the narrative might be to other situations by providing enough information (1) to reassure readers that there is no sleight of hand about the text and that it is the outcome of an honest, systematic and thorough inquiry (see also Chapter 5) and (2) to allow readers to get a fair picture of exactly what is being reported so that they have a rich or thick description and are not forced to try and make sense of morsels of information. Researchers can help readers to generalize by providing full descriptions of methods and the research setting and by being considerate of the readers. They usually have expertise and understandings of the topic of research which are more advanced than readers', so they have a duty to indicate how their findings might be more widely applicable, either to other cases or to theory. Notice that this is about offering readers an interpretation and, in all honesty, researchers should say that it is an interpretation and the reasons for treating it as a plausible interpretation should be clearly set out.

Generalization from social research is at the heart of growing government interest in evidence-based policy and practice. The idea is that thorough reviews of all the relevant social research literature identify best practice which is then codified as guidelines or benchmarks that apply to all schools, hospitals, young offenders' prisons, nursing homes for the aged etc. This is sophisticated generalization from many, sometimes hundreds of research studies and, as with positivist research studies, the underlying assumption is that the general claims that come from the reviews should be accepted because expert reviewers have scrupulously used trustworthy methods to reach their conclusions. The technique of meta-analysis, which is more fully explained in Chapter 4, is a mainstay of generalizing from many research studies and, although it was designed as a way of aggregating the findings of quantitative inquiries, Light and Pillemer (1982) suggest ways of combining qualitative and quantitative data. I also said earlier that it is possible to generalize from case study research, so it is a pity that most meta-analyses routinely discard the majority of research reports that they find because the reports are not positivist studies that meet design and reporting standards that are quite alien to non-positivist research traditions. The relationship between generalization, benchmarking and social policy is elaborated in Chapter 9.

This account has argued that generalizability is about readers making sense of research reports. Figure 2.3 illustrates this claim that the main difference between generalizing from quantitative and positivist research and generalizing from qualitative and small-scale studies is that there are conventions that allow quantitative researchers to say how reasonable it is to generalize their findings to larger groups. Others cannot do the same, but (1) readers will generalize as they make sense of the research reports anyway, (2) researchers can be considerate and provide a rich enough account to help readers make their own inferences about generalizability, and (3) researchers may also invite readers to share their interpretation of the generalizability of their findings to other cases and/or to theory. Notice that points (2) and (3) make hermeneutic, *verstehen*, interpretive or qualitative research much more demanding for the researcher than quantitative, positivist research with its 'generalizing by numbers' conventions (which are perfectly fit for *its* purposes). This account of generalization is continued in Chapter 5 when sampling issues are explored and briefly resumed in Chapter 6.

A Pragmatist Account of Social Research

Social research has many concerns, which are indicated by this list contrived around the mnemonic of the five vowels:

- Action: how can inquiry improve social practices?
- Evaluation: how good is social practice or theory?
- Is: description of the way things are, appear to be or are said to be.
- Ought: the world of the critical, asking why things are as they are and who benefits, as well as exploring ways of improving things as they stand.
- Understanding: which includes interpretations and explanations of why things are as they are, why people think and act as they do, and so on.

One implication is that it is idle to look for any one set of rules for doing social research. It is more a matter of pragmatics, which means judging which methods seem to have the best chance of being fit for the purpose of making sense of the topic to be studied in ways that are fit for the research purpose or concern. Of course, there are binding rules for some purposes and some forms of inquiry and all researchers are expected to maintain standards of honesty, diligence and mindfulness, as described in

	Research purpose	Sampling strategy and generalization
Researcher makes claims about generalizability: the text is authoritative	Quest for findings that will be trustworthy as a representation of the situation for the whole study population Assumptions of a stable world that can be reliably captured through well-conceived research	Random sample. Size as large as possible. See Oppenheim (1992), for example, for advice on sample size. Researcher makes strong claims about the generalizability of the findings Structured sample. Used where there is a danger that random sampling might lead to key groups being unrepresented. The larger the sample, the greater the confidence when generalizing from it, although some say that structured sampling is not as powerful a basis for generalization as is random sampling 'Opportunity sampling' is when it's not possible to control sampling. Researchers are on shaky ground if they try to claim the findings are generalizable, although their samples are likely to be large enough for their claims to be more seductive than those of interpretive researchers with smaller samples
	Mixed purposes – as above *plus* a wish to understand better people's reasoning, feelings, motives etc.	If the survey is the most important element, the principles above apply. If the exploration is the most important, refer to those below. Note that this may involve a radical mixing of paradigms, which is discussed in Chapter 6
	(1) to narrate or describe events, practices, cultures etc.	Research methods typically used for these purposes preclude small-scale researchers from using large samples. Besides, the emphasis on the contexted and situated nature of knowing, feeling and doing implies that there are limits to how far researchers *could* generalize, even if they had large samples to work with
	(2) interpretive purposes – to try and understand meanings, feelings, reasons for behaviour, beliefs etc. In neither case need researchers assume stable reality that can be validly (or reliably) represented	Tendency to use opportunity sampling, look for good informants and increase sample size by snowballing. Where resources allow, researchers continue to add to the sample until they stop hearing anything new They also aim to hear stories and accounts from different perspectives, so they seek out people who may have a different slant on what happened, how things are etc.
	Evaluations and action research	Investigators do not make it a priority to generalize from the case in hand. When they do so, they incline to the approach sketched below
	Exploratory – getting into a field	Methods and sampling can be eclectic, so the researcher might suggest that readers draw their own conclusions and lessons. The findings are context-dependent but that is no reason to assume they have no meaning: sensemaking is taken as a form of generalization
Reader makes inferences about generalizability: the text is to be interpreted	Looking for counter-examples	A sample of one person, case or event is enough to show that some research generalizations can be too sweeping. In as much as they make sense of them, readers are generalizing from case studies and other microstudies, whether they are aware of doing so or not

Figure 2.3   *Research methods and generalizations (after Arksey and Knight, 1999)*

Chapter 5. This pragmatist position means that all researchers have to make claims about why their inquiries should be trusted and about their preferred interpretations of what they have found. That can seldom be done by following rules and usually depends upon sensemaking and claimsmaking, both of which can be understood as pragmatic activities. An implication of this chapter is that research questions are not only developed by the thinking and writing processes described in Chapter 1 because they should also reflect a considered view of these superordinate questions about metaphysics, standpoints, forms and concerns.

But if all social research is, in that sense, pragmatic research, small-scale research is super-pragmatic. Well-funded research teams can make sure that what they do is very close to their research design because they have money, staff, expertise, time and, sometimes, prestige enough to be able to get a match between intention and execution by brute force. Small-scale researchers are vulnerable and exposed and become used to finding themselves having to make the best out of situations which compromise the research design. It is not at all unknown for the whole design to collapse in the face of recalcitrant reality. Chapter 7 develops the theme that small-scale researchers need pragmatic adaptability and Chapters 3 and 4 survey commonly used research methods.

3

Face-to-Face Inquiry Methods

The humanistic psychologist Abraham Maslow said something on the lines of, 'Give a boy a hammer and everything's a nail.' Here I take it to mean that researchers who only know a couple of methods will use them indiscriminately and inappropriately. This chapter and the next draw attention to alternatives to the questionnaire lump hammer and the interview claw hammer. They also indicate some of the things that each main inquiry method is good for, as well as those for which they are as appropriate as a hammer is for putting in screws.

The greater part of this chapter is about face-to-face methods. Chapter 4 covers other methods. This distinction is rather artificial because some methods – experiments, for example – could go in either chapter. However, it is not a pointless one because the research medium – face-to-face or paper-based – tends to make a difference to the inquiry process: sometimes a profound difference. Obviously, in face-to-face work the researcher can have quite an effect on participants. This has been seen as a source of contamination and researchers whose work mimics the principles of natural science inquiry will try to eradicate researcher effects. There is a considerable literature on these effects, explaining how participants have reacted differently to male or female, older or younger, posh or plain, same race or other race researchers. People working within this tradition are also alert to the ways in which small deviations from the standard interview schedule or rules of procedure can introduce sources of variation that compromise the reliability of the findings. Boxes 3.9 and 3.10 show some of the ways in which these researchers will try to design all human variations out of the procedures, using standardized voice recordings at pre-set volume levels so that there can be no question of some of the sounds being at a different volume, pitch or pace. This is an approach that treats the variations that can come from face-to-face interaction as threats to scientific rigour. Good science kills all known threats, fast.

There is an alternative view that has been particularly, but not solely, associated with feminist inquiry. This is the view that good research depends upon researcher and participants developing trust and empathy, which are necessary if participants are to speak freely and, perhaps, to work with the researcher to tease out fresh understanding and bring some embodied or embedded things into words. Here researchers are valued for their subjectivity. Where those taking a natural science stance on face-to-face research want to know how the researcher could contaminate the inquiry (and how to disinfect them), those anxious to understand participants' subjective worlds want to know how researchers can best become accepted by them. Rather than compelling interviewers, for example, to stick to the script, researchers in this tradition value interviewers who can improvise well, who have an ear for what participants imply, not just for what they say, and who will improvise prompts or questions to add meaning to those implications. In one research tradition, face-to-face contact may be necessary but may taint the work, while in the other the researcher *is* the main research instrument and the inquiry would be stunted if it were not possible to do subjective, human, face-to-face work.

So, whatever the approach, face-to-face inquiries force researchers to think about the role and effect of the researcher to a much greater degree than with inquiries at a distance. A second reason for making this fuzzy distinction between face-to-face inquiries and those at a distance is that researchers can improvise in face-to-face work. Now, the preceding paragraphs have made it quite clear that for many researchers, improvisation is a sin and flexibility a curse. For others, though, face-to-face work offers the chance to change the direction of a whole inquiry to accommodate new insights, comments made by participants, prompts or patter that turn out to work well. They can also jettison things that aren't working. A researcher who is dependent on a questionnaire and realizes that it is not being completed as expected (and let's assume that this researcher was scrupulous enough to have piloted it, so this is not the result of carelessness) is stuck with hundreds of useless answers. A face-to-face interviewer can change the question. At worst, someone working within a natural science approach would have to start again. The point is that once the flaw has been spotted, change can be made. With research at a distance, the researcher watches helplessly as the enquiry keeps heading on to the rocks.

Some methods, notably interviews, can follow natural science practice and make the interviewer not just a voice reading a script, *and* they can be a warmly intersubjective means of exploring human experience. A case could be made for putting interviews and some other methods as well in this chapter or the next because the distinction between face-to-face and at-a-distance methods may be convenient but it is also irredeemably fuzzy.

No book can give exhaustive advice on any one technique, although it can help investigators to decide which are fit for the purpose of trying to answer a given research question. I have tried to do this by offering a summary of what each method involves, along with an outline of problems that may be encountered and benefits that can be had. In many cases this is illustrated with examples from the recent research literature, which are contained in the boxes.

Instrument Structure and Question Formation

Fixed-Response Questions and Highly Structured Instruments

This section explores a fundamental issue in the design of research instruments (questionnaires, interview schedules, Likert scales are all research instruments): whether an instrument is highly structured and contains fixed-response items or is lightly structured and open-ended. For example, questionnaires, interviews and observations can all be more or less structured. Take interviews. One structural dimension would be the degree to which the interviewer is required to follow a script and ask questions exactly in the set sequence. The second dimension concerns the way in which individual questions are asked. In a highly structured interview the questions would all be fixed-response questions; the sequence of questions, along with the opening 'patter' and the 'thank you' at the end, would all be prescribed; and the interviewer would be *required* to follow the script exactly. In a highly structured observation, the investigator would be following a script that said who she was to observe, when and for how long. She would probably complete an observation grid by ticking only the categories on it that applied at each observation point. A highly structured questionnaire would rely on fixed response items such as:

How many cigarettes did you smoke yesterday?
None   1–5   6–10   11–15   16–20   21–30   more than 30

It is very important to appreciate what is going on when a technique is used in a highly structured form. The payoff is that the researcher gets clear, unambiguous, easy-to-process and easy-to-analyse data, as Chapter 8 explains. Even a small-scale study can collect large amounts of highly structured data because they are cheap to get and cheap to handle. Some people see another advantage, namely that the data can then be run through statistical analysis software and some very impressive charts, tables and probability figures can be produced, making the whole study seem scientific, respectable and important. But highly structured inquiries muffle informants and turn them into respondents. (Replies to open-ended questions inform the researcher, but replies to closed or fixed-response questions are just responses; consequently we distinguish between informants [open-ended questions] and respondents [fixed-response questions].) In the case of highly structured interviews, the respondents only get to talk about the things that the researcher thinks are important and there is no scope for them to talk about other things that may be far more significant for them. This an inescapable feature of highly structured inquiries: they reflect the researcher's theory of what matters. If that theory is based on a good literature review and upon serious, open-ended pilot research, then highly structured inquiries may be fit for the research purpose. The big problem is where highly structured observations, for example, are based on a common-sense view of what is important. For example, early classroom observation schedules were easy to use because they had just 10 categories with which to code all observations. They were also problematic because most of the categories concerned teacher behaviour and assumed whole-class teaching: the naïve educational theory was that what mattered in the classroom was what the teacher was doing and that this would be some form of didactic performance. Later, highly structured schedules assumed that what learners did was significant, that learning could happen when the teacher was not addressing the learner, that learners could learn in many ways and might learn in groups, and that the teachers' actions *and* words were also important (Galton et al., 1980). They were also much harder to use, which meant that it was harder to assume that all observers were using them in the same ways.

Not only do highly structured instruments lock respondents into the researcher's theory of what matters, but the fixed-response questions reduce their ability to convey the complexity of their experience, perceptions or feelings. The question 'Do you feel angry when you see beggars in the street? Yes/No' can only get a response shorn of the complexity of emotional reactions to different people begging in different places at different times. There are limits to how far fixed-response questions can be extended to record something of that complexity. Partly the limits come from the difficulty of anticipating all possible variations of response, but that can be substantially overcome by good, lightly structured pilot work and a good literature review. The main limitation, though, is that the interview script, questionnaire or observation schedule quickly becomes so long that it is unusable.

Lightly Structured Inquiry Methods, Receptive and Spontaneous Understanding

Needless to say, there are problems with lightly structured approaches, although they let us hear about or see the world without gazing through the peephole of theory with spectacles that are only sensitive to a narrow spectrum of data. (Some people refer to 'unstructured' approaches, although there is a sense in which all inquiries must have some structure: Hammersley and Atkinson, 1995). But lightly structured instruments produce data that are much harder to handle (see Chapter 8) This is related to a distinction between receptive and spontaneous understanding. Consider interviews. Highly structured interviews tap into people's receptive understanding, whereas open-ended questions and free-flowing inquiries discover what is on people's minds at the time (spontaneous understanding). I often find that if teachers are asked, 'What are the characteristics of an effective teacher?', they will typically describe four or five behaviours but forget to say that an effective teacher is one in whose classes children learn. However, if they are directly asked about this by a fixed-response question that taps receptive understanding, they all agree that it is not just a characteristic of an effective teacher but one of the most important. Open-ended questions, then, tend to get incomplete responses. If they are used in lightly structured interviews – ones in which the interviewer follows the direction taken by the informants – then it is also unlikely that any two informants will have been asked the same set of questions, simply because the interviews will have grown in different ways. So, not only is it hard to make sense of sets of lightly structured interviews (because each is different), it is also hard to be confident that they have given a full picture (because they record what was at the front of informants' minds.)

Box 3.1 The safety of Prozac (From The *Guardian*, 30 October 1999)

A study compared the suicide rates of people on 10 different anti-depressants, and found that far more killed themselves on Prozac than on other drugs. It found that there were 187 suicides per 100,000 depressed patients per year on Prozac. Lilly [the drug manufacturers] argues, however, that suicide rates among people with depression run at about 6000 per 100,000. But those figures apply only to hospital patients with acute depression. Among the depressed population in the community, the published studies show that the suicide rate is only around 30 per 100,000. That implies that of every 100,000 people prescribed Prozac *by their* GP 157 will kill themselves because of it.

In clinical trials patients may not spontaneously report problems. During the trials of Prozac only 5% reported sexual problems but it is now known that half of those on the drug will report changes in sexual functioning if asked about it. And how are they supposed to report a side-effect, such as akathisia, that they've probably never heard of? The answer is to draw up a checklist, which is a more structured method of getting at receptive understanding. Patients in trials should be asked if they are suffering from any of a range of possible side-effects. One study has shown that patients who are asked to tell a doctor if they have any side-effects are up to six times less likely to report them than others who are asked whether they have experienced any of those in a checklist.

Box 3.1 illustrates this. The suggestion that inquiries cover both spontaneous and receptive understanding is one that could be incorporated in many small-scale studies. In most cases it would mean using low-structure methods to explore a topic, area or issue and then using a more structured method to check out the extent to which the picture that emerged with low-structure methods is recognizable in a larger group. This more structured inquiry could allow the researcher to make strong generalizing claims. If the research questions only involved exploring and understanding the perspectives, actions or feelings of a small group, then the researcher might quite fairly be uninterested in structured interviews, questionnaires or observations.

It is sometimes thought that it is possible to have unstructured observations. A response is that they are simply ones where the investigators have not appreciated the ways in which common sense and the scripts and schemata that they routinely use to interpret perceptions are acting as a filter on perception itself. If observations are not structured in the sense of being mindful attempts to see things with a fresh gaze then the researchers will observe realities that are as much reflections of themselves as anything else. Mindful observation has a structure, even if it is a set of reminders to try and observe through fresh eyes that helps to displace the hidden structure of researchers' habitual patterns.

Special Concerns in Face-to-Face Research

The Suzy Lamplugh Trust aims to create a safer society and enable everyone to live safer lives. One way in which it does this is by researching, developing and implementing personal safety strategies: for more details, visit <http://www.suzylamplugh.org/about/index.htm>. Research in familiar surroundings, in schools and other public organizations, offices and shopping malls is normally low risk, but even in those sites there can be dangers. Elsewhere, safety should be taken seriously. Visits to people's homes can be dangerous (if in doubt, go in pairs; take a mobile phone; tell someone where you will be, give them a phone number on which to contact you, and say when you will return); some urban areas are obviously risky and cameras or videos can attract unwanted attention. The Trust's advice includes 'trust your instincts and never assume it won't happen to you', and 'if the worst happens your first priority is to get away from a difficult situation as quickly as possible'.

Apart from the obvious dangers, novice researchers should realize that some research hurts: it can hurt the informants, although ethical practice is designed to avoid that (see Chapter 7).

Face-to-face work is also special because you, the researcher, are plainly part of the data development and collection, whereas you are anonymous in a Likert scale or web questionnaire. Patton (1990) has argued that as far as interviewing goes, the researcher *is* the instrument, and others (Lather, 1991; Knight and Saunders, 1999) have argued that the researcher and the informant together create the interview. Even with clipboarding (otherwise known as 'intercept interviews', where the researcher accosts people leaving a soccer game, entering a music store, or in bus queues), the way the researcher looks, stands, moves and speaks affects people's willingness to waste their time answering fixed-response questions. Match your dress and appearance to what your potential informants expect and prepare by getting someone to watch you at work and then advise on your body language and the messages that you inadvertently send out.

Long interviews, focus groups, nominal group techniques and simulations are some of the face-to-face techniques that depend on the researcher's interpersonal skill for their success. For example, 'If what people have to say about their world is generally boring to you, then you will never be a great interviewer. Unless you are fascinated by the rich variation in human experience, qualitative interviewing will become drudgery' (Patton, 1990: 279). Similarly, 'The researcher's empathy, sensitivity, humour and sincerity are important tools for the research.... How the researcher asks questions depends on how he or she feels about the topic or the interviewee. And what the researcher hears from the answer may depend on his or her mood and prior experience' (Rubin and Rubin, 1995: 12).

The demands can be summarized by two, perhaps three, words: listening, empathy and, perhaps, sympathy. Good listening is something that takes effort and practice. One part of it is not talking: I am pleased when I get interview transcripts back and find that on some pages I have not said a thing. Another is paying attention closely enough to be able to feed back to the informant a summary of what has just been said, both to check whether your understanding of it is appropriate and to serve as the basis for the next question. It also means thinking about what might be unspoken, suggested by the words but not explicit in them. This shades into empathy, in the sense of entering into and appreciating another's perspective. If researchers do not understand how things might look from informants' perspectives then they are limited in the questions they can ask and in the sense they can make of what they hear. A good imagination and a rich life both help researchers to empathize, but good knowledge is just as important. Although I do not want to go as far as to say that insider research is superior to outside research, midwives understand midwifery, and researchers who are midwives know questions to ask and have ways of hearing that outsiders are unlikely to have. In the same way, some researchers argue that only women can understand women's lives. This idea that insider research is privileged because only insiders can have sufficient empathy to understand properly has been criticized, and I return to it in Chapter 7. Outsider researchers can lessen the gap between them and insiders by making sure that they have done enough pilot fieldwork and reading to have a good working knowledge of that which they are investigating.

For some people empathy and sympathy are the same, although that is a contentious position in psychology (Goldstein and Michaels, 1985). Others take it to be seeing another's position or view while sympathy involves sharing it. For them, sympathy involves identification whereas empathy is a more detached understanding. Empathy can be seen as a neutral or 'objective' appreciation of another's position: as a historian I needed to empathize with Stalin but I did not sympathize with him. Had I sympathized with him and let that influence my work, then I would have been vulnerable to criticism from other historians. The intricacies of the empathy/sympathy debates need not concern us. The point is that some researchers argue that sympathy is necessary, especially those who believe that they should be in the business of helping the victims of unequal power distributions in society. Their view is that only by sharing and endorsing the standpoint of the people in the study can the researcher directly or vicariously appreciate that condition with the consequence, for example, that only women could do feminist research. Furthermore, sympathy (and not a straight-faced empathy) is, they say, necessary if researchers are *really* to get the trust of the people they are trying to learn about. Those who have these views are unlikely to be worried about the loss of objectivity because they will deny that research should be neutral in the face of social inequalities and that it can be value-free.

All researchers need empathy in the sense of being able to appreciate the reasoning and perceptions of the people who are the subjects of research. Face-to-face researchers also need to get the co-operation and trust of those involved in the research in order to create the research data, which means paying attention to the semiotics of dress and body language; taking time to build interpersonal comfort; listening; and empathizing or, perhaps, sympathizing. Again, Chapter 7 supplements this summary.

Observation

Observation is a mainstay of ethnographic research and, at the other extreme, of time and motion studies, which means that there is no shortage of introductory books, such as the one by Harvey and MacDonald (1993), that describe ways of doing it. Box 3.2 describes an ethnographic participant observation (it is a nice question whether there can ever be observation that is strictly 'non-participant'.) Few small-scale researchers would be able to commit the time to immerse themselves in a culture in the ways that Mader did, but the report is of value as an indication of what can be involved in lightly structured observation. Atkinson and Hammersley (1994) identify four ways in which the level of participation, and hence the nature of what can be observed, can vary. These are shown in the left column of Table 3.1, and in the other columns the participant observation studies summarized in Boxes 3.2–3.4 are described in terms of those four dimensions.

Ethnographers, who do a lot of participant observation, may use checklists to remind themselves to pay especial attention to some features but this does little to simplify the complexity of the barely structured data they collect, which raises considerable problems in terms of analysis (see Chapter 8). Some are helped, perversely, by difficulties of data collection which force them to depend on notes made after the event. These research journals are invariably more organized than contemporaneous, on-the-spot notes, which somewhat reduces data analysis problems. Where they can directly record speech, Atkinson and Hammersley (1994) warn of the temptation to treat transcripts of these words with 'hard' discourse analysis that makes the findings look spuriously precise and falsely scientific.

Table 3.1 *Levels of participation in ethnographic studies*

Levels of participation in ethnographic studies	Mader	Horvat	Sassatelli
Whether the researcher is known as such by all or some people in the setting	Full disclosure to all	Disclosure to informants and 'gatekeepers' – gym managers and school officials	
How much and what is known about the research and by whom			
The researcher's involvement on the margins or at the centre of group activities	Central to 4 women's activities	Accepted by the students	Fully involved as group member
The extent to which the researcher takes up a group persona (crudely, 'goes native')	Moves in and out of persona	Too old to do so	

Box 3.2 An ethnographic study among the Bush Cree (Mader, 1999)

This ethnographic study centres on four Bush Cree women on a Reserve in Northern Canada. It took more than three years, involved four visits to the Reserve of up to 10 weeks, joining tribal summer pilgrimages, weekly phone calls and presentations of Mader's emergent understandings and impressions to members of the band. There was no hurry about the research. 'I was able to join Reserve life a little. I made friends. I worked. I played. I watched. I listened. I helped out. I noticed how readily people gave things away. I joined in that too ... People told me stories about their youth ... My story for theirs, my time for theirs' (98). Mader emphasizes that this relaxed pace allowed her to join in ordinary things and to learn through being involved in the commonplace, which helped her to see that in Bush Cree society 'the ordinary brings pleasure' (98) and brings learning too.

In so far as it is possible to identify distinct research techniques, her use of photography stands out. She took over 900 photographs of the community and exhibited them, inviting comments from community members which became integrated into her research thinking. Subsequently she invited each of the four Bush Cree women, as her collaborators, to identify four photographs that were paradigmatic – which captured something quintessential about Bush Cree life – and to talk about each choice. Eight of the 16 photographs were subsequently enlarged to poster size and, with short explanations, were used prominently as sources in her PhD dissertation which was constructed as a narrative – as a form of story – not as a more conventional report. Her interpretations and writings had also been shared with members of the community and teachers in it, both as a form of member verification and to enrich her emergent understandings.

She acknowledged that the lightly structured inquiry and interpretation process meant that 'What I have just written can be argued away' (113), and replied that (1) what she wrote resonated with the tribe, who accepted it; (2) her narrative could be appreciated in much the same way as the story of King Arthur or Ulysses, as a tale with meaning that is independent of its factual accuracy; and (3) it had practical value because it underpinned a programme she developed for people who taught in Bush Cree schools.

Box 3.3 An ethnographic study of African American girls in an elite high school (Horvat and Antonio, 1999)

'Our goal in this project has been and continues to be to understand the [school name] experience from those many different perspectives and to shed light on how this experience influences the African American students in the study' (324). The researchers drew upon Bourdieu's concept of 'habitus', a notion similar to but more dynamic than 'culture'.

Fieldwork involved some 100 hours of observation mainly in the senior school lounge, which concentrated upon six African American girls in a predominantly white, elite high school. The fieldworker, Horvat, was a white married woman aged 30. She attended school functions, collected documentary and pictorial material and interviewed each girl, a parent and a best friend, as well as the principal, the school counsellors and the school's three black employees. She used the evidence of hugs, tears and warm and friendly greetings as evidence that she had established a rapport on the basis of being a woman who shared her experiences with the girls.

Throughout the work she practised 'a formal, systematic monitoring of self' so as to help her to 'manage her own subjectivity. To this end she wrote self-reflective memos, shared manuscripts of analyzed data with study participants and discussed emerging themes with colleagues familiar with the project' (321). The other researcher, Antonio, was not involved in data collection but was active in data analysis. His different background (immigrant, working class) was useful in a process of data analysis in which they actively engaged 'each other with challenges to possible biases that may be a product of our specific life experiences' (323). He also took a 'grounded theory' approach to data analysis, trying to derive themes from repeated readings (see Chapter 8), whereas Horvat independently analysed the data with codes that she developed from the research questions that concerned the usefulness of Bourdieu's concept of 'habitus' for understanding these girls' experiences. An agreed set of 27 codes was then applied and verified by comparing the two researchers' work. What emerged was not 'truth' but 'Our most accurate and thorough representation of the perspectives that were gathered during these interviews and many hours of on-site observation' (324).

The conclusions were that the price these girls paid for the promise of greater social mobility was 'the pain and anguish they endure by living their lives as outsiders within the race-and-class-defined dominant habitus of the school organization' (318). In the words of one informant, it was the habitus of 'a snob, rich, white, girl, bratty snob school' (329).

Box 3.4 Participant research and body culture within fitness gyms (Sassatelli, 1999)

What happens in fitness gyms can be understood at a macro-level as investment in body presentation as a way of constituting the self in a consumer culture where the body is one sign of consumption. However, the researcher was interested in a micro-level of analysis that would allow him to explore, from the bottom up, how and why body definitions are achieved. A conclusion was that, 'Body definitions are not simply embodied by the gym or reproduced by its clients, but continuously and actively negotiated and

continued

transformed' (244). In other words, close-up research suggested that matters are more complex and variable than the grand theories imply.

Details of the research methods are skimpy and contained in a footnote, which is also the case with the study in Box 3.6. Both studies come from a journal that is influenced by post-structuralist ideas and the message I get is that the construction and deconstruction of meanings are more important than methodology. Sassatelli spent several hours a day for six months as a client of two Florence gyms engaging in different exercise regimes with different instructors. The gyms differed in size, clientele, facilities and the ranges of activities. Instructors and gym managers were informally interviewed. A number of clients were identified by theoretical sampling (chosen because they had patterns of participation that matched different theories of why people should go to exercise gyms) and involved in semi-structured interviews. Observation of clients' expressive behaviour and glances while they were working in the gym was the basis of the ways in which participants construct special spaces in the gyms which then allow them 'to forget, partially and momentarily, other external relevances' (237). Specialist periodicals and fitness magazines were also consulted.

Still photographs are also widely used in observational work, as in Mader's study (Box 3.2), which describes an interesting approach to handling the mass of data contained in 900 photographs. Other ways of interpreting images are described in Chapter 4.

The low cost of remote sensing devices makes it possible to let video cameras do the observing. When cameras are concealed – *and where that is ethically acceptable* – then the researcher gets unobtrusive evidence about what happens when subjects are unaware of being observed. Such covert surveillance can be a sinister device for eavesdropping on what was intended to be, and should have remained, private, but it can also be fairly innocuous. For instance, the CCTV footage from city and store surveillance videos can be like gold dust to researchers interested in crowd behaviour, the semiotics of body language, consumer psychology, geographical nets, leisure, and parenting behaviours, to name just half a dozen (see also Chapter 4 on unobtrusive research methods). Ethical problems become more pressing if researchers use the video footage so that individuals or groups, whether they can be named or not, could be harmed as a result. Moreover, the ease of data capture can be deceptive. Traditional methods of data capture may be more time consuming, but the observer's need to make sense of what is happening *while it is happening* acts as a preliminary form of data reduction (not everything can be recorded by those methods) and of data analysis (observation schedules enormously simplify the task of analysis). Collecting data by letting the webcam run just defers the complex analytical task of sensemaking, although it has the possible advantage that once captured on film the observation can be re-viewed and agreed interpretations hammered out. For many researchers the main value of video observations is that that they are a rich record to which reference can be made as, when and if needed. So, when uncertainties arise about data collected by more traditional observational methods, then the video or digital record may help to resolve them, assuming the camera was pointing in the right direction.

At the other extreme is highly structured observation involving an observation schedule, often in the form of a checklist with instructions about what to observe and when. Mention was made earlier of Galton and colleagues' (1980) observational work in elementary classrooms. Although the researcher's gaze is easily captured by the teacher's actions, in Galton's ORACLE study observers also had to look at equal numbers of boys and girls chosen at random from the low-, medium- and high-ability groups in each class. Prompted by a pre-recorded signal played through an earpiece attached to a cassette recorder, the observer noted the behaviours of each pupil 10 times and the teacher's 45 times in each observation session. The checklist, which had been developed from a review of the literature, discussion and pilot work, required observers to record the *behaviours* they saw at each observation point. The observations were intended to be low inference, so as to maximize inter-observer reliability: the observers ticked what they saw and were not asked to make an inference that, for example, talking with another pupil meant that the child was or was not working. The result was a very detailed record of the frequency of different behaviours in an observation session. The study amassed 47,000 observations of 58 teachers and 84,000 observations of 489 pupils. In both cases, highly structured observations made by trained observers who achieved inter-observer reliabilities that were typically greater than 95% produced a large amount of 'objective' data that could be analysed in sophisticated ways with advanced statistical techniques. The ORACLE study is open to the charge that it was blind to the meanings of the behaviours it tallied. Some attempt was made to forestall that criticism by collecting plans of the classroom layout, notes of curriculum content, pedagogic methods, apparatus and resources, critical incidents and learning activities, along with prose accounts of the observers' impressions and reactions and a teaching styles questionnaire completed by each of the 58 teachers.

Three potential difficulties with highly structured observations have been implied: the work is only as good as the explicit and tacit theories on which the observation schedule is based; it depends on reliable observers making low-inference observations; and in describing behaviours it can miss the meanings. Nevertheless, it has attractions for small-scale researchers because a relatively small amount of observation time generates a large amount of impressive-looking data that can be genuinely revealing by showing patterns that had been below participants' thresholds of awareness. Consider most workplaces, for example. How accurate are people's beliefs about what they really spend their time on?

Semi-structured observations can be seen as a compromise or as a cop-out. They are likely to be structured in the sense that the observer has a checklist of open-ended questions that indicate key things to watch for and keeps a timed record of observations. They are usually 'unstructured' because the researcher keeps running notes of what she sees happening, albeit with the checklist in mind. On the one hand this lacks the fullness of ethnographic immersion and on the other it lacks the rigour of structured observations and their power to show unexpected patterns of behaviour. The data are harder to handle than those produced by checking the boxes and may not be much simpler than data from lightly structured observations. Yet observations like these are common in pilot studies and are the mainstay of many evaluation, audit and inspection systems: the quality of prisons, for example, is judged by experts in the field who observe with guidance notes and open-ended observational questions in mind. Naturally, they use documentary, statistical and interview data as well.

Interviews

If questionnaires were once the default research method in social science, interviews appear to be their successor. Like any default model, interviews are popular for good reasons but there is the danger that their popularity leads them to be used unthinkingly and, sometimes, inappropriately.

Here interviews are defined by face-to-face interaction. Other ways of questioning people, including e-mail and web inquiries, are treated as questionnaires (so they are in Chapter 4). Telephone interviewing, though, is covered in this chapter. Falling video-conferencing software prices are making it a feasible inquiry method for small-scale researchers but at the time of writing there were no signs that they were taking it up. The earlier section on face-to-face work has already identified many of the distinctive demands of interviewing. Chapter 7 in this book has more to say about encouraging informants to speak freely and should be consulted. Chapters 7–9 in Arksey and Knight (1999) go into a lot more detail on the practicalities of interviewing, and Gillham (2000b) has written a concise, user-friendly guide to interviewing that is well suited to beginners.

Remarks earlier in this chapter will have made it very clear that interviews can be highly structured and used for purposes when reliability, in the sense of consistency of interviewing practice, is a necessity. In those cases, where the aim is to collect data from many respondents which can be captured in numerical form and statistically analysed, the interview schedule will have been very carefully designed and piloted. The interviewer will only be an instrument for the administration of the schedule. When it comes to drawing up a schedule to use in interviews such as those, the advice in the next chapter on the development of questionnaires and rating scales should be read and used. Alternatively, interviews can be organized around open-ended questions and be lightly structured. The differences between highly structured, fixed-response interviews and freewheeling conversations are far greater than is implied by the fact that both can be called interviews. Table 3.2 brings together some of the more importance points of difference between structured and less structured approaches to interviewing and questionnaire-based inquiries. It should be studied alongside the earlier coverage of heavily and lightly structured inquiries and fixed-response and open-ended questions. Boxes 3.5–3.7, which contain examples of published semi- and lightly structured interview studies, put flesh on those sections, and on Table 3.2. Box 4.4 reports a study that used a fixed-response interview schedule in telephone interviewing. Bryman (2001) gives a good account of structured interviewing practices.

There is no need to go into detail here about the development and piloting of highly structured interview schedules, since the advice in Chapter 4 on questionnaire design and measurement applies to interviews like these, which are really nothing more than read-aloud questionnaires. However, one thing that does not come across sufficiently strongly in Table 3.2 is that even when interviews are likely to be exploratory, conversational and free-flowing, they still need to be carefully planned. One pitfall of lightly structured interviewing is that good rapport, plenty of empathy and skilled listening can get the interviewer carried off on a flow tide of goodwilled disclosure. That risks leaving the researcher uninformed about things that might be of considerable research interest but which, in the flow, got overlooked. Although that might be acceptable very early in an inquiry when the territory is being mapped, at other times it is likely to produce embarrassing gaps in the research conversations. At the very least, then, it helps to have a list of prompts or key questions and some would say that except for these preliminary inquiries it is necessary to have an agenda. The principled, as opposed to the pragmatic, case for a conversational agenda is that the set of prompts itself amounts to a theory, explicit or tacit, of the subject being investigated. Asking about some things indicates a belief that they are important, and lurking behind those questions are assumptions – often crude ones – about why they are important. Equally, not asking about things indicates that they are unimportant. So, if lightly structured or conversational interviews are not guided by an agenda there is every chance that, by default, naïve or unexamined theories will shape them when the interviewer asks questions on the spur of the moment and fails to ask about anything that does not press itself into consciousness. In this way the whole inquiry could be based, unthinkingly, on naïve theories and end up only adding fresh data to existing common-sense understandings of the phenomena in question.

The processes of identifying research questions and surveying the literature should have done a lot to displace or reshape naïve theories but, by themselves, they may not be sufficient to ensure that lightly structured interviews draw on the more sophisticated understandings that have resulted. In order to create an interview agenda or set of prompts, revisit the literature review and use it to construct a working account of the

Table 3.2 *Characteristics of structured, semi-structured and lightly structured questionnaires and interviews (after Arksey and Knight, 1999: 8–9)*

Structured (fixed-response questions, in a set order)	Semi-structured (fixed- and open-response questions)	Lightly structured (some prompts/questions, flexible sequence)
Quick to do. Danger, with questionnaires, of respondents ticking faster than they can think	Interviews are usually longer and may be very long. The same goes for questionnaires, although people seldom spend as much time on them as they would on speaking face-to-face with someone	
Large samples possible and they are usually expected: the positivist logic of surveys demands them	Time taken on interviewing and the complexity of transcription and analysis tend to restrict sample size. Besides, interpretive research tends not to see sample size as a key indicator of research quality	
Samples are often randomly selected (as with CATI), or are structured to get large numbers of people with certain characteristics (people who shop at Woolworths, use Lycos, or read *The Times*). Often the sample is the largest number of people who can conveniently be found and persuaded to participate. The longer the instrument is, the more advisable it is to sample in the manner of lightly structured inquiries (as in right column)	The time demands mean that a greater commitment is needed from informants, making it harder to get them. This, and the greater time taken to capture and analyse data, mean that samples are generally much smaller. Opportunity sampling and 'snowballing' are common, as are targeting people in positions that make them likely to be good 'key informants', and simply using whoever can be dragooned into participating. Remember that interpretive research does not usually take sample size as a key indicator of research quality	
Questionnaires constrain respondents' answers. Interviewers follow a script or schedule exactly	Respondents given a mix of closed and open questions. Interviewer will use judgement to improvise	Interviewer improvises around a list of topics of discussion. Questionnaires seek free comments around those topics or questions
The instruments are largely blind to things not covered by the schedule. So, the instrument pretty well defines what is discovered. Where the questionnaire or interview schedule is soundly based on theory and research, has been piloted, and really does help to answer the research questions, this is not a fault	The researcher seeks the informants' stories and perspectives and is far more open to complexity, ambiguity and things that had not been anticipated or considered	
Validity depends on the validity of the questions, individually and as a set. (See Chapter 5 for a discussion of validity)	Validity partly dependent on the quality of the questions, partly on the creativity of the informant (see the column to the right)	Validity is related to the quality of the prompts and questions and to the informants' commitment. In interviews the skill of the interviewer and the amount of the time available also matter

(Continued)

Table 3.2 (*Continued*)

Structured (fixed-response questions, in a set order)	Semi-structured (fixed- and open-response questions)	Lightly structured (some prompts/questions, flexible sequence)
Reliability of data collection is dependent upon interviewer training, supervision and strict rules of working. Less problematic with fixed-response questionnaires and literate respondents	Reliability takes second place to validity. Usually, evidence that the interviewer's actions or the prompts on a questionnaire were appropriate is a proxy for formal evidence of reliability	
Few data capture and transcription problems with the fixed-response questions; even fewer if answers are directly captured by electronic means	Full transcription desirable, although headline summaries of interviews are often used, with the taped record serving as a reference point. Very time consuming	
Easy to analyse	Some parts easy to analyse, some hard	Usually hard to analyse
Reliability of analysis seldom a problem, in the sense that there is seldom room for argument about whether the analysis is a good summary of the data	Hard to analyse reliably. Plausibility of analysis a better concept than reliability? With interviews it can be difficult to decide what a section of conversation is about, let alone to agree on the key messages it contains	
Respondents' anonymity can be easily guaranteed and there's little danger of individuals being identifiable in any report (this approach usually has large samples and collects data that could not easily be associated with any respondent)	The open-ended responses mean that it is unintentionally possible to identify an informants by publishing distinctive views experiences etc.	Informants tend to be more cautious about their responses in face-to-face situations than if they have anonymity. Small sample size and distinctive features in the data can make it even harder to avoid identifying individuals in a report, so compromising the promise of anonymity

---

Box 3.5 Semi-structured interviewing and the responsibilities of counsellor supervisors (King and Wheeler, 1999)

Although counsellors expect to be supervised, the legal position of supervisors, the extent of their responsibility and expectations of what they should do are all unclear. This exploratory study used semi-structured interviews to redress the 'paucity of research and information on this issue' (218). The choice of method was seen to be particularly appropriate to counselling, in which lightly or semi-structured interviews are the main clinical technique.

Twelve key questions were identified through a literature review and pilot interviews suggested that they made a suitable research instrument. Some of the informants in the pilot interviews said that being interviewed had 'sharpened up' their thinking, suggesting that meaning was not simply being revealed by the research but to some extent being created through it.

The main study involved 10 high-profile people in the counselling profession who were interviewed for about an hour each at home or at work. Interviews were taped and transcribed. The researchers began to see

continued

categories in the data and following the precepts of grounded theory (see Chapter 8). They kept trying to construct thematic categories that covered most of the relevant interview data. In the end, they arrived at 10 thematic headings. Their conclusions were that there were several reasons why 'either expectations of supervision should be played down or something akin to "consultative support" should be adopted, or the responsibilities of supervisors need to be [made] more formal, with more power and authority conferred upon them' (227). They recommended that the British Association for Counselling introduce codes of ethics for supervision.

Box 3.6 Semi-structured interviewing, body modification, fashion and identity (Sweetman, 1999)

The study was intended to illuminate the significance of the growth of body piercing and tattooing: 'It is suggested that for many body modifiers, an involvement in tattooing or piercing represents not so much an appropriation of the cultural detritus adrift within Baudrillard's "carnival of signs", but rather a reaction to such superficiality: an attempt to lend corporeal solidity to expressions of individuality' (52–3).

Thirty-five informants were recruited through tattoo conventions, advertisements in tattooing and student magazines, and snowballing (asking one informant to suggest other people to approach). The aim was to represent a range of body modifiers and piercers. About 40% of the female informants and 70% of the men were loosely classed as 'heavy modifiers/piercers'. There were 15 women (aged 19–40) and 20 men (20–60), including a company director and unemployed people. Informants, like most members of the body modification community, were mainly white.

The interviews were semi-structured and lasted between 20 minutes and three hours. Seven were conducted by phone. As is quite common in small-scale studies, the report provides no details of the source of interview prompts or questions, of the length and conduct of the interviews, or of analytical techniques. The interviews were supplemented by informal observation at tattoo conventions and by the popular literature on body modification.

The conclusion is that for the more lightly pierced or tattooed informants, their body modification was an 'incorporation of "the exotic" into the "supermarket of style"' (70). For the others, modification was not a matter of fashion but 'a form of "anti-fashion" ... valued in terms of ... contrast with more superficial, sartorial accessories' (70).

Box 3.7 Conversational interviewing, crack dealing, gender and arrest avoidance (Jacobs and Miller, 1998)

Crime is deterred by the likelihood of capture, which means that criminals' strategies for avoiding arrest are of interest to criminologists. The researchers asked whether women's arrest avoidance techniques were different from men's and, if so, what that might indicate. They concentrated on crack dealers. (Many researchers find it easier to get funding to explore

continued

issues of broad significance by linking them to areas of public policy priority, such as the war on drugs and AIDS research.)

Other research had indicated that self-reports are the best source of data about serious criminality and that they are certainly better than impersonal surveys. Although this suggested that interviews should be the method of choice, they decided not to follow a common line of inquiry and interview jailed crack dealers, reasoning that they might behave artificially (and there would be an irony in asking the jailed about arrest avoidance). Through snowballing they recruited 25 women informants, observing that 'the most we can claim is that the sample appears to be representative, in general terms, of the population of female crack dealers known to the interviewees' (554). Informants received a small payment. The researchers suggested that informants enjoyed the opportunity to correct the faulty impressions held by 'the straights'.

The interviews began with basic questions about how the women operated and then developed naturally. In later interviews the researcher asked about themes that had begun to emerge in these conversations. Interviews took place in the areas where the informants dealt. The interviewer was accompanied by a guide with credibility as a fair dealer. Since tape recorders were associated with police evidence gathering, the interviewer took notes, accepting that 'imperfections are an unavoidable part of fieldwork' (555).

phenomenon in question. For example, if the study will be essentially a descriptive one, exploring the strategies that single working mothers use to try and reconcile the demands of caring and working, then existing research describes strategies that other women have used, which can be the basis of a set of interview prompts. If the study is explanatory, aiming, for example, to explore why self-confident young women are less likely to be employed than self-confident young men, then the literature (for example, Feinstein, 2000) contains hypotheses which point to areas to explore in conversations with young unemployed people. Ideas from the literature are only starting points though. Draft lists of prompts, lead questions or agenda points should be refined by (1) discussing them with colleagues and supervisors and (2) using them in one or two pilot interviews. Piloting will quickly show whether the list is a manageable one (and because lists often have to be memorized it is advisable to follow the finding that most people can only remember 7±2 pieces of information and keep lists to 5–9 prompts). Piloting should also show whether the prompts are useful and, perhaps more important, good pilot interviews can identify topics that need to be added to the list but which had been missed by the literature review. When that happens, either it means that the pilot interviews have identified a fresh theme, which means that the study may end up making a novel contribution to thinking in the area, or it says that something was missed in the literature review, which means that more work needs to be done on it.

Telephone Interviews

Telephone interviewing is an attractive way of doing survey work now that almost all homes in highly developed countries have phones. This means that almost-random samples can be computer-generated (this is known as computer-assisted telephone interviewing or CATI) or, as long as the researcher can be relaxed about the exclusion of ex-directory subscribers, numbers can be picked at random from the phone book. More structured sampling can be done by choosing phone numbers on the basis of postcode or of asking to speak to anyone in a household who has certain characteristics (is older than 70, goes out to work every day, travels by bus). Lavrakas (1987) suggests that it is possible to get a 90% response rate from those of the target group who can be contacted, which compares very favourably with questionnaires, where the mean response rate appears to be about 50% (Baruch, 1999) and can drop as low as 11.6% (Heard and Vyse, 1999). This means that telephone interviewing can be cheaper *per completed response* than postal questionnaires and clipboarding.

This technique is suitable for people who do not read easily and the interviewer can help any respondents who are unsure about any question. It is more widely used for fixed-response questions in highly structured surveys than for less structured, open-ended inquiries. That may be because informants cannot be seen and the visual cues that are so important in establishing an interviewing relationship are lost. In fact, the interviewer has little guarantee that the informants' minds are really on the questions and not distracted by TV, children, pets or the dinner that is burning and, in any case, informants may be reluctant to spend the long amounts of time that lightly structured interviews often need. There is a consensus (Frey, 1989) that open-ended questions are harder to manage over the phone and that answers tend to be less complex and shorter than they are in face-to-face conversations. The section in Chapter 5 on self-report studies has something to say about the case for researchers telephoning informants to collect daily information updates as opposed to relying on them completing daily activity logs.

Action Interviews

In some studies the interview comes after informants have engaged in some standard task. One aim is to reduce the distance between the sorts of explanations we give when asked in general terms about something and what actually goes through our mind in action. The second is to see how people think in certain situations: when buying a house, teaching primary science or working in a team. Piaget's work on the development of human knowledge was based on the clinical method of giving children tasks to do, watching and then asking them to talk about what they did and why. Other times he asked them about common childhood activities, such as the games they played. Clinical interviews might also begin with photos or a video clip of the informant and the request that she or he comment on the images, describing, for example, thoughts, feelings, actions and reasons, and making some evaluation of his or her performance. Orland (2000) used a similar approach when she asked student teachers to draw a line of any length or shape to denote significant 'felt experiences' in their lives as beginning teachers. These lines – some looping, others with wave patterns, many with explanatory remarks added – were good prompts for individual reflection and for discussion with the researcher by means of which important but subliminal theories were 'surfaced'. It is a simple technique that can be widely applied and which can easily be modified or extended.

Alternatively, an activity, test or simulation might be the basis for a debriefing interview. These interviews have the complexity of texture that comes from being closely tied to a vivid instance, but the corresponding costs are (1) that it is hard to extract general meanings and themes from them and (2) that those that are extracted can be fairly easily criticized. For instance, Piaget's account of the development of human knowledge has been widely criticized on the grounds (1) that when the same inquiries are made about somewhat different tasks or situations, different levels of response can be found, and (2) that the interview data can be interpreted in competing ways and are, in any case, too insubstantial to support an account as ambitious as Piaget's. With the more structured interviews and questionnaires used in surveys, it is possible to get more reliable data from a larger number of respondents, although validity often becomes more questionable, especially for researchers who consider that since knowledge is situated and context-related, then research is only valid if it too is contexted. These issues are more fully reviewed in Chapter 5.

It is widely accepted that the thinking that comes across in general statements (espoused logic) is rather different from the thinking that is used in practical contexts (logic-in-use). In general terms I may think analytically but when the car breaks down I kick it rather than systematically explore the source of the fault. Schön's (1983; 1987) accounts of the ways in which professionals think and learn are frequently cited here. Crudely put, his work implies that retrospective accounts are to a greater or lesser degree the constructions of espoused logic. They tend to be simplified, tidied up and selective and may be understood as stories about how things ought to have been, not about how they really were. This view of espoused logic is similar to Weick's (1995) notion of sensemaking with its claim that we don't know what the talk is until we've done the walk: thought follows action just as much as it precedes it. For researchers who want to make a difference to people's practices, the fact that interviews tend to be saturated with espoused logic is a substantial problem, because it means that they are not finding out about the sort of thinking – the logic-in-use – that is really operating as people act. This does not mean that it is misguided to investigate espoused logic. It is a claim that researchers who want to affect practices need to understand both why people think they act as they do (espoused logic) and how they think when they are acting (logic-in-use).

One way of getting close to people's logic-in-use is to explore it as soon as possible after they have acted and to make sure that the interview is firmly grounded in reflection upon that recent, vivid action. Even when it is not possible to do an interview soon after an action, it is still possible to evoke something of logic-in-use by asking informants to recall an example of the research topic and to refer to that throughout the conversation. Informants can be asked to identify more than one critical incident, which helps the researcher to get a sense of the ways in which different contexts affect thinking and doing. However, there remain concerns that even when interviews are soon after a critical incident and even if recall is stimulated by watching a video of the incident or looking at Polaroid photographs, the responses are still overlain by tidied-up sensemaking. For this reason some researchers want to talk to people about what they do as they do it. Although this on-the-fly or contemporaneous interviewing looks to be highly valid, it is unusual for people to be questioned as they act and it is not clear what the relationship is between this talk and informants' 'real' knowledge in use. Tomlinson (1999) has used psychological research to argue that not all of our tacit knowing can be brought to consciousness and Donnelly (1999) has complemented this with his analysis of Heidegger's philosophy. Even so, researchers who want to get close to practice need to think of ways such as these to anchor informants' conversations in specific instances and to try to make those instances ones that are as fresh as is possible. Specificity and recency are the guides to interviewing about actions. Interviews about beliefs can also be enhanced by exploring how those beliefs operate in specific circumstances, especially in recent or memorable circumstances.

Nominal Group Technique

Nominal group technique (NGT) is similar to q-sort and concept mapping (both covered in Chapter 4) in that it (1) identifies informants' views, concerns, beliefs etc. and (2) gets them sorted into an order of priority. An example is contained in Box 3.8. Padgett and Imani (1999) also used NGT to explore differences between participants' attitudes before and after a day-long attitude change programme. Despite a suite of films, talks and discussions, 21 land-use managers who had responsibility for assessing the environmental impact of federal agencies' actions became *less* sensitive to issues of social justice during the day (as measured by NGT scores), even though the hapless researchers made it clear that the land-use managers were legally obliged to take these issues seriously.

Box 3.8 Nominal group technique and planning a communication education programme for older people (Hickson et al., 1999)

The Australian government favours education programmes that help old people to sustain their health and independence. These researchers wished to develop a programme to help older people maintain their communication skills and social networks but first wanted to establish old people's wants and needs. Since this study, which used NGT, found that professionals and old people had very different perceptions, the research was timely.

NGT groups should ideally have between five and nine people. In this study there were 36 elderly informants in seven groups and 10 professionals in two groups. Sessions lasted some two hours. The stages were:

1   The researchers put the three questions that most concerned them to the informants.
2   Each person was asked to reflect silently on the questions for five minutes.
3   Each person reported aloud one of his or her answers, which was written on a whiteboard, until all answers had been heard to all questions.
4   The ideas were discussed and clarified with the group.
5   Participants suggested ways of clustering similar ideas under one heading.
6   They were asked to select up to three points that were particularly important to them and put those three in rank order.
7   The researchers did more work on clustering the ideas and then used the informants' rankings to put them in order of importance.

The outcome was an education programme that was firmly grounded in the needs and perceptions of the clients, not in the different beliefs of the professionals.

Focus Groups

A focus group is a set of people invited to respond to researchers' questions, findings from earlier studies, policy documents, hypotheses, concerns, views etc. Researchers often use them to explore provisional findings either by summarizing them to a selection of participants or by bringing the findings to other groups of stakeholders in the inquiry. Both strategies help researchers to hear how well their interpretations fit with informants' understandings and both provide chances for them to ask for explanations of unexpected findings and to clarify details. Groups tend to have four to eight members who may be a cross-section of the population, or who may have been chosen to represent groups such as retired women, 16- to 18-year-olds, or clients of the probation service. Informants may be paid for their time.

The results of these focus group discussions *prove* nothing, not least because the number of informants is usually small and group dynamics can mean that dominant individuals can obliterate alternative points of view. Groups can be hard to manage and the discussion can loop around on itself and some issues can get quite brief attention. It can be difficult to get a good recording and it is often so hard to try and match tape-recorded comments to individual informants that it is not worth trying. Video recording solves that problem but if you want to be able to link statements to individuals, perhaps you should be using individual interviews, NGT or q-sorts, not focus groups.

Focus groups have their uses. They are a low-cost way of getting a sense of the range of informants' perspectives and of getting some, tentative purchase on which groups of people hold them, how strongly and why. As long as the results are treated only as material for thought, reflection and further investigation, they can be valuable and relatively inexpensive. They can also be used to pilot and refine research instruments, as well as to explore provisional findings. A more substantial treatment of focus group inquiry is the set of six books in the *Focus Group Kit* (edited by Krueger and Morgan, 1998) which is a comprehensive, practical and accessible treatment. Greenbaum (1998) is an alternative.

Memory Work

This method, which has been reported by feminist researchers, focuses on 'How did we get to be the way we are and how can we change?' (Schratz and Walker, 1995: 42). I see this as a process made up of six main parts.

1   Four or five people form a self-selected group and agree to explore a theme related to their self-identities for personal or research purposes. They are co-researchers and collaborators (see Heron, 1996 for much more on collaborative research).
2   Individually, they write a story, usually focusing on an incident connected to the theme. For example, if the theme was social class and the way it has affected our identities, then I might write about the day I realized that I would never have a turn to be King. The text is written at leisure, may be quite long, should be in the third person ('she saw', 'he said'), should be descriptive, not explanatory, and should include details that come to mind, even if they appear to be irrelevant.
3   The group meets and turns to one of these memory texts. Schratz and Walker list prompts that others have used which direct attention to metaphors; gaps, silences and blind spots; the taken-for-granted assumptions; the writer's tacit or practical theories. Writers are not allowed to comment or explain. They listen and see how their memory texts are understood.
4   When all the texts have been analysed, which is likely to take several meetings, the group looks for similarities between them and for anomalies. Here they are creating new understandings from their explorations of the written memories, which have been their data.

5   Each person rewrites their texts. The process may bring up memories
    and data that would otherwise have been suppressed and may evoke
    new understandings of how the self has been constructed.
6   The original texts and the revisions are compared in the group setting.

This is not mainstream (or 'malestream') research because it is much
closer to the confessional practices of self-help and self-improvement
programmes that draw upon Maslow's and Rogers' humanistic psy-
chologies. However, it is possible to see ways in which participant
researchers who are deeply trusted (see Chapter 7) might be able to use
techniques like this to explore the ways in which aspects of identity and
self are constructed and changed. Crawford and colleagues (1992:
Chapter 3) give a fuller account. Haug, who pioneered this approach,
cautions that 'this method … does not work in every case. Some members
of the group had extreme difficulties with it. It cannot moreover be
applied at random to any given topic' (1987: 72).

Experiments

In crude terms, experimentation is about studies in which one experience
(the control) is compared with another (the experimental experience) that
is the same in all respects except one. This could be represented as

$$O_1 \ x \ O_2$$

Where O_2 is the baseline measurement, x is the experimental intervention,
which might be brief or long, simple or complex, and O_2 is the post-
experiment measurement. The effects of the intervention can be calculated
by subtracting the score at O_1 from that at O_2. There are a number of problems with this, though, not least of which are problems of measurement.
If the same test is used before and after intervention there is a possibility
that the experimental subjects would do better the second time because of
practice or, if children are involved and the intervention has been a
lengthy one, simply because they've developed. There is also an assumption that the measure will be sensitive to all of the changes that might be
attributed to the intervention, although this is often not the case. It is also
assumed that the measure or instrument has good test–retest reliability,
which means that people who are not involved in the intervention would
generally give the same answers at O_2 as they did at O_1. That may not
be so. The most common response to problems like these is to use a
two-group design, represented as:

$$A: \ O_1 \ x \ O_2$$
$$B: \ O_1 \ O_2$$

Both groups are measured before and after the intervention, although only group A gets the treatment. This certainly controls for instability in the measurement instrument but it introduces a lot of complications. We have to be sure that groups A and B are equivalent in every way to begin with, so that the strong claim can be made that any difference between them at O_2 can be attributed only to the intervention. But if group A comprised men and group B women, differences might be due to gender and nothing to do with the intervention, *or* the intervention might only have 'worked' with one group, not with the other (which might be a treatment × gender interaction). There are basically two ways of trying to balance A and B. One is to allocate people to the groups at random. The section on sampling in Chapter 5 explains that quite large groups are likely to be needed before we should be confident that random allocation has produced two equivalent groups. Small-scale researchers are often unable to use large samples or to allocate people at random to the intervention or other group. A common alternative is to allocate the people involved in the experiment in a way designed to produce two matched, or equivalent, groups. The ideal way to do this is to create matched pairs of people who are identical in respect of every variable that might influence scores on the measurement instrument and then allocate, at random, one of the pair to A and the other to B. The large samples needed to construct two equivalent groups by allocating people to one or the other completely at random are not needed, although researchers have to accept that it will seldom be possible to pair up all the people involved in a study and some will have to be left out of the analysis. The biggest problem lies in the idea of matching. Can it be assumed that it is sufficient to match on the basis of age, sex, socio-economic status, race and IQ? Or might it be necessary to match for physical health, beliefs about self-efficacy, extraversion and libido, for example? When matching there is a fundamental assumption that it is possible to identify all the variables that might affect responses to the innovation, to measure them accurately and match people accordingly. I always feel uncomfortable when people say that I've been matched with someone in a research project, and doubly so if I find out who the other person is: in those cases, I feel my individuality and only see the differences.

Assuming groups A and B are acceptably similar does not deal with the objection that an intervention – any intervention – is likely to have an effect since it is widely known that you can give people chalk tablets for headaches and some of them will report improvement. A good design should control for these placebo effects, as shown here:

$$A: \quad O_1 \; x \; O_2$$
$$B: \quad O_1 \; p \; O_2$$

The placebo, or control experience, should be as similar as possible to the innovation without actually being the innovation. For example, when

I wanted to explore the effects of a certain approach to teaching history, one group got an afternoon a week for a term of history taught in the innovative way, and I taught the same material with as much enthusiasm to a matched group in the same school for the same amount of time: only the teaching approach differed. There are circumstances where it is useful to know about the relative impact of an innovation, something similar to the innovation and no treatment at all. A three-group design might be used (shown below). The principle can be extended to four or more groups but it becomes progressively harder to recruit enough subjects and allocate them, on a matched basis, to the different groups.

$$
\begin{array}{ll}
\text{A:} & O_1 \; x \; O_2 \\
\text{B:} & O_1 \; p \; O_2 \\
\text{C:} & O_1 \; O_2
\end{array}
$$

Rather than vary the treatment, or innovation, it is possible to explore the differential effects of a treatment by varying the composition of the groups. For example:

$$
\begin{array}{ll}
\text{Social groups A or B:} & O_1 \; x \; O_2 \\
\text{Social groups C or D:} & O_1 \; x \; O_2 \\
\text{Unemployed:} & O_1 \; x \; O_2
\end{array}
$$

If funds permitted, this design could be complicated by adding placebo groups and groups getting neither the intervention nor the placebo treatment.

One way around the problem of matching groups is to use the same people to study the effects of two (or more) treatments. Suppose that a researcher into sleep disorders was interested in the effects of herbal sleeping tablets (T) as opposed to relaxation techniques (R). An experimental design would be:

$$
\begin{array}{ll}
\text{A:} & O_1 \; T \; O_2 \; R \; O_3 \; \text{etc.} \\
\text{B:} & O_1 \; R \; O_2 \; T \; O_3 \; \text{etc.}
\end{array}
$$

Although administering the treatments to the two groups in a different order helps the researcher to identify interaction effects (so that R may leak into T, when they are in that sequence, or the experience of T may prejudice subjects against R when they are in that order), the tendency is to avoid these designs because of the danger of contamination and learning effects. There are times when the researcher has few subjects and no choice but to use within-subject designs but they tend to be seen by followers of natural science approaches as a design of last resort. They are more commonly used in quasi-experiments, which are sometimes called field or natural experiments. There is more on quasi-experiments later in this section.

In real-life situations, researchers cannot control all of the relevant variables and quasi-experiments or field experiments have to suffice. You might want to see whether children being taught to read by one method do better than those taught by another. A true experiment is not likely to be possible and double-blind trials (where the researcher does not know who gets the treatment and who gets the placebo) are certainly not feasible. The treatment – a new approach to reading – is complex and the researcher has problems being sure

1 That the children really get the new approach as intended (this is unlikely since plans get changed by individual teachers in classroom practice).
2 That there is no' leakage' caused by teachers in the control group using parts of the new method in their work.
3 That both groups get teachers with similar experience, enthusiasm, time and resources.
4 That both groups of children were equal in terms of their reading performance before the trials started. Ideally that would involve large numbers of children randomly assigned to the control or experimental condition. In practice, the best that can be done is to identify children of similar reading attainments in the control and experimental classes and compare the end-of-treatment scores of the two matched groups. However, matching on the basis of one measure does not control important variables, such as socio-economic status, which are also likely to have an effect.
5 That the fact that one group is made up of enthusiasts for the innovation (after all, they adopted it) does not introduce a major source of error. In fact we know that volunteers and early adopters differ in many ways from non-volunteers and late adopters.
6 That the measure of reading achievement, which is the dependent variable, is a worthwhile and fair measure of the learning of *both* groups.
7 That nothing happens during the experiment that jeopardizes the findings. Suppose the experimental group's reading materials were about dinosaurs and in the middle of the experiment the BBC's popular *Walking with Dinosaurs* series was screened.

Note that these and other threats to quasi-experiments threaten experiments as well. Arguably, the main difference between 'true' and 'quasi' experiments lies in the amount of success the researcher has – and wants to have – in designing these threats out of the study. The classic discussion of them is by Campbell and Stanley (1963). It can be expensive trying to forestall these threats but at least in field or quasi-experiments the results should say something about what is possible in ordinary settings and have some interest to practitioners. True experiments, however, are routinely criticized on the grounds that the price of trying to control all sources of variation except the one that the researcher is deliberately manipulating (the independent variable) is artificiality. Boxes 3.9 and 3.10 contain summaries of two experiments. It is worth asking what practical use either has, what significance their findings have and, quite simply, who is likely to care about them. Bryne (1998) argues that most social systems are complex (see Chapter 6 for elaboration) which means that it is inherently impossible to make strong predictions about their exact outcomes. It is possible to say something about probabilities, especially those within a 'prediction horizon', which may not extend far into the future, but greater certainty is not possible. What, then, is the value of experimentalism if it 'only works when the world is linear and when causes are simple and single'? (1998: 65). A response is offered by the psychologists Keating and Miller who argue that: 'We need to recognize the tension between tightly controlled studies [such as experiments – PK] which reduce or eliminate complexity by removing context, and studies that embrace a wide range of processes and contexts, but at the risk of being uninterpretable … At the simplest level, it requires the incorporation of experimental, correlational and developmental models' (2000: 386). Bryne implies that attempts to improve experimental design are of limited value in a world that is overwhelmingly complex, uncertain and contingent. Keating and Miller suggest that the answer, which will often be outside the scope of small-scale studies, is to combine experiments with other methods that are more congenial to complexity and mess. Both positions mean that the decision to use experiments has to be carefully made in the light of the sorts of claims that the researcher hopes to make. That is, of course, true of all research methods.

Box 3.9 An experimental study of reading speech and hearing print (Borowsky et al., 1999)

The experiment was designed to contribute to an understanding of how, in basic reading, phonological (sound) and orthographic (print) features interact. The literature review established two views that had research evidence to support them: (1) print features feed forward into the sound systems, so there is no feedback from sound to print (saying does not help seeing, but seeing helps saying); (2) 'there are fully recurrent connections between the orthographic subsystem and the phonological system' (297) (saying helps seeing, seeing helps saying).

Four experiments were conducted. In the first the subjects saw a clear grapheme shown on a computer monitor for a set period of time (the letters *na*, *da*, or *ta*) and heard a pre-recorded phoneme played at a set volume (*na*, *da* or *ta*) while a white noise generator was operating at 70 dB. In one condition the grapheme and phoneme were the same (*ta*, *ta*), in the second they were incongruent (*da*, *ta*), and in the third the grapheme was irrelevant (*na*, *ta*). The 36 possible combinations were presented in randomized sequences. In experiment 2 the noise generator was set at 69 dB. In experiments 3 and 4 the phonemes were not degraded by the white noise generator

continued

but the graphemes were more (experiment 3) or less (experiment 4) blurred. In all cases, subjects had to press one of two buttons to give their response, the data going directly into the computer. Twenty-four undergraduates did experiment 1 for course credit and another 38 did experiment 2 on the same basis. Twenty-four students were paid $5 each to do experiment 3 and another 24 were paid to do experiment 4. Each experiment took about 20 minutes per subject and the experimenter was present throughout.

Experimental conditions were rigorously controlled. For example, the make and model of the computer monitors and speakers are given and we are told that the output of the white noise generator (model number given) was measured on a 'Radio Shack digital sound level meter (model 33–2055) directly in front of one of the speakers' (299). The phonemes were carefully 'matched on place of articulation (i.e. alveolar) … (spoken by a male) … [and] recorded in 16-bit mono, at a sampling frequency of 22 kHz and … 500 ms in duration' (299).

The data were analysed using ANOVA and Student's t-test to establish the probability that variations had merely happened by chance. The analysis established that it was acceptable to combine the data from 1 with 2 and from 3 with 4 (in other words neither the sound nor the visual degradations made a statistically significant difference to the results). The pattern of results was consistent with theory 1, namely that saying does not help seeing, but seeing helps saying. The authors considered that the results might be of interest to those concerned with dyslexia and in basic reading.

Box 3.10 An experimental study of the representation of facial expression of emotion (White, 1999)

The question was whether facial emotions are (1) interpreted holistically, in which case the positioning of the mouth and eyebrows both have to be read, or (2) identified independently, on the basis of less information, much as, for example, hair colour is identified. If facial emotions are independently identified then subjects seeing an upside-down face should be able to identify an emotion as quickly as they identify any other independent feature, such as hair colour (inverting the face is intended to control the effect of our being used to making rapid judgements of facial emotions). If emotional decoding is holistic and involves correlating information from mouth and eyes, then it should be slower than the recognition of hair colour.

Sixteen student volunteers saw 16 pictures. Four were simple sketches of angry faces, four were neutral, four happy and four sad. Each set of four sketches comprised a face with eyebrows and mouths and one without (the 'expression condition'); one with dark hair and one with light (the 'hair condition'). Eight subjects saw each upright picture for 200 ms; eight saw them inverted for the same time. They pressed one of two microswitches ('Yes' and 'No') to indicate (a) whether faces in the expression condition had brows or mouths, (b) whether those in the hair condition had dark hair.

The dependent variable was the response time (RT), which was automatically recorded and statistically analysed using Student's t-test and ANOVA. RTs were longer for inverted faces in the expression condition, which was interpreted as evidence for proposition 1, that facial emotions are

continued

> holistically interpreted. There were also shorter RTs for angry and sad faces, which White suggests may reflect an evolutionary predisposition to identify anger quickly and then the systematic mis-coding of sadness for anger.
>
> The applications and wider significance of this study did not draw themselves to my attention.

The findings of quasi-experiments are compromised because the researcher cannot be confident that only one factor, the intervention, can explain any change between O_1 and O_2. Nevertheless, they-can be attractive propositions for small-scale researchers simply because changes in practice – the introduction of a new system of ward hygiene, for example – are always being introduced and come ready-made as topics for dissertations and projects. The design would typically have the form:

OLD SYSTEM O_1 NEW SYSTEM O_2 NEW SYSTEM O_3

O_2 would give information about the new system in its early days and O_3 would show how it bedded down. Of course, each set of observations would involve different patients but, unless there were good reasons not to, the researcher would assume that one set of patients is much like another.

Laboratory experiments can appeal to small-scale researchers because it is relatively easy to take a published experiment, observe that the research subjects all had certain characteristics (in psychology experiments they will often have been students who were getting course credit for participation) and repeat it with subjects of a different age, sex, class, gender, nationality etc. There is a view that this is important and that the social sciences suffer because too few studies are repeated, with the result that too many claims are based on rather slim empirical foundations. Alternatively, you might see ways in which the experimental controls or treatments could be criticized, which then justifies doing a modified version of the original. If you are looking around for a small-scale study to satisfy course requirements it is worth considering consider experiments and field experiments on the grounds of:

1 Feasibility: many experiments involve relatively small numbers of subjects and collect fixed-response, numerical data, which are usually easier to handle than responses to open-ended questions (see Chapter 8).
2 Slipstream: like a racing cyclist tucked into the slipstream of the rider ahead, those who replicate or modify someone else's study are helped by their slipstream. They benefit from their precursor's literature review and a ready-made research design that only needs to be tweaked.
3 Structure: the structured nature of quantitative data analysis means that it is generally far simpler than qualitative data analysis, *as long as*

you have taken a course in statistics (see also Chapter 8). There is also a strong convention governing the writing of experimental reports. This structure, which can feel constraining, even inappropriate, can also be very supportive to the novice researcher and ease the writing-up task (see Chapter 9).

However, unless natural opportunities for quasi-experiments present themselves, or unless it is easy to organize a laboratory study, experiments can be difficult. The difficulty lies not so much with design and measurement issues as with a scarcity of people who are prepared to play along with the manoeuvres experimenters want to make. For example, a student devised an elaborate experiment that depended on using IQ scores to allocate 48 out of a population of 150 school children to one of eight matched groups, each of which was to get different classroom learning experiences. Aside from massive problems with matching, it was entirely unrealistic to expect that any school would co-operate in these quasi-experimental shenanigans.

4

Research at a Distance

To repeat a point made in Chapter 3: a major difference between face-to-face research and that done at a distance is that in face-to-face work the researcher has the choice of improvising ways to patch up defects in the research design that only become apparent when the investigation is under way. For example, in a semi-structured interview the researcher may realize that an important line of inquiry has been overlooked and simply improvise appropriate probes and incorporate them into future interviews. That is seldom an option when the research design is locked up in fixed-response schedules, scales, q-sort cards or tests. Validity, in the sense of addressing everything that is relevant in terms of the research questions, has to be designed in and, because these small-scale inquiry methods often produce numerical data, the instruments' reliability also needs to be established before they are used on respondents. Mistakes that have got embedded in a questionnaire or measurement scale are expensive. Piloting is the best way of reducing the chance of making them. Piloting also helps you to find out how best to present the instruments to participants. Their only contact with your inquiry may be through the piece of paper which is your questionnaire, scale, or q-sort instructions. Whether they respond or throw it away depends a lot on the opening patter (which promises confidentiality and explains what the research is about, who it's for and why it's important) and on the sense that the questions, instructions or scale makes (if the readability level is too high, response rates will plummet). Once launched, research at a distance is out of your control. Get it as right as possible before launching it. Second chances have to be purchased and most small-scale researchers cannot afford the time and money costs.

Measurement, Rating Scales and Lookalikes

This section starts with the features and development of measurement and rating scales. With literate respondents who are likely to complete them, rating and measurement scales can be sent out and treated as a special form of questionnaire, which is what the next section is about. In other cases they are administered by a trained researcher and the section in Chapter 3 on doing face-to-face research is more appropriate. A distinction should be made between scales and other instruments that might look the same but which are less sophisticated. These psuedo-scales or lookalikes have not been carefully developed to have:

- Consistency, which means that the scale has been designed to measure one or more known constructs. For example, the Myers–Briggs personality test has been designed to profile personality (and *only* personality) in terms of four Jungian dichotomies: introversion, extroversion; feeling, thinking; sensing, intuiting; judging, perceiving. The 100 forced-choice items in the tests are there because extensive research has shown that they (1) measure personality and (2) profile it in terms of the eight Jungian types. This is quite different from a questionnaire containing items that may look similar but which (1) have not been tested to establish which of the eight types each relates to, (2) have not been examined to see how sensitive the questionnaire is to each of them, and (3) do not combine to make a scale that has both power and concision. You might visit <http://www.teamtechnology.co.uk/tt/t-articl/mb-simpl.htm> for a non-technical indication of how the Myers–Briggs indicator works. For a critique that says the indicator is, like many others, little more than a parlour game see <http://skepdic.com/myersb.html>. Spoto (1995) questions whether a simple scale such as this can do justice to the complexity of Jung's thought.
- Validity. It should be a fair measure of the construct. For example, it is very debatable whether IQ tests are a fair measure of intelligence, unless we define intelligence as that which IQ tests measure (Sternberg, 1997). Again, there are problems in claiming that some reading tests are valid measures of reading. They may be good tests of word recognition, of word attack strategies and of how well someone can sound out words. Whether those achievements are 'reading', which some would see as a form of sophisticated thinking, is another matter.
- Reliability. Measurement demands reliability, although it is possible to make a fetish of it. The level of reliability that a measure should have rather depends on the purposes for which it is intended. Nevertheless, scales will usually include many questions directed at the same thing because reliability increases with the number of measurements. On the other hand, few take up more than two pages because long scales deter respondents, although well-piloted scales should not have to be any longer.
- Interval-level scores. The concept of interval data is reviewed in Box 8.1. For present purposes it is enough to say that it is possible to devise scales on which there is a case for saying that the difference between a score of +3 and +5 is as great as that between −1 and +1. These data are of interval-level quality, which makes it possible to analyse results with powerful statistical routines that are sensitive to fine differences in the responses.

Box 4.1 Attitude scales and a study of authoritarian and paranormal beliefs (Heard and Vyse, 1999)

The authors said that there is a lack of research testing a claim that superstitiousness and belief in the supernatural are characteristics of the authoritarian personality. They explored this through the Authoritarianism–Rebellion Scale (which seems to have been quite well established) and the Tabacyk Revised Paranormal Beliefs Scale which comes from an unpublished dissertation. With the exception of test–retest reliability figures, no evidence was provided that it met the four criteria that define a scale, and its assumption that Christianity is a paranormal belief may be literally true and practically misleading.

The sample of 85 was obtained through (1) a mailshot to 250 staff and students, selected at random, who were members of a small, predominantly white liberal arts college; (2) by soliciting in the library and student centre; and (3) by giving course credit for participation to students taking introductory psychology. The three methods combined had an 11.6% response rate.

Fixed response data were analysed by computer and the two scales were generally found to correlate with each other. The conclusion was: 'this study provides some evidence for a relationship between paranormal beliefs and authoritarianism, but in the absence of corroborative evidence, no strong conclusions can be drawn' (124–5).

These four characteristics are hard to achieve and small-scale researchers would often do best to use an existing scale rather than consider developing their own. Box 4.1 implies that using scales is no guarantee that the study will be a good one.

In many cases it will be acceptable and illuminating to ask a set of questions or items that look like a scale but do not constitute a scale because the consistency of the set is unknown, the reliability is uncertain and the statistical routines designed for interval quality data ought not to be used.

All scale and psuedo-scale development begins with a substantial set of items that have been written to address the main components of the construct in question. Suppose a scale was wanted to measure adults' self-theories. Some 10 or 15 items would be written for each of the eight main aspects identified from a search of the literature. The most common type of scale is a Likert scale where the items are presented as statements that respondents might strongly agree with or strongly disagree with. An example is in Box 4.2.

To discourage people from mindlessly ticking the boxes, some of the statements are 'reversed'. For example, the statement 'My personality is a significant influence on my academic performance' could easily be reversed to disrupt a tendency to tick only the far right boxes. Ideally these statements should capture a good spread of responses and attract neither extreme responses, nor ones clustered around the middle column. Some researchers try to extend the range by using seven response cells but it is not clear that this brings any great benefits and it may be asking

Box 4.2 A fragment of a draft Likert scale exploring undergraduates' self-theories

What do you think about your experience in higher education? (Respondents had been told that ++ meant 'strongly agree' and -- meant 'strongly disagree' etc.)

	--	-	?	+	++
20 I do not enjoy my academic work					
21 My personality is a significant influence on my academic performance					
22 If there is a difficult task to be done, I put myself forward to tackle it					
23 My academic work is largely shaped by what the teaching staff tell me I ought to do					
24 I do not find that academic work stretches me intellectually					
25 I see higher education as an opportunity to develop new skills					

respondents to make artificially fine grained distinctions. Others try to discourage people choosing the middle column by providing just four (or sometimes six) response cells to force an agree/disagree choice. In the full version of the scale, extracts from which are in Box 4.2, we wanted responses to the same statements in two contexts. The order of the statements in section B (life in general) was different from that in section C (higher education) in order to discourage any corner-cutting.

This bank of draft items should be piloted with a large sample that is representative of the target group. The self-theories items were *first* piloted on 187 undergraduates. Large though that number may seem, it is often on the low side. For example, undergraduates' self-theories may vary according to the subjects they are studying because different academic subjects may attract people with somewhat different characteristics. If there are four main subject groups and all four were equally represented within the pilot sample, there would be fewer than 50 respondents from each group. If, in addition, gender is an important variable, then there are likely to be fewer than 25 women or men in each group. Pilot data should be based on as large a sample as possible, which is another reason why small-scale researchers are best advised not to try developing their own scales or lookalikes.

With the responses collected and entered into a statistics package, it is possible to identify those statements that are most closely correlated with the scale as a whole (or with any subscales) and discard those which, because they do not correlate well, seem to be measuring something else. It may be that a scale designed to measure attitudes towards the police can be reduced from 79 pilot statements to a scale of just a dozen or so. Here is a major difference between true scales and lookalikes: true scales are internally consistent because items that do not correlate highly with the total are discarded, whereas psuedo-scales, which are concerned to capture the range of responses, keep them. Those who develop Likert scales or psuedo-scales usually act as it the data were of interval quality, although it is unlikely.

Box 4.3 An extract from a grid used in rating the professional standing of occupations

Trait	Medicine	Law	Police	Nursing	Teaching
Above average pay					
Commitment to the work					
Systematic theory or codified knowledge base					
Authority over the client					
Controls entry to the occupation					

Box 4.3 contains a fragment from the sort of informal grid that is widely used in small-scale research. The main advantage of this format is that it allows a great deal of information about the relationship between two sets to be captured on one page. Greater discrimination can be had by inviting respondents to tick or to use ? for possible or marginal cases. Repertory grids are an attempt to bring grids more into line with the requirements of scaling. Kelly's repertory grids may look the same but in their original form there two differences: (1) the categories are elicited from each respondent rather than coming from the literature or from the researcher, and (2) the grids were originally intended to be custom-made for each informant, although they are now widely used in surveys.

Suppose the researcher's interest is in 18-year-olds' constructions of masculinity. A set of stimuli intended to evoke gendered reactions would be put together. It would include male and female photographs and could also include objects, advertisements, video clips, short quotations and sound recordings. It is easier to manage if all of the stimuli can be laid out on a table. The informant is then asked to look at any three of them and identify a way in which two are the same but the third is not (examples might include 'muscular', 'fit', 'caring'). That becomes the first construct. The process is repeated until no fresh constructs are generated. This list of constructs is then systematically applied to each stimulus in turn, so that the researcher ends up with a grid showing (1) what constructs are salient in this informant's thinking about masculinity, and (2) which are used more often in response to the stimuli. The main strength of this technique is that the constructs are supplied by informants and have a validity that is quite different from any the researcher supplied. The drawbacks are the amount of time involved in the individualized approach and the problems of making comparisons between different informants. For this reason many researchers would prefer to (1) give all respondents a grid whose categories are based on a literature review or (2) treat the individualized work as a pilot and then analyse and reanalyse the different categories that have been produced by different informants to get a set of grounded categories that could then be used in a standard grid administered to all respondents. Once a common grid has been produced, factor analysis or other statistical techniques can be used to increase its internal consistency, although this rather flies in the face of Kelly's intention, which was to capture diversity.

The approach to item design used in Likert scales has been widely copied by researchers developing rating scales. Some ask for judgements, feelings, behaviours and suchlike to be captured on five-point scales. For example, people may be asked whether they think that something is 'very likely' through to 'very unlikely'; whether something makes them feel 'very sad' through to 'very happy'; and whether they like something 'very much' or 'not at all'. A common rating technique simply asks respondents to give a number on a 1–10 or 1–20 scale where 10 or 20 is good. It is often used in student evaluations of university teaching, which is something that has probably been investigated more than any other topic in North American educational research (Marsh and Dunkin, 1997). It is frequently found that (1) these are psuedo-scales and lack internal consistency; (2) it is doubtful whether the data are of interval quality; (3) there are validity problems when some aspects of teaching are missed from the instrument; (4) reliability is compromised when students are asked to make global rather than focused judgements and when there are too few items relating to each major dimension of teaching; (5) because of these four limitations, it is unwise – and possibly damaging – to compare one teacher's scores with another's or with any norm, mean, median or mode; and (6) responses can be very illuminating when interpreted in context, which might include discussion with other teachers and with a sample of the students. In spite of these common deficiencies, teaching evaluations are widely misused in the high-stakes business of deciding promotion and merit payments.

A variation is to ask the question or make the statement and then ask respondents to make a mark on a horizontal line that is 100 mm long to indicate where they stand in relation to the statements or qualities that are at each end of the line. The distance in millimetres between one end of the line and the mark is measured and used as the statistic for that item.

Ticklists simply get respondents to tick statements they agree with and tell them to ignore others. These can be used to direct researchers' attention, so that a good practice inventory could guide a moderately structured observation of customer service and a set of statements might be used to explore respondents' reactions to Prozac (see Box 3.1) or to identify forms of exercise that they took yesterday.

Sorting is another common rating technique. The principle behind one approach to sorting, Thurstone scales, is that a large number of judges sort large numbers of statements into 11 piles. When all judgements of all statements are aggregated it is possible to see (1) a rank order, (2) which areas cause the most disagreement, (3) whether certain groups of judges tend to rate statements in distinctive ways, and (4) whether the judgements tend to show clusters amongst some of the statements. Simplifications to the sorting technique make it attractive and it is the basis of the q-sort procedure described later.

Associative techniques are illustrated by considering Bogardus' social distance scaling. He asked respondents to say whether different groups of people would be acceptable in each of several more or less intimate social roles or positions. In this way it is possible to identify those people or groups who are regarded as 'more like us' and 'least like us'. The technique can be extended to identify those people who might work best together and those least likely to do so. It can be modified by asking people who, in a group, they would like to work with on various tasks, to have as a friend or to socialize with. This can then be represented visually as a sociogram with the most chosen person located in the centre and others arranged around that focus. For example, it might be argued that workplace cultures are quite fractured, which means that change agents need to understand where micro-cultures are favourable to change and where they are not. Sociograms could show patterns of association and influence in the department which could then be matched up to data collected through repertory grids, Likert scales, checklists, questionnaires, interviews, observations etc. In the process, change agents could also see who would be the key people, the gatekeepers, who it would be most urgent to win over to the new policy or practice. Unfortunately, it is hard to draw sociograms for large numbers of people and it may be easier to display the data in a matrix or to calculate indices to describe each person's popularity, influence or value as a team member. At this point the idea merges easily into the techniques of clustering that are dealt with in a later section on concept analysis.

Dissociative techniques are not really distinct techniques but a set of distancing devices intended to counter respondents' common wish to censor what they say so as to put themselves in a good light (the halo effect). Shaw and Wright (1967) refer to some of them as 'disguised' techniques and Oppenheim (1992) writes of 'projective' techniques. One approach is to ask participants to respond to many of the instruments described in this chapter and the previous one as if they were someone else. That persona is often someone similarly placed to respondents, the intention being that they will simply project their own views, behaviours or ideas on the imaginary person without first censoring them. Variants invite them to make up stories to fit images presented by the researcher; to suggest how someone in a picture might be feeling or thinking and why; to complete a half-told story; to suggest characteristics that match a picture of a product, place, school, house, portrait etc.; to say what a person would be best advised to do in response to a problem; and so on. These manoeuvres to evade the halo effect can, of course, be used with most research techniques and it can be very interesting to explore the differences between the answers people give about themselves as subjects and those they give when operating under distancing techniques like these. They can also be used to explore sensitive topics: child sexual abuse may be more easily investigated in play with anatomically correct dolls than by direct questioning, and filling in the blank speech bubbles in strip cartoons can substitute for direct inquiry about adolescents' sexual health practices.

Questionnaires

Some writers describe any highly structured set of questions as a questionnaire, regardless of whether it is read by respondents at their convenience or read to respondents by a researcher who is not allowed to offer any help or guidance beyond rereading any question that causes problems. I want to distinguish between the two and call self-administered sets of questions or scales 'questionnaires' and reserve 'interviews' for face-to-face encounters, even when the interviewer has virtually no discretion in using the scale or schedule. This has the disadvantage of concealing the substantial similarities between self-administered questionnaires and highly structured survey interviews, but it also signals that the choice between survey interviews and self-administered questionnaire is not a trivial one. To give one, often overlooked example, once a questionnaire or rating scale is printed and mailed out, the researcher can do nothing except receive the responses. Errors are beyond redemption. On the other hand, a faulty interview schedule will be quickly identified, especially in telephone interviewing, and although the interviewer may not have the power to change it, the person who designed the study can. There is a cost – material collected before the problem was corrected may have to be junked – but it is far less than the cost of a faulty questionnaire.

E-mail inquiries and web-based conferencing software are blurring my distinction. For example, my colleague Paul Trowler and I sent e-mails out on various lists asking people to click on a website address and then answer either three or eight open-ended questions, depending on how busy they were. We could refine our questions after the questionnaire had gone out on one list and before sending it to another. By using a dozen lists we got enough replies to help us in our thinking about the research topic and we were subsequently able to ask informants for clarification and for suggestions about other people who might help. Our experience was that this method would not have been fit for any purpose except exploration because for every person who clicked and completed, at least another 50 probably deleted the e-mail on sight.

Low response rates are likely to be the bugbear of attempts to base systematic inquiries in cyberspace, although response rates to conventional ways of delivering questionnaires are not encouraging. Box 4.1 describes a study with a rate of 11.6%, and Baruch (1999) reports that his analysis of 175 studies (83% of which originated in the USA) showed (1) that response rates in 1995 were about 50%, (2) that 20 years earlier they had been close to 65%, and (3) that the range of response rates is widening, which means that quite a lot of studies are now based on a 30% response rate and few on a rate higher than 70%. Since those who complete questionnaires (or let themselves be observed, interviewed or experimented with) are by definition different from those who decline, these low response rates suggest that social research is fast approaching the point of routinely drawing conclusions from work with unrepresentative minorities. Furthermore, Jenkins (1999), writing about fixed-response questionnaires designed to measure (yes, measure) quality of life points out (1) there are dangers of false precision when scores get reported to three decimal places; (2) it is debatable whether the fixed-response questions are a valid representation of people's diverse perceptions of quality of life; and (3) that once people realize that their answers can be used to ration care and decide upon priorities for treatment they will complete the questionnaires strategically, not objectively. To problems of low response can be added problems of strategic responses.

Questionnaires can include all sorts of ways of getting a written response. On my loose definition, any of the scales, lookalikes and other inquiry methods mentioned in the previous section could be loosely called a questionnaire or incorporated into one. Questions can be written in a variety of forms, from sentence completion items that involve either selecting phrases from the set provided by the researcher (good for reliability) or writing in one's own (better for validity), to ticking a box if you watched television yesterday (and if you did, there would usually be follow-up questions asking that you tick boxes to quantify how long you watched and to pin down what you watched). So, neither interviews nor questionnaires are homogeneous research methods. Even so, the distinction between face-to-face and impersonal inquiries does allow some common differences to be identified, which is the theme of Table 4.1. Boxes 4.4 and 4.5 describe two questionnaire studies to illustrate ways of using fixed-response and open-ended questions. There is no shortage of books that provide a good introduction to doing survey research based on

Table 4.1 *Questionnaires and interviews (after Arksey and Knight, 1999)*

Characteristics	Self-administered questionnaires using fixed-response or open-ended questions	Interviews using open-ended questions or promts
Provide information about	Attitudes, motivation, accounts of behaviour, opinions, events	As for questionnaires, but far better at exploring these things in depth, learning about the informants' perspectives and about what matters to them
Best at	Surveying and generalizing: checking how far the researcher's hypothesis or world view is shared by the sample and getting an idea of how common or widespread attitudes etc. are among different groups	Sensemaking and understanding: exploring the stories and perspectives of informants, asking 'Why?' Necessary when subjects neither read nor write easily and willingly
And	Open-ended questions allow the researcher to ask for informants' stories and perspectives	Can also be used to do what questionnaires do
Sample size	Can be very large because highly structured responses are quite easy to capture and analyse (especially if they are electronic responses). Since the aim is often to generalize from the sample to the population, samples often need to be big	With the exception of phone and intercept interviews, the time cost of interviewing, data capture and qualitative analysis ensures that sample sizes are restricted: better for in-depth work with fewer people
Richness of response	Nuances cannot easily be detected and highly structured instruments allow for thin responses only. Short (and superficial?) is the norm and long questionnaires that could get richer responses are rarely acceptable	A dialogue between researcher and informant is possible, allowing nuances to be captured (especially where video recording is used), questions to be clarified and adapted, and new ones to be improvised. Long interviews are often reported in research papers
Anonymity	Sensitive questions may be more acceptable in anonymous questionnaires	Can be awkward for some people to say some things in face-to-face settings; consequently there's a real danger of only hearing from the confident members of the target group

(Continued)

Table 4.1 *(Continued)*

Characteristics	Self-administered questionnaires using fixed-response or open-ended questions	Interviews using open-ended questions or promts
Time costs (design)	Devising questionnaire (checking validity and reliability), piloting to check whether people (1) will fill it in, (2) appear to understand it, (3) seem to be 'faking good'	Devising interview guide (checking validity and reliability, or their equivalents). This may be quicker with interpretive research. Piloting to check that the interviewer (1) can interview and (2) use these prompts/questions
Time costs (doing)	Distributing questionnaires (e-mail is cheapest but there's a growing risk that e-mail questionnaires will routinely get junked as 'spam')	Arranging interviews (less of a problem with clipboarding and telephone surveys Establishing trust and rapport (less of a problem with surveys) Allowing time for diversions during the interview (less of a problem for surveys) Travelling, getting lost and hanging around (unanswered calls in phone interviews, refusals in intercept interviews) Limit number of interviews to guard against interviewer fatigue
Time costs (data capture)	Usually swift, especially where data are directly entered into a computer or optical mark readers are used	Transcription of data (frequently estimated as seven to ten hours transcription time per hour of audiotape: videotape can be worse)
Time costs (data analysis)	Usually swift. However, any open-ended questions are difficult to analyse, whether they are used in interviews or questionnaires	Substantial: see Chapter 8 Novice researchers frequently underestimate the time needed for coding and analysis
Cash costs	Mainly cost of printing, distributing and retrieving questionnaires. At face value the cost per questionnaire is relatively low. *But* low response rates, which are typical (Baruch, 1999) can make it an expensive method per returned response	Interviews with open-ended questions are expensive: hire of interviewers (perhaps), travel costs, tapes, batteries, transcription of tapes. Phone interviews possibly cheaper than questionnaires on a per response basis, especially if calls are preceded by a letter telling the sample about the research project and the forthcoming phone contact

Box 4.4 A questionnaire survey of drink driving and deterrence
(Baum, 1999)

Does random breath testing (RBT) have deterrent effects?

A total of 430 Australian respondents were interviewed by telephone. They were selected at random by computer using the CATI technique outlined in Chapter 3. Up to five attempts were made to contact each number. When contact was made the interviewer asked to speak to someone aged 16–70 and the interview only went ahead if the respondent's English was sufficiently good and if the informant had consumed alcohol at any time in the past six months. The sample was compared with census data and found to have a similar age profile, although younger people were slightly over-represented.

Interviews took between 10 and 12 minutes and were conducted by trained interviewers supervised by an administrator. Respondents were asked whether they had driven after drinking and about their alcohol consumption. They were then asked to respond to statements such as 'The risks of drink driving are over-rated' and 'My friends would think I was stupid if I drove after drinking' (255) on a 10-point scale. The items were designed to explore the relationship between self-reported drink driving behaviour and five variables.

The responses were analysed using non-parametric statistical routines to identify those that were most strongly associated with drink driving. It was found that heavy drinkers were more likely to drink and drive, they felt that the risks were over-rated ($Rs = + 0.277$) and they doubted that their friends would think this behaviour stupid ($Rs = -0.193$). The researchers concluded that RBT has unstable deterrence effects.

Box 4.5 A questionnaire survey of the effect of the prison environment on inmate drug taking behaviour (Swann and James, 1998)

'Prison has the potential to discourage continued drug use. However, the very nature of the environment means that it may equally, although indirectly, encourage drug misuse' (p. 253).

A semi-structured, self-report questionnaire was chosen as the means of inquiry since it preserved informants' anonymity. Eighty-five inmates at one male category B prison completed fixed-response questions about their drug taking before entering prison and while in it. Open-ended questions explored the reasons for their behaviours. Nine inmates helped design the two questionnaires (which helped improve validity and technical quality) and then distributed and collected them. While all 85 completed the fixed-response questions, only 55 did the open-ended ones.

The sample was not representative of male category B prisoners because a disproportionate number (51) of them were in prison for drug-related offences. Nonetheless, the authors considered that the findings well illustrated the problems of promoting abstinence in prisons. They found that (1) 82% used drugs while imprisoned, including two who had not previously used them; (2) some wanted to abstain from hard drugs but not from 'puff', which meant that they were not attracted by the official solution of creating a drug-free wing; (3) 52.9% felt that the pressure to use drugs

continued

> inside was greater than outside, not least because of the tedium of prison
> life; and (4) prisoners' lack of trust for the warders was a bar to their asking
> for help.

questionnaires and similar instruments: Harvey and MacDonald (1993),
for example, give well-founded advice, Gillham (2000c) has written a
succinct guide for novice researchers and Bryman (2001) provides, as
always, good advice.

Questionnaires, measurement scales and suchlike are commonly used
when big samples are needed because the research aim is to answer
questions about large groups. Well-funded researchers, such as the team
that produced the British report *Social Services: Working under Pressure*
(Balloch et al., 1999), may be able to do a couple of thousand interviews
but small-scale researchers who want to make generalizing claims will
rely on questionnaires and measurement scales. For example, Griffith
et al. (1999) investigated levels of stress among British schoolteachers and
factors associated with it. On the basis of replies from 780 teachers
(a 53.5% response rate) they were able to conclude that 'similar challenges
may be more or less stressful depending on the individual's perception of
his or her social environment' (1999: 527). Three points are worth high-
lighting. First, their 'questionnaire' comprised four distinct items, three of
which were established and validated measurement scales, the fourth
being a questionnaire about sources of social support in the workplace.
Secondly, their choice of instruments was driven by a well-developed
hypothesis that offered an explanation about the incidence of stress
amongst teachers: this was not a haphazard exercise in data dredging
driven by a belief in serendipity. Thirdly, 780 teachers is a big sample, but
when it comes to making statements about female secondary teachers or,
even worse, young male primary teachers, the numbers get to be quite
small and chance factors are more likely to be behind the patterns in the
data. In that light, a sample of 780 is not really very big. Small-scale
researchers using survey instruments will often have to settle for closer to
150–200 responses.

Although it is impossible to overemphasize the advantages of using
instruments that others have developed, especially if they report the work
they did to establish reliability and validity, small-scale researchers will
often want to create their own schedule, one that is customized for the
particular audience. Even then it is worth thinking seriously about lifting
questions from published scales and questionnaires, principally because
it provides a way of associating your findings with what has already been
established. It is not only experiments that can or should be replicated.

When investigators develop their own scales and instruments there
are some large pitfalls to avoid. The main one is that anyone can come
up with a Likert lookalike or questionnaire that some people will

answer in some fashion by using nothing more than common sense and investing five minutes of time. Good questionnaires and scales either have been used by others and shown to be fit for the purpose or are the product of an approach based on thought, theory, technical skills and piloting.

First, it is essential to have *thought* about why a questionnaire is an appropriate way of addressing the research questions. For example, if the study is an interpretive one, then a questionnaire might reasonably be used to collect background and biographical data; a rating scale could establish informants' views, attitudes or practices in preparation for open-ended interviews or observation. It would be inappropriate to claim that a study was interpretive and rely on fixed-response questionnaires or scales: interviews would be the method of choice.

Secondly, good questionnaires, like other instruments, rest on a good working *theory* of what ought to be explored and why it might be significant. Otherwise, the instrument is made up of haphazard probes. In such cases some probes will be quite irrelevant (why ask respondents' age unless there is reason to believe that age is a significant factor in your inquiry?) but most will be sensible enough. The lack of theory shows up mainly in the questions that do not get asked. This is where a literature review is justified, even for very 'practical' inquiries such as action research projects. The literature review should give the researcher a fairly complete map of the factors that could bear on the research questions and conceptual issues to be kept in mind when addressing them. For example, when studying the effectiveness of a police force, it is important to realize that the concept of effectiveness has contested meanings and can be measured in different ways. A questionnaire that is insensitive to that is defective. In the same vein, a rating scale that asks how effective police are at doing different jobs would be faulty if jobs that one group – beat officers, local politicians, ethnic minority people, senior officers, old people – thought were important were missed from the list. And if earlier research had identified factors that were correlated with how people viewed the police's effectiveness, then it would normally be necessary to follow that up in the questionnaire. The researcher who has a defensible theory of what should be investigated is less likely to do a study that is weak because key areas have been ignored.

Thirdly, *technical skill* is needed. This refers to the ways in which questions and statements are worded, response categories are designed and everything is then brought together.

- Readability tests should be used to establish that the questionnaire is not too hard for the audience. Questions should be as short as possible, clear and in plain English. It is as important to make sure that the preamble or 'patter' (which tells respondents what the questionnaire is for and why it matters, assures them of confidentiality, says how long it is likely to take to do, and thanks them for their time) is readable and written in the active voice using 'I' and 'you'.

- There may be a decision to be made about whether to invite respondents to choose on a scale with three, four, five or more points.
- If respondents are asked to choose from lists – to tick phrases that describe their views, for instance – try to keep the lists as short as possible. Long lists deter. If you want them to rank the options they have chosen, it is more friendly to ask them to identify their first, second and third choices than to suggest that all choices be ranked.
- There are times when questions have to be global, which means that they ask about views, beliefs or behaviour in general. Many researchers prefer the sort of accuracy that comes from asking people to respond with a specific case in mind: ask how many times they remember doing, saying, hearing, seeing, feeling or thinking something yesterday, in the past hour, or the last time they visited or did/saw something. The drawback is that the researcher may get a false impression of *an individual's* exercise behaviour. Suppose the questionnaire asked about exercise taken yesterday but yesterday was too wet for that informant to go running, even though he normally runs five days a week. That is only significant, though, if the investigation is concerned with individuals. Surveys are usually interested in *groups*, in averages across large samples and people who normally run but didn't run yesterday are cancelled out by ones who ran yesterday but who might not run today or tomorrow.
- The order in which questions are arranged can have an effect on the answers: ones at the beginning and end may be answered differently from those in the middle, especially if the instrument is long (and boring). The test is whether two orderings of the same set of questions produce different patterns of response. Since it would take quite a large pilot study to explore that, it can be simplest to distribute at random two versions of the same questionnaire or measure. This is not possible when the instrument has to be set out in a certain sequence to funnel inquiries from specific cases through to questions about attitudes to the cases taken as a whole.
- Presentationally, there should be plenty of white space on the page (clutter is a deterrent); the font size should be no smaller than 12 point; there should be plenty of room for respondents to write in answers to open-ended questions; it should be shorter rather than longer; and it will often be laid out so that OCR software can be used to read the responses.

Fourthly, questionnaires and other home-grown instruments must be piloted, even if the best that can be done is trying drafts out on a few friends. The *piloting* should have three purposes: (1) to see whether people can complete it in a reasonable time, (2) to see whether their responses suggest that there may be problems with some questions or items on a rating scale, and (3) to make you think carefully about how you will code and analyse the data. The more widely it can be piloted the less likely it will contain assumptions about activities, values or thoughts that are culturally skewed: you might have lunch, I have dinner; you might drive to work, I catch the bus; you have a Christian name, I have a first name; and so on. The greatest benefit comes when it is possible to talk to people who completed a pilot version about why they answered as they did and whether they can suggest improvements or additions.

Diaries, Logs and Journals

Questionnaires are often used to collect data about behaviour but there is a concern that they are not very accurate. For instance, I am not entirely sure how long I watched television yesterday and I would be unlikely to spend too long working it out for a questionnaire: I would just tick the box that seemed to be about right and move on to the next question. Where researchers want more accurate data than they can get from these retrospective accounts and when observation is not feasible, then structured diaries or logs are an alternative. A log might be a sheet for each day, activity or target event with a set of instructions for completing it. What participants are asked to do depends on the research questions. One might require them to check each time they smoked a cigarette and then complete fixed-response questions about their feelings and motivations at the time. Another could ask them to record what sort of work they were doing by entering a code into a grid dividing the day into 15 minute segments. A third could involve the experience sampling method (ESM) of writing a description of one's emotional state and what preceded it every time a pager went off. Happe and colleagues concluded that:

> Both diary and ESM formats are quite flexible, including open-ended questions, fixed-format responses, and checklists, and can typically take but a few minutes to complete ... Advantages ... include greater accuracy, fewer problems of recall, improved ability to determine the order of events, and the ability to capture events of low salience that are easily forgotten ... [diaries and ESM] generally yielded higher reports of behaviors and events than other data collection methods. (2000: 103)

It can be difficult to get volunteers for something as intrusive as diary research, and because it is quite demanding it is all the more likely that volunteers will not be entirely typical of the target group at large. Besides, behaviour may be influenced by the diaries themselves: if smoking behaviour is monitored the respondent may try to 'fake good' by cutting consumption. It is also expensive to brief respondents on how to complete the diary and to keep them on task: one approach is to send new diary sheets out weekly and to ask for completed sheets back daily, so that any fall-off can be swiftly spotted and the respondent can be 'remotivated'. Happe and colleagues (2000) compared daily self-completion logs with telephone interviews. Both approaches used the same set of questions. The study lasted for eight weeks and involved 48 people who reported their drinking, drug use and sexual behaviour daily when phoned by a member of the research team and 52 who mailed in their paper diaries. The only differences in the data were that the reported alcohol and vegetable consumption of the telephone group was higher. Telephone reporting was about 50% more expensive, largely because of the extra costs in staff time. However, rapid developments in voicemail technology, combined with touchtone phones, mean that it is possible to envisage automated telephone interviews using fixed-response questions as an alternative, for some purposes, to self-report diaries.

For some researchers diaries are highly structured logs but for others diaries are a way of collecting more open-ended data. Little more needs to be said about using this technique to get a running commentary from informants on their perceptions, reaction and feelings, except that (1) without the structure provided by the daily log sheet, ESM or phone call it is probably harder to get them to write diligently, (2) the data will be as rich and uneven as all open-ended data with corresponding problems of data analysis.

Research diaries were mentioned in Chapter 1. In some form they are kept by many researchers, regardless of whether they are working from a traditional, more or less positivist position or from an interpretive one, although different positions do imply keeping rather different sorts of diary. All researchers should ensure that there is a good project archive, not least because it is very useful when writing a research report to have reminders of why a questionnaire contained *those* questions in *that* form, or of how a sample was selected. Researchers dealing with open-ended data need records, whether in diary form or not, that describe the analytical categories used and show, through examples, how the categories were actually used. This is developed in Chapter 8.

Interpretive researchers who see themselves as research instruments, as necessarily subjective players in the research game, will also know that they should be reflexive in the sense of carefully considering how their participation in the research has contributed to the stories they wish to tell (see Box 3.3 for a reminder of this). It is far less important for more positivist researchers to reflect on their part in the research process because they are supposed to be neutral observers of other people's realities and, as a consequence, their personal reactions are of no significance in the scientific process. But those investigators who believe that the researcher cannot be separated from the research need to keep diaries to help them appraise their part in the research. They will often make extensive use of that material when they make the case that although they have not been neutral, 'scientific' observers, their work is authentic, careful and trustworthy, a plausible and serious representation of a systematic inquiry. In principle, then, their diaries should be as open to inspection as any other research data that they create, always respecting the limitations imposed by the ethical need to sustain confidentiality.

Q-sort

This method is widely used to get a better understanding of individuals' personality, beliefs and attitudes (Block, 1978) and to investigate group functioning (Peterson et al., 1999). Although there are other ways of doing research in these areas, notably semi-structured interviews and observations, q-sort is attractive when the researcher wants an approach that is more tightly structured, replicable and 'objective', and where there is value in using statistical routines to process the data and make fine comparisons between the respondents. This method is considered in this at-a-distance chapter because it is important to get the documentation right, as with questionnaires and scales. However, that does not imply that the researcher should not be present when q-sorts are done. On the contrary, people generally find it much easier to do q-sorts if a researcher is to hand to coax them through what is quite a complex procedure. The researcher can also learn from watching people as they do q-sorts and interacting with them.

Box 4.6 Q-sort in an evaluation of a drop-in youth centre (Mercier et al., 2000)

'The role of the evaluation would then be to make known these assumptions [about the characteristics of a good drop-in youth centre programme], to synthesize them into a consistent theoretical format, and to examine their congruence with the programme as implemented' (p. 76).

Eight people working in a Montreal drop-in youth centre brainstormed 188 ideas in response to a question about ways in which it could contribute to the prevention of a variety of risks to young people's well-being. Ninety-eight were chosen at random, and then ranked on a seven-point Likert scale and sorted into themes by each person. *The Concept System* program (see Trochim, 1999) produced cluster maps which were discussed by participants who named the 10 clusters and suggested ways in which the clusters could act upon each other to bring about juvenile risk reduction.

In addition, a computerized literature search helped to identify features of good programmes. Five focus groups made up of people who used the centre were also convened. These 40 clients were a convenience sample. The groups were of the same sex, language and age. They spent up to three hours responding to five key exercises. Transcripts of the focus group sessions do not appear to have been made but analysis of the recurrent themes was still possible.

Findings from the three inquiry methods were tabulated and it was agreed that they converged on broadly similar conclusions. This then formed a template to be used (1) in the evaluation, which now had a model of desirable practice against which to judge the centre, and (2) by the centre managers, who began to plan to align provision with the model.

The process depends on having a valid set of questions or statements relating to the topic of study. These can be generated by substantial literature reviews or by brainstorming with focus groups and other informants, as in the case reported in Box 4.6. There should be plenty of statements, in the region of 100. Longer lists are common, although researchers often shorten them to no more than 100 in the interests of manageability. Random selection of the statements to retain is less desirable than collapsing several similar statements into one *simple* replacement. The quality of this listing process determines the quality of the research (which is, of course, true for all scale, questionnaire and other fixed-response instrument development). The research will be blind to any aspects that are missed off the statements list.

Each of the retained statements is then printed on a card with its opposite. For example,

The group acts impulsively
(i.e. the group responds emotionally and rarely makes contingency plans)

versus

The group acts in a methodical and deliberate manner. (Peterson et al., 1999: 132)

Respondents then sort the cards into three piles. One contains all cards for which the upper statement is true, another all those for which the lower statement is true, and the third contains the rest. Then comes a second sorting stage when the cards have to be arranged into sets (nine is common) with cards quasi-normally distributed amongst the categories. Table 4.2 shows the distribution pattern to which respondents had to conform that was used in the study done by Peterson and colleagues (1999: 119). In studies using fewer or more cards, similar patterns of card distribution should be used. Notice that the first of the three piles is decomposed into four sets containing a total of 41 cards. If there were fewer than 41 cards in the first pile, cards were added from the third pile containing 'the rest'. If there were more, some were rejected and added to 'the rest' pile.

The second pile, containing cards for which the lower statement basically held true, is also subdivided into four sets with cards chosen from (or added to) 'the rest' to get a subtotal of 41. The remaining 18 cards constitute set 5. Sorting the cards into nine sets makes it possible to apply ordinal statistics, while specifying how many cards should go into each set makes it possible to compare the rank orderings of different respondents. The major attraction of q-sort lies in this potential for comparison and statistical analysis. The main drawback is that there may be difficulties finding respondents willing to make fine judgements about 100 cards. The other limitations of fixed-response instruments also apply, although Peterson and colleagues say that they 'are not advocating the abandonment of existing methodologies. We simply wish to advocate the GDQ [q-sort] as an additional research tool' (1999: 124). A summary of their study is in Box 4.7.

Concept Mapping

Tony Buzan's *Use Your Head* (1974) popularized mind maps™ as a way of organizing and communicating ideas, and of structuring information so

Table 4.2   *A q-sort template for 100 prompt cards*

Category	Label	Number of cards in this category
1	Upper statement is extremely characteristic	5
2	Upper statement is highly characteristic	8
3	Upper statement is quite characteristic	12
4	Upper statement is slightly characteristic	16
5	Neither upper nor lower statement is characteristic	18
6	Lower statement is slightly characteristic	16
7	Lower statement is quite characteristic	12
8	Lower statement is highly characteristic	8
9	Lower statement is extremely characteristic	5

Box 4.7 Q-sort in organizational research (Peterson et al., 1999)

The researchers took an existing q-sort that had been used in studying elite political decision-making teams and modified to apply to group decision-making in organizations in general.

Based on their command of the literature, they grouped the 100 items into eight subscales. They acknowledge that more or fewer scales could have been identified and that cluster analysis (which is described in the section on concept mapping in this chapter) could have been used to identify sub-scales as an alternative to relying on their command of the literature. The researchers' expertise also sensitized them to 10 patterns of group dynamics that researchers had identified. They collaboratively worked out the q-sort patterns that would follow from taking the perspective of each of these 10 group dynamics patterns. Again, this was a work of expert judgement and open to challenge by others with a good grasp of the research literature.

In a conventional q-sort study the investigators would have used the cards with groups of respondents, recorded which set each card was placed in and statistically analysed the information from the 100 cards. This would have shown how different respondents who had been involved in decision-making groups saw their groups' decision-making and allowed some statistically based assertions to be made about similarities and differences between groups. In fact they did something far more intriguing.

They argued that people who were steeped in a case study could then do a q-sort from the perspective of someone who was a part of the case study. So, for instance, a q-sort could be done of decision-making at the Chrysler Corporation in 1980–1 based on immersion in two published accounts of what happened. At least two investigators who were steeped in the two main histories of those years did q-sorts to rate the 100 statements in terms of how well they thought they described Chrysler decision-making in 1980–1. High levels of inter-rater agreement were obtained ($r = +0.79$). The process was repeated for two other key points in Chrysler's history and the q-sorts for the three periods were compared, showing that decision-making processes and group dynamics had changed between 1980 and 1990.

This method of doing q-sorts vicariously offers researchers the chance to bring a common, reliable analytical framework to bear in trying to extract themes from case studies of similar phenomena. It also provides a basis for

continued

looking at changes, assuming that the evidence is sufficient to allow q-sorts to be done for different points in time, as was the case with the Chrysler example. Finally, q-sorts can, in theory, be done from the perspective of different participants in the same story, so that Chrysler could have been looked at from the point of view of top management, middle management and shopfloor workers.

as to help creative thinking, decision-making and problem working. They can also be used to capture data. Informants need to be shown examples of mind maps and to have the concept explained to them before being asked to make their own mind maps to represent a story, incident, relationship, concept, experience etc. Sometimes they are given a set of cards containing prompts that they might wish to use and sometimes they are invited to start by brainstorming as many ideas to do with the topic as they can before beginning to organize them. Buzan's *Mindmanager*™ software at <http://www.mindmanager.com/product/index.html> allows this to be done on screen, which makes it easy to save maps with word-processing software, whence they can be loaded into a program such as Atlas-ti for analysis (see below for more on image-based research and Chapter 8 for Atlas-ti).

There are several ways of handling the completed maps, although they are better thought of as works-in-progress, which means they can be very useful in longitudinal research and in before-and-after studies. One tactic is to make them the basis of a conversation or interview, another is to score them for their complexity (number of distinct ideas, number of nodes, number of principal branches, number of links between main branches etc.), and a third is to note all the points down and to infer a weighting for each one – a point on the edge of the map might be less important than one near the centre. That third means of analysis makes it clear that mind maps can be treated as a visual, more flexible analogue of q-sort procedures. That comes through very clearly in Trochim's concept mapping software *The Concept System* at <http://www.conceptsystems. com/>. In *The Research Methods Knowledge Base* (Trochim, 1999), he argues that concept mapping is particularly useful for planning and evaluation, because it helps to identify people's main concerns and their relative strengths. Box 4.6 illustrated the use of concept mapping for both purposes. Assuming that the researcher has already identified informants and has a clear question in mind ('What would be the signs that we were doing a good job for our clients?', 'What do we need to do if we are to be leaders in our field in three years time?'), then there are six main stages:

1   Get responses to these questions – by having participants brainstorm ideas, identify points in focus groups or choose from options that you have identified in the literature. Trochim suggests keeping the total

below 100. When more ideas, suggestions and statements are put forward, a random sample may be chosen or the researcher may discard near duplicates. It is possible not to involve informants in generating the statements but instead to present them with ones taken from the literature and start with step 2.

2   Rate the statements. This is usually done by asking informants to rate each statement on a Likert scale; q-sort is an alternative.

3   Sort the statements. With each statement, idea or concept printed on a separate slip, informants are asked either to group them into as many sets as they wish, or to do a q-sort. The researcher must keep an accurate record for each informant of which statements are grouped with which. The individual grouping data are then transferred to a matrix which maps the combined grouping decisions of all of the informants.

4   Use statistical analysis software to identify different clusters of statements and to display a map showing the relationships between all of the statements. In theory there can be one cluster or as many as there are statements, which means that it is an act of deliberation to choose which of the options offered by the software is the best for the purpose. Trochim's advice is to choose too many clusters rather than too few.

5   The clusters need to be described and then named. If possible, the informants, or some of them, should be asked to comment on whether the clusters make sense, on whether statements seem to be in the wrong clusters, and on the names that could be given to them. If it is hard to name a cluster, that may be a sign that a different level of analysis should be tried.

6   The ratings from the Likert scale or q-sort are now added to the cluster maps to identify the clusters which informants had rated as the most significant.

Evaluators could then use this map to guide their inquiries, as in the case in Box 4.6, and action researchers could use them to help them decide what interventions would most closely address the priorities identified by stakeholders.

Image-Based Research

One study that relied heavily on images as research data has been described in Box 3.9, and images were referred to in Chapter 3 as aids to recall in clinical interviews and as ways of capturing observational data. The assumption in that chapter was that researchers could learn much by creating images themselves in face-to-face settings. Here, for the sake of completeness, it is worth noting that images can also be helpful in other ways. Earlier in this chapter images were identified as possible stimuli in repertory grid research, and experiments (Box 3.10), tests and questionnaires can all ask research subjects to respond to visual materials.

Dissociative techniques often use images. For example, respondents could be asked to complete sentences to indicate how they would expect someone who is shown to them in a picture might respond or act, or they could complete a grid, fixed-response questions or ticklist on the same basis.

There is also a lot of scope for treating images, such as newspaper photographs or cartoons, as raw material for inquiries. For example, the nineteenth century 'science' of phrenology held that character and racial quality could be scientifically inferred from close, objective study of facial characteristics, and one reason why police forces began to take mugshots was to help scientists define the outward signs of inward corruption. Turning away from this mumbo-jumbo, researchers who work with images might ask how cartoonists depict trade unions or about the taken-for-granted messages embedded in magazine photographs of middle-aged people, or how television advertisements show adolescents, and so on. But this image-based research is not an easy way of confirming what is in print. First, it notices things that do not show up in print. For example, teachers in newspaper cartoons published in England in 1976 are frequently shown wearing gowns and looking staid and rather seedy. This depiction has little contact with reality and is certainly not present in the printed word but it is a persistent and apparently very significant symbol. Exploring the meaning of these visual signs can lead researchers to more complex understandings of the discourses about teaching as a profession in the 1970s, and putting them alongside cartoons from the 1960s, 1980s and 1990s as well gives a powerful grip on questions about change in teaching's public standing. Secondly, image-based research is not easy because, as Chapter 8 indicates, images are information-rich and difficult to analyse in any systematic way. It takes a great deal of thought, discussion and persistence to find a way of sustaining a systematic gaze upon large sets of images, and that leaves aside questions about how the set is selected in the first place. This research is so new in social science that there is little to guide the researcher, which compounds the difficulties (but see Simco and Warin, 1997).

Box 4.8 Image-based research into the role of environmental complexity in the well-being of the elderly (Davidson et al., 1997)

'The elderly are more likely to remain autonomous within an environment that provides adequate nutrition, rest, and sufficient complexity to stimulate and challenge without being overwhelming' (5). The study investigated the association between the complexity of old people's living environments and their physical and mental well-being. Established, reliable and valid rating scales and physiological measures were used to assess well-being, which left a need to 'define and quantify … environmental complexity so that it could be empirically studied and manipulated with greater precision' (5).

Thirty-two people aged 67–96 who were living in two types of housing (community and congregate) were recruited. For each person a Polaroid
continued

picture was taken of the living room; kitchen; two other rooms; and a frequently used outdoor site. A rule-based measure of the complexity of each space was produced by counting the number of objects in each picture. Each type of object was also rated in terms of its shape, texture, colour and pattern and whether it was moving or static. The ratings were summed and then multiplied by the number of objects of a similar sort. These subtotals were then added together to provide a score for each picture. Totalling the scores for each of the five pictures produced a complexity score for each person's living environment.

Although the researchers cited Shannon's well-regarded information theory and although they went to some length to be consistent and careful in their quantifying, the results are based on a number of assumptions that might be challenged: for example, is complexity well captured by this adding-and-multiplying technique? Such reservations are supported by alternative measures of environmental complexity and aesthetic quality which involved judges rating rooms on 100 mm lines with the poles identi-fied as 'not at all complex' and 'extremely complex'. Judgements on those scales indicated that there was a 20% difference in the environmental com-plexity of community as opposed to congregate housing, whereas the mea-surement technique showed a 100% difference.

Statistical analysis showed that people living in more complex environ-ments scored higher on some measures of well-being, but it was not clear whether this meant that people who were fit and active created more complex environments or that complex environments help people to stay fit and active.

Some investigators have tried to devise 'objective' ways of analysing images, as can be seen in Box 4.8, but that depends on a common-sense theory of signs with which few experts would agree. Although image-based research does not need an advanced theory of signs, it is neces-sary to realize that a sign, such as a photograph, is interpreted and interpreted as a sign by an observer. The popular view may be that every picture tells a story but a philosophical view is that the sign has no meaning without an observer (in that sense the observer creates the sign) and the observer does not simply 'read' the sign in some objective fashion but creates significance. Object, significance and observer are bound together: all three are necessary (Hookway, 1985; Hausman, 1993). So, image-based researchers need to establish that the people the signs were intended for do notice them and interpret them in the ways that they, the researchers, suppose. There is more likely to be a fair match when researchers have done pilot work and gone deeply into the literature but neither guarantees that any one understanding would be appreciated by others. For that reason scrupulous researchers do face-to-face work with informants who are typical of the images' intended audience in order to see how their understandings fit the researchers'. Unfortunately too many rely on their own scholarship and disdain audience studies.

Furthermore, understandings are better based when researchers have considered the context of production. Published images are carefully chosen and have been produced under certain constraints and for reasons that are rarely apparent to the casual gaze. Understanding what got produced, the conventions and constraints of creation and the process of selection and editing helps researchers to attribute significance to the images. In the case of published images, they may have been created for artistic or more purely representational purposes. They will embody tacit or explicit viewpoints, for example defining certain incidents as significant ones either because they are typical or because they are not. There may also be a moral intention, perhaps of the 'look how these people suffer' type (Becker, 1974). There is just as much need to think about production with images, such as snapshots, that are created for private use. Notice the conventions that govern the poses, expressions and organization of people in the picture and consider the significance of the occasions that are photographed and the artefacts displayed in them.

When it comes to creating images as a way of recording in social science inquiries, common problems include:

- Reactivity: people may play to the camera. This can be reduced when the photographer or artist has become almost taken for granted.
- Getting access: filming identifies people and makes it harder for researchers to guarantee anonymity, which makes it wise for some people to steer clear of image-based researchers.
- Sampling: once in place, some researchers may be happy to film or draw things that seem to be typical and/or untypical. Others prefer rules such as 'use a roll of film an hour'.
- Framing: all data capture frames reality, abstracting pieces for further study. While a picture may be worth a thousand words, it is helpful to have another thousand words of notes that fill in some of the context that the camera or sketch misses.

In short, image-based research is a many-layered process of sensemaking in which attention swings between the image, the conditions of production and the meanings that audiences might have attached to them. The quality of understandings that can be had from images is related to the ways in which other sources of data, such as documents and conversations, can be brought into play with them.

Documentary Analysis

Most research studies use documents to clarify policies, expectations and issues but it is entirely legitimate for a study to be based on analysis of documents alone. It is possible to treat documents, especially official documents, as unproblematic statements of how things are or were. That is suitable for some purposes but most researchers working with official documents quickly realize that they are shot through with subjectivity. For example, what counts as unemployment in today's official British statistics is not the same as 20 years ago; murders by poisoning are under-represented in early twentieth century crime figures because poison was harder to detect; and reports of sexual and racial crimes say as much about what is regarded as crime, by whom and why as they do about patterns of criminal behaviour. Understood like that, it quickly becomes evident that there are many similarities between the interpretive skills of the image-based researcher and those of the documentary researcher. In both cases, meaning is not self-evident, the contexts of production are significant and the audience's reactions cannot be assumed on the basis of the investigator's slick hermeneutics. It follows that documentary sources are, as historians well know, open to many readings and that inquiries can be written in many ways. Rhodes (2000) has shown how the same story about organizational change can be presented from three perspectives: his paper tells the story from a feminist perspective, then in terms of critical theory and finally as a deconstructive reading. Boxes 4.9 and 4.10 show something of the ways in which texts can be treated in discourse analysis, although it will quickly become obvious that this is far more than an approach to documentary research, being a general way of making understandings.

Box 4.9 Deconstructive discourse analysis: feminist deconstruction of heterosexual orgasm (Potts, 2000)

'This article could begin by asking why conduct a deconstructive analysis of (the experience of) orgasm? Who could benefit – if indeed there could be any positive outcome – from such a manoeuvre?' (55). In this research, 'all accounts are treated as "texts"; they are not representations of any underlying truth about orgasm … but rather they permit access to current discourses employed by participants to construct and "make sense of" orgasmic experience at the turn of the century [in the style of] feminist deconstructive discursive analysis' (60).

The method was to make a close reading of the utterances of 47 New Zealanders who, in same sex groups, talked about normal sex, sexual health and the significance of orgasm. The researcher identified them through personal contacts and snowballing. She led the group discussions, guided by a semi-structured schedule. She participated in the discussions, arguing that the concept of a neutral researcher made no sense. As far as this summary is concerned, the emphasis is not on data capture but on the technique of discourse analysis. Full interview transcripts were produced but it does not appear that the conventions for capturing inflections and hesitations that are shown in Box 4.10 were used (that is, discourse analysis at the most fine-grained level).

This examination of the discourse was deconstructive in that it was intended to challenge the common practices of (1) representing the world in terms of polar opposites such as orgasmic and non-orgasmic, or intercourse and foreplay, and (2) valuing the first term in the pair over the second, such

continued

as masculine over feminine, or reason over intuition. Potts' readings of the texts led her to claim that 'there is a potential space for "sex" which has no pre-set goal in mind (or body) ... but which enjoys the possibilities of desire – sex which is not *just* a mode of suspension, deferring an inevitable endpoint, but sex which pleasures in the "sexiness" of desire: sex without a primary orgasmic mission ... Destabilising the traditional opposition of intercourse/foreplay, sex would take place as *interplay*: a celebration of the unfixedness of both intensification and diminution of pleasure' (70).

Plainly this is one reading of the texts she collected and she made it clear where her reading comes from. Notice, too, that she makes a manoeuvre that is typical of deconstructive analysis, namely to identify a third way which is not presence (orgasm), absence (foreplay or non-orgasm) or any point in between (tantric sex, perhaps), but which is deconstructive of the dichotomy itself (and in this case she says that it could be called sexual interplay). This form of discourse analysis looks for alternatives to the prevalent discourse of polar opposites.

Box 4.10 Discourse analysis of retrospective accounts of drunken behaviour (Giles, 1999)

Recollections of drunken behaviour involve creating accounts because the drinking has blurred or obliterated recall of events. The ways in which these recollections are constructed shows how identities can, individually and collectively, be constructed, managed and preserved.

The paper is mainly based on a transcript of a group interview with five male students, which had been loosely guided by a set of prompts and cues to the informants. The method of data collection is of less interest here than the close discourse analysis of the data. A tape of the interview was transcribed in standard Jefferson style for fine-grained analysis, which is illustrated by this extract from page 399:

88	DG:	What's (Sven) like when he's pissed?
89	Dan:	Fuck↑ing cra↓zy (.5 *laughs*) turns into a madman (1.0 *laughs*)
90	Steve:	Like the Incredible <u>Hulk</u>.
91	Dan:	Couple of weeks ago he tried to take a <u>crap</u> on a <u>car</u> down <u>here</u> (*laughs*)
92	Sven:	[( )] pre<u>tend</u>ing [( )]
93	Dan:	Yeah we started (.) weeing on cars and it (.5)
94	DG:	So I know [where <u>not</u>] to park round here then
95	Dan:	[progressed]
96	Sven:	It's because I get carried away with mad crazy ideas, y'know (.) I'm just a ↑<u>follower</u> actually (.5 *laughs*) I'm just a <u>follower</u>

Lines are numbered, pauses are measured where possible, stress is <u>underlined</u>, ↑ and ↓ indicate rises and falls in pitch, [ ] enclose overlapping speech, and laughter is recorded. This level of transcription is very demanding and very costly, so it is reserved for research methods that depend on microscopic textual analysis. In this paper, Giles intensively analyses what is going on – in the crapping on a car routine, for example – in order to make claims about the ways in which identity is constructed and negotiated by the individual and the group. The line numbers allow him to make precise references to support his argument.

Discourse analysis and deconstructive readings might equally have been mentioned with interviews in Chapter 3 (since the texts often come from interviews, as in the cases in Boxes 4.9 and 4.10), or in Chapter 8 (because they can be treated as methods of data analysis). Returning to the theme of documentary research methods, Box 4.11 describes a small survey of the ways in which schools marketed themselves, and Box 4.12 summarizes an analysis of newspaper stories about child abuse. Bryman (2001) has a good chapter which has more to say about the range of documentary sources and their treatments. Now that newspaper archives are available on-line and can be interrogated with search engines, it is surprising that more of this sort of documentary research is not done. Done electronically, it has two big advantages for small-scale researchers: it is cheap, and it can be done from anywhere with a phone socket. Even older microfilm and paper research is cheap, usually manageable and often a lot more convenient than fieldwork.

Box 4.11 Analysis of secondary school prospectuses (Hesketh and Knight, 1998)

Knight had previously analysed 100 high school prospectuses published in 1991 and (1) investigated the degree of compliance with government regulations about the information schools should publish, (2) identified the discourses schools used to position themselves favourably in the market-place for students. The 1998 paper revisited these themes in an examination of the 1996 prospectuses produced by 59 of the original 100.
  Methods of inquiry were broadly similar to the original study which had used prospectuses from all secondary schools in one mainly rural area and from two divisions of an urban area 250 miles away. The set of prospectuses was analysed in five ways.

1 Quantitative, computerized analysis of prospectuses' readability showed that nearly three-quarters were too difficult for the average adult.
2 A comparison of each one with a list of government requirements found that most of the 1991 prospectuses did not comply with the law. Most of the 1996 ones did.
3 By law the prospectuses should all have covered some common themes. Close reading by both authors of key sections suggested that nearly all of the schools made very similar claims, even though there were substantial differences in the communities schools served, in the students' academic achievements, and between the comprehensives and the selective schools in the sample. This was unexpected.
4 Photographs and other images were also examined in terms of their contents and tone. Again, the authors found no systematic differences between schools.
5 Each prospectus was appraised in terms of its production quality (professional through to cheapskate). Again, there were no systematic differences between schools.

continued

Method 1 involved scanning text into a computer which then did the readability calculations. Methods 4 and 5 were also quite undemanding. Methods 2 and 3 took a lot of time and would have been exhausting if the authors had used discourse analysis to explore in detail the complex meanings in each text. However, their view was that it was sufficient for a 6000-word article to compare texts in terms of the messages that were apparent on a close, literal reading. Done this way, the inquiry was a small-scale study that took the two authors three months of part-time work – perhaps 30 person days in total. More detailed analysis of images or texts would have made the project substantially more demanding.

Box 4.12 Analysis of media representations of child abuse (Wilczynski and Sinclair, 1999)

The research questions were (1) how is child abuse covered in the Australian press, and (2) is there a difference in tabloid and quality press coverage? Electronic searches identified 1302 child abuse stories in two sets of newspapers in 1995. These stories were located by searching headlines and by using key word searches of the index to these electronic archives. The authors recognized that there could still be some stories that both search methods had missed.

Stories were coded in a standard way. Illustrations were coded simply in terms of their main subject, and higher-inference judgements about meaning were avoided. Counts (for example, of the number of column inches given to cases) were analysed with a statistics package. All other data were thematically analysed (see Chapter 9) by the authors, who shared and compared their analytical notes. No inter-observer reliability estimates are given.

They found that (1) the press focused on hard news cases to the exclusion of analysis of the 'broader social and systemic context of abuse' (267); (2) severe and atypical cases got disproportionate coverage; (3) abuse cases were individualized and often treated in titillating ways; and (4) the few research-related stories were in the 'quality' paper. In sum, 'The sample findings confirmed that the print media coverage of child abuse is largely stereotypical and superficial' (278). It is not clear who needed this confirmation.

Unobtrusive Methods

When information has to be elicited from people, problems arise because research participants are not representative of people at large, because they forget or 'fake good' and because the research itself can affect that which it is intended to study. Unobtrusive methods involve the inquirer acting rather like a detective and looking for clues in the way things are and in what people do and say unthinkingly: the research evidence is in the traces they leave. For example, the bibliographies that students append to their papers tell a different story to that which could be inferred from the wear and tear on library resources. The former represent students as polymaths but the physical condition of library books suggests that they are, as a group, making heavy use of some sections of a few books and even fewer journals. Such erosion measures are one indicator of patterns of use. Accretion measures, like the counts of discarded hypodermic needles reported in the study in Box 3.7 and garbology (rummaging through refuse), are others. Graffiti are another form of accretion data that are widely used to understand sexual, racial, political and religious attitudes that might otherwise be hidden from view. They can also be read as markers of territory and as signifiers of ingroup identities. Observation of signs, such as tattoos (Box 3.6), of gestures, and of the use of public space provides more unobtrusive information, as can studies of public notices, such as advertisements, obituaries and cartoons, whether they appear in print, in public spaces, or on television, radio or the web. Lee (2000) gives a clear summary of the proliferating possibilities for research using non-obtrusive methods, including investigations in cyberspace.

Unobtrusive methods can seem whimsical, eclectic and playful, qualities not regularly associated with social science research. It can also be hard to be confident about what the measures mean. There is a lot that can be learned about schools from the state of pupils' toilets (washrooms) but it is not clear whether dirty facilities mean that the users are savages, that there are too many users for the facilities provided, that cleaning and maintenance are usually inadequate, or that they are inadequate only at the point of observation. For these reasons unobtrusive methods are generally incorporated in mixed-method designs (see Chapter 5). Even so, 'Many researchers ... feel that the best data are those produced, designed or created for a specific purpose' (2000: 140) and unobtrusive measures do not intrude upon the majority of research reports.

Post-empirical Research

The idea of post-empirical research is a playful one because it combines postmodernism's sceptical attitude towards claims that empirical work can deliver certainties with ideas about knowledge that pre-date the seventeenth century's intellectual revolutions. A post-empirical position is that research questions seldom need fresh data to be collected. It makes at least as much sense to (1) use the copious data that almost invariably already exist and/or (2) think. It follows that the assumption that research equals empirical inquiry is rejected. Consequently, greater importance is placed upon conceptual and theoretical work (reconsidering what data might mean) and on secondary data analysis (analysing existing data with different questions or fresh techniques). Of course, sometimes research questions do hinge on empirical inquiries and it is frequently wise to do some empirical work to clarify the context in which evidence is to be deployed and about which thinking is to be done. But too often researchers turn to fieldwork like a child to a comfy blanket or well-used toy. Machado et al. argue that 'a variety of well-known problems in psychology reflect a pattern of unhealthy growth due to a disproportionate emphasis on factual investigations at the expense of theoretical and conceptual investigation' (2000: 2). Cushing (1998) points out that the same set of formal findings may be honestly interpreted in quite different ways, as is the case in quantum mechanics, and Wolpert (1993) insists that science is a counter-intuitive activity which involves good inquiries and good thinking. These all reassure me that research-as-thinking is at least as important as research-as-data-creation.

It is salutary to consider how understandings are created in other disciplines. Take history as an example. Historians of modern times are faced with new data becoming available as archives are opened up and have the problem that the recent past has left so many sources that many have not been well explored. Yet even in modern history, it is notable that understandings are not, in the main, changed by the release of new sources, although the sources may change the footnotes. New understandings of Truman, Churchill and Mao have sprung from new ways of thinking, not from new sources. If history is a never-ending process of reinterpretation in which every age writes its own stories of the same past, then the reinterpretations come not from new sources as much as from the new cultures of the present. Today's scholars look at the partition of the Indian subcontinent in 1948 through lenses spattered with modern stories of religious venom and ethnic cleansing; they see the British empire with the words of the Stephen Lawrence inquiry (or the Rodney King case in the USA) in their minds; and their take on post-war planning is overlain by modern discourses of individualism, markets and workfare. For historians of older times the record is much smaller and very unlikely to change significantly. Once I was expert on early modern England. In my academic lifetime several understandings have emerged and competed and, although they have invariably been supported by a good command of the archives, they have sprung from different ways of thinking, seeing and feeling, not from the discovery of new sources. Although history is commonly understood as a quest for truth that fails to achieve scientific certainty because its facts are largely missing and contaminated by bias and subjectivity, my picture is of a discipline that is essentially interpretive: it is more about different ways of reading the same texts than it is with unearthing new ones.

Post-empirical research in the social sciences takes this sort of history as its inspiration and tries to learn by means of good thinking about what is already available rather than by expecting salvation to come from new texts created by empirical inquiries. It could involve any or all of the following sorts of inquiries.

First, there are *literature reviews*. Serious literature reviews that draw together what is already known are not as common as you might expect. For example, I find it hard to understand why any empirical work on ways of assessing undergraduate learning should be funded when there is an enormous archive of data that has never been systematically reviewed. What we need is not so much fresh work as a good grasp of what has already been achieved. An illustration of this is that a major study of 681 research publications on formative evaluation and children's learning 'shows conclusively that formative assessment does improve learning' and that the possible effect size of 0.7 is 'amongst the largest ever recorded for educational interventions' (Black and Wiliam, 1998: 61). The point is that the review showed what was already there if only people had recognized the significance of looking for it. Again, there is not a great deal in the British literature on higher education about ways of responding to increased student diversity in the classroom, but there is a substantial North American literature. Upcraft's (1996) review is, in my opinion, a better guide for British teachers than more poorly funded, small-scale empirical work would be. There is also the strategy of reviewing research in a nearby field. If we want to know more about the management of workgroups such as subject departments in universities, then it is very useful to look at what we know about high school departments and about communities of practice in commercial and business organizations (Knight and Trowler, 2001). There are differences of setting, just as there were national differences in the diversity work, but I judge the similarities to be such that lessons can be learned – and faster and more cheaply than they could be learned by initiating a set of empirical inquiries into departmental leadership in higher education.

Secondly, Black and Wiliam's study was a special type of literature review known as a *meta-analysis*, which is a very systematic review of the literature that depends upon reanalysing all the statistical data so that the findings of many studies can be combined. The advantage is that findings in one small study that might barely be statistically significant and have fairly modest effects may turn out to be far more powerful when data from a dozen studies are combined. That is exactly what Black and Wiliam's study did. The disadvantages are that it is impossible to do this with qualitative studies, or only possible with what some would see as pure trickery (Light and Pillemer, 1982); reports often leave out some of the statistics that are needed in meta-analysis; and inquiries that failed to find statistically significant differences rarely get reported, with the result that published studies present a skewed picture of the research experience. Rosenthal (1991) suggests ways of coping with these deficiencies. This work of synthesizing and interpreting what is already established is a vital part of post-empirical research and is also accessible to small-scale researchers. See also Chapter 9.

Thirdly, few topics have been so thoroughly investigated as what makes for a good school and how that knowledge could be brought to bear on ineffective ones. School effectiveness is a field badly in need of syntheses of research findings (which has begun to happen) but it is also, as White pointed out in 1997, one in which good thinking is more urgently needed. As a philosopher, he observed that a number of empirical research findings were truisms, logically necessary or unhelpfully vague. Much the same could be said of research into effective penal institutions, social work teams, police stations, community medical practices, midwifery units and so on. *Philosophical inquiries* can make two main contributions to social knowledge. One is by bringing the philosopher's craft to bear on social science common sense. The problem with much of what is accepted by social science is that, like common sense in general, it is insufficiently coherent, systematic and critical – not so much at the level of the design of individual inquiries but in terms of the way that social problems are framed and the means of addressing them are conceptualized. This view of common sense comes from the work of Antonio Gramsci who argued that common sense is disjointed and contradictory, and in his pre-war Italy it was also systematically corrupted by political and religious assumptions that operated against ordinary people's interests, *even though* their common-sense view was that these assumptions were natural and correct (Entwistle, 1979; Nemeth, 1980). In this way they were prisoners of false consciousness – of their own 'common sense'. Philosophical inquiry can offer the freedom of good sense and social science could benefit from bringing it to bear on social questions. A second contribution philosophy can make is the speculative one of reasoning about where empirical work might be necessary and productive.

Fourthly, if research is systematic inquiry, then *reflection* might be seen as a form of research when it is understood as deliberate thinking with a view to developing understandings. It can be distinguished from philosophical inquiry because it does not take a philosopher's training to do it, although that can also be seen as a weakness. Reflection in, on and for practice has been widely regarded as a good thing, the hallmark of the reflective practitioner (Schön, 1983; 1987; Eraut, 1995; Moon, 1999). Despite this enthusiasm for it I do not accept that any learning can be regarded as reflection and hence as some form of research. As with Parker, I fear that 'any kind of *thinking about one's practice* tends to get described as "reflective" … [but it is not] just *any old example of thinking*' (1997: 34). For reflection to be research-like it needs to be systematic, which means that it needs to challenge the thinker to consider explanations, analyses and evaluations that do not come easily and habitually to mind. One way for this to happen is to make reflection a shared activity so that colleagues help the thinker to appreciate different ways of sensemaking and claimsmaking. Another, which can be used alongside it, involves using a set of prompts to raise questions and issues that might otherwise have been missed. Writing of nursing and midwifery, Taylor (2000) provides three sets of prompts. Table 4.3 shows the main concerns that the prompts address but does not include the detailed questions that help to make reflection a groundbreaking activity rather than an exercise in self-grooming. Where reflection is systematic, sustained and involves challenge, whether in the form of prompts or of critical friends, then there is a case for saying that it is a form of research in its own right. Indeed, what was described in Chapter 3 as memory work could be regarded as a very systematic communal work of reflection.

These first four points have mainly been about the development of better understandings. A fifth and alternative post-empirical position is

Table 4.3   *Prompts for reflective inquiry (after Taylor, 2000)*

Technical reflection, concerned with problem-*solving*, gaining competence in well-defined skills. Think like a positivist	Practical reflection, concerned the human sides of practice – with interacting and communicating. Think as a sensemaker	Emancipatory reflection, concerned with ways in which people are caught in practices and ideas that may not be in their best interests. Look beneath the surface and think critically
1 Make initial assessment of the problem and work out a provisional explanation or hypothesis	1 Take on a critical incident which illustrates which illustrates a problem of practice and describe fully what happened, how you were involved, felt etc.	
2 Analyse the assumptions that sustain the problem and also think through the implications of your alternative	2 Interpret the critical incident, analysing your hopes, fears, feelings, values and actions, as well as those of others	2 Deconstruct the experience: consider whose interests were served by what happened and why things happened that way
3 Evaluate the arguments, develop your position and organize the evidence you have in order to support it	3 Sensemaking: what can I learn from the different interpreta- tions I explored?	3 Extend this habit of asking how power flows can trap people and try to work, speak and act in emancipatory ways

that data collection should come second to a concern for *action*, as it does in action research and some versions of feminism and critical theory. Gramsci held that thought and action should be entwined so that 'to have a philosophy is, above all, to act in a manner that conforms in principle with that philosophy' (Nemeth, 1980: 85–6). This is close to the pragmati- cist position that valid concepts are ones that effectively describe the world of actions. Both of these positions could allow the claim that, rather than have data collection as a priority for action, researchers should have action as a priority since the adequacy of understandings is mainly to be established through action. More data can never, on this view, substitute for action as a test of knowledge. If that argument is plausible, it follows that action research, evaluations and case studies, as forms of research with a particularly close connection to action, are called for but – and this is important – only in as much as they are designed to address the specific needs of the situation *and* to explore the adequacy of understanding. The evaluation topic, case under study or action research project would be valuable for what was done on its own terms *and* for the ways in which understandings were developed by it. This is close to the position taken by Heron (1996) and Levin and Greenwood (1998).

This closing advocacy of small-scale research that is not dependent on going out and hewing more data is complemented in Chapter 9 by atten- tion to what has been called 'a crisis of representation'. For some, though, the meanings of the research need no reporting because they *are* in the actions that have been taken: practice is their testimony. The next chapter takes up a question that is more pressing at this point, the question of which methods are best.

5

Research Design: Bringing It All Together

Earlier chapters have pressed the argument that the most important thing in small-scale research is to be mindful about the sorts of claims that the research is intended to enable, although the message may have become submerged by the more technical focus of Chapters 3 and 4. This chapter reinstates the concern with mindfulness and gives guidance on putting methods together to design a study that is fit for the research purpose. Mindful research thinking can produce designs that look lopsided when judged by classical positivist standards but which are admirable, efficient and effective ways of getting at the research questions. Indeed, Cronbach and colleagues considered that 'Balanced and complete designs are a default option for the evaluator who cannot judge what information will be of most use' (1980: 278), adding that, 'Merit lies not in the form of inquiry but in the relevance of information' (1980: 7). And, although much of this chapter will say that mixed-method designs have a lot to be said for them, the opposite position – a single method, well used for the right purpose – is worthy of respect. If there is a problem with single-method designs it is that social inquiries are usually about phenomena that are complex, fuzzy, shifting and multifaceted, so that mixed methods are needed to capture that complexity. The point is, then, that questions about which method or methods to use in a research design can only be answered by reflecting on which one or ones have the best chance of allowing the researcher to make with confidence the sorts of claims that she or he wants to make.

This chapter has four main sections. The first, carried by Table 5.1, is a résumé of the 21 methods described in Chapters 3 and 4. The second is about the claims that might be made on the basis of the study – about generalizing from it – and about sampling issues. The third summarizes the case for multi-method designs. The fourth is a formal treatment of the need to satisfy yourself that this will be a careful and credible study that really does explore what you claim to be clarifying: it is about the reliability (or honesty), validity (or appropriateness), doability and ethical standing of the design.

Table 5.1 A palette of research methods (those that tend to yield data that are largely in numerical or quantitative form are lightly shaded)

Method	Often used for …	Be careful about …
1 Observation, using detailed schedule	Establishing what does happen. This is important because (a) most studies examine people's beliefs about what they do, and (b) what they really do tends to be different from what they say (and think)	All instruments embody a theory of what matters, so when investigators have to follow it completely, there's a danger of missing things not captured by the schedule. Concentrating on behaviour at the expense of subjects' feelings, meanings and thinking
2 Survey interviews, inc. CATI	Testing theories and exploring how common something is, how widely views are held, what people think they do, what people say they will do etc.	Similar to structured observations
3 Highly structured questionnaires	See method 2 survey interviews.	Response rates often low
4 Experiments and field, natural or quasi-experiments	Powerful methods of investigating causes, effects and other relationships Opportunities for natural experiments arise every time one group of people adopts new practices, beliefs, structures etc.	The need to control variables can make true experiments seem very artificial With quasi-experiments many variables are not controlled, which means that the findings do not have as much power as the researchers would wish
5 Rating scales, tests and measures, including IQ tests and other psychometric measures	Off-the-shelf instruments are convenient and have known levels of reliability and validity, which make them very attractive. The numerical data make it feasible to do statistical analyses and identify patterns within large samples	Off-the-shelf tests may not fit a given research situation very well and so be misleading if they are used Numbers can mislead by making findings look more authoritative than they are Constructing your own tests or scales is a complex, long and technical business

(Continued)

Table 5.1 (Continued)

Method	Often used for …	Be careful about …
6 Likert 'scales'	For properly developed scales, see above A convenient format for responses and an efficient way of identifying differences amongst groups of people	As ever, the numbers that can be derived from Likert scale responses need to be treated carefully Seven-, five- and three-point response formats can be indiscriminately used in social research
7 Repertory grid technique	Used as Kelly (1963) intended, this is attractive as a way of uncovering the constructs that individuals apply to the researchers' stimuli When participants respond to stimuli with constructs supplied by the researcher it's an effective way of identifying different patterns of use	In Kelly's form this is a slow procedure and, since different people use different constructs, data analysis can be slow Responses to sets of constructs supplied by the researcher are limited in the same way as responses to any other highly structured instrument
8 Nominal group technique, concept mapping, q-sort and Thurstone scales	NGT and concept mapping typically get participants to make statements in response to the researchers' prompt – a scenario, problem, issue or question. All methods then arrange the statements into clusters and show which statements and clusters are the most important	Where participants generate the statements it is possible that they will only list things at the front of their minds and miss other important points Difficulty getting people to engage with what can be long and complex tasks The sorting is only as good as the set of statements There is some danger that the clusters formed by statistical analysis (and concept mapping) can be treated as real phenomena, rather than as interpretations of participants' statements
9 Sociograms and distance scaling	Mapping networks of friendship, affinity, working relationships, ideas etc.	Rigidities caused by asking all informants to identify the same number of friends, work partners etc. General – or global – questions cause problems because people have different friends etc. in different settings False precision when results are portrayed visually or put in numerical form

(Continued)

Table 5.1 (Continued)

Method	Often used for ...	Be careful about ...
Unobtrusive methods		
10	Corroborating conclusions based on self-reports and for substantiating judgements that cannot be based on other sources because of difficulties of data collection	Interpretation of the data
11 Semi-structured observation	As for method 1	The dangers of structured observation should be reduced, but unless interviews or questionnaires are also used, information about thought and meaning will be nothing more than the observer's inferences
12 Semi-structured questionnaires	An attractive-looking way of combining fixed-response probes and requests for an explanation: 'Please explain your answer'	Response rates Written responses to open-ended questions can be hard to interpret
13 Observing by being there: little structure	In the exploratory stages, getting a feel for situations, what people do and what matters. Also in some ethnographic research where it's important not to let preconceptions, in the form of structured instruments, cloud the fieldwork	Hard to compare observations made without a common agenda Easy to miss subtle things of significance because the observer's attention is caught by blatant features of the situation
14 Lightly structured interviews	The mainstay of social research. Used a lot in early stages of inquiries and also when feelings, meanings and thinking are to be investigated	Data capture and analysis are frequently lengthy and expensive What the interviewer and informant create together is not acceptable to those concerned with the classic concept of reliability
15 Focus groups	Very useful for identifying the range of ideas, concerns, feelings etc. that people have. Widely used in marketing and other areas to get a sense of the sorts of things that concern people, that they talk about, prefer, dislike etc.	Focus groups provide data that should be used to inform thinking, not to determine it. They represent the ideas in currency but are not very good for showing how strongly those ideas are held, by whom and when
16 Action interviews	A common way of trying to explore what people think and feel when they are doing something – an approach to documenting 'logic-in-use', the procedural knowledge used when people take action	A major reservation is that this artificial procedure does not really capture logic-in-action, because that's locked up in practice and can only imperfectly be captured by propositional knowing or espoused logic. Procedural knowledge is often tacit and cannot easily be made explicit

(Continued)

Table 5.1 (Continued)

Method	Often used for …	Be careful about …
17 Memory work	Personal development and 'self-help' work that can also be used to explore identity construction	This is a collaborative research enterprise demanding great sensitivity and skill. It is intensive and time consuming. What emerges has been constructed by all participants
18 Diaries, logs and journals	The best substitutes for observations of behaviour or active interviews	Requires a great deal from informants How reliable are self-reports?
19 Analysis of images	Richness: images contain information that would usually be absent from other media Study of the creation, presentation and publication of images can be a powerful way to show cultural norms	It is a long and complex business to analyse video recordings, which are not as objective as they might seem Many readings of images possible
20 Analysis of documents	Exploring past events, states etc. Checking the security of claims, accounts and interpretations in the present	Documents are often incomplete and inaccessible. They are not 'objective' witnesses; they often tell an 'official' [male] story A variety of readings is often possible
21 Post-empirical approaches	A reminder that sometimes the best way of answering research questions does not mean generating fresh data	

A Palette of Methods

The methods summarized in Table 5.1 and outlined in Chapters 3 and 4 are likened to colours on a palette because:

- Most of the methods can be used in a more or less heavily structured way, which is analogous to colours being lightened by adding white or darkened by adding black.
- Methods may be mixed, although just as mixing colours from very different ends of the spectrum can produce some rather unpleasant results, so too methods as diverse as experiments and lightly-structured interviews should only be mixed with care.
- Methods may usefully be placed alongside one another, so that lightly-structured interviews help investigators to see better how to design an experiment, which in turn leads to survey work.
- Artistry determines what is used and where. This is not research by numbers and so the comments about the uses and disadvantages of each method are not instructions but hints to researchers-as-artists about things to keep in mind.

Good research involves creatively designing ways of using inquiry methods to face the research questions.

Sampling, Generalizations and Research Methods

Sampling is about choosing who or what is to be studied. The way in which the sample comes together affects the sorts of claims that can be made about the meanings of the findings, about their significance for the world in general. The inquiry methods chosen are not independent of sampling decisions but they too influence the confidence with which investigators can claim that their findings can be respected as representative of things in the population at large. When researchers say that their findings are trustworthy in this way, we say that they are generalizing from the sample to the population. This is classically the aim of the scientist. Mendel, the founder of genetics, generalized from his work on cross-breeding tens of thousands of pea plants to make claims about inheritance in peas in general and, by implication, living things. Other researchers may feel that their work is just as scrupulous but, perhaps because they could not get the right kind of sample, or because their methods were not reliable (see below), or because what they were investigating was context-specific and/or changeable, they ought not to claim that their findings can be generalized to the population. That, as Chapter 2 suggested, does not imply that the findings have no meaning and no significance for others, nor does it mean that generalizations cannot be suggested. It simply means that researchers need to make it clear that claims about the findings are plausible statements about possibilities and probabilities. And where researchers are interested in close study of one or a few instances, they may report their conclusions, explain why they think they are important and invite readers to judge for themselves the extent to which they speak to other cases, events or people.

This section, then, returns to the concerns of Chapter 2 but with the aim of elaborating them in terms of designing an inquiry. Sampling comes first because although in an ideal world investigators would use samples that matched the sorts of claims they wished to make, in practice the samples we use are not those we might have wished to use. But, whether a sample is freely chosen or not, it constrains the claims that can be made about the significance of the research findings for a wider world.

Sampling

If we want to know why people in an area no longer shop in the town centre as they did 10 years ago, we could ask them. Since it would be impossible to ask all of them, we would sample, which involves assuming that the sample will be truly representative of the population *in terms of our inquiry*, which is not to say that it need be representative in terms of political views or religious beliefs. If simple random sampling is used, we make the assumption that picking people at random from the population provides a sample that will be essentially representative of the population in all respects, including the one in which we are interested, shopping behaviour. Chance factors make it possible that the sample will not be truly representative, although the larger the sample the less the probable error. The question is what would be an efficient sample size, one that is sufficiently large to be trustworthy and sufficiently small to be affordable. The answer involves a calculation based on three things. First, we need to know the size of the population about which we wish to generalize. In the case of the study of downtown shopping we might say that the population is all adults within a 10 mile radius. A rough estimate of this population could then be taken from census summaries (up to 10 years out of date) or electoral registers (which only show those adults who registered). Secondly, we need to decide what level of error is going to be acceptable: will we be happy if we can be 95% confident that our finding is ±2% of the true figure for the population?

Suppose, in addition, that the survey was made up of 10 questions and that answers were to be summed to provide a total 'town centre shopping attractiveness score' (TCSAS). In that case, where there is also a numerical variable involved, the third factor to consider when calculating sample size would be the standard deviation of scores on that variable. This needs explaining. The standard deviation (SD) is an efficient way of describing whether scores tend to cluster together around the mean (average) or whether they are dispersed. A mean score of 50 with an SD of 5 indicates that some two-thirds of scores lie between 45 and 55. The same mean score with an SD of 25 indicates that the scores are widely scattered, with two-thirds falling between 25 and 75. The bigger the SD the larger a sample needs to be. So, when a study captures behaviour or attitudes in the form of a numerical score, sample size should take account of the SD. In the case of the TCSAS score the pilot study data will provide an SD score to use in calculating the ideal sample size for the main study. The mathematics of the calculation are straightforward and many books on survey research and sampling set them out (see Henry, 1990 for example).

The same principles are applied to calculate the sample size needed to make trustworthy judgements at a certain level of precision. Suppose we are interested in the idea that girls score more highly than boys on an empathy index and that we are interested in detecting differences between the groups as small as two points on a 27-point scale. This can be entered into the sample size calculations, allowing us to choose a sample that is big enough to be sensitive to a difference between the boys and girls of just two points.

Although this may seem rather remote from the needs of small-scale researchers who often have to make do with what they can get (opportunity samples), it should not be. Small-scale researchers may do survey work which, when simple instruments are used, can involve large samples. Researchers who do surveys often want to generalize, so they should know how big their samples need to be if their claims are to be convincing at a given level of confidence and precision. Others may be less interested in claiming that their findings are representative of a population but will often want to suggest that readers should take their conclusions seriously. The researcher who understands the relationship between sample size and the confidence with which generalizations can be made is able to explain how findings based on a smaller sample might best be understood. Above all, awareness of the principles behind random sampling can help to develop a suitable humility. People who have been immersed in intensive, small-scale work can easily grow a subliminal belief that everywhere else is similar. It may be, but sampling theory reminds us how many cases ought to be studied before we should be confident that the instance is representative of the world in general.

Random sampling (the first method) is not feasible in most social research inquiries. Telephone surveys (CATI) are the main exception. There are many alternatives (Patton, 1990 has a good list), the most common of which include:

1 Theoretical sampling involves selecting people who meet a given criterion: they may have a first degree, experience of unemployment, membership of a political party. Getting a manageable sample will then involve one or a combination of the following methods. This is sometimes known as 'multistage sampling'.
2 Systematic sampling (choosing every 10th, 50th, 79th case, record, incident, person etc.) The sample size and intervals (10th, 50th, 79th) are calculated on similar principles to those for random sampling.

3 Stratified sampling (choosing equal numbers of obstetricians, hospital midwives, community midwives, health visitors, care assistants, and new mothers and fathers in a study of mother and baby care from booking-in to three months after delivery). With random sampling the voices of minorities are muffled by the louder voices of majorities but it may be very important to hear what they have to say. Social workers make up 10% of social services staff in England (Balloch et al., 1998) but their role is so pivotal that it would be a serious mistake to study social service provision on the basis of a random sample of 100 people involved in service provision. There would only be 10 gatekeepers – the social workers – in that sample. Better to consider a stratified sample containing more social workers.

4 Site sampling is based on identifying groups of people, such as primary health care teams, small businesses or adult education classes, and then sampling everyone in the site or group, or using stratified sampling. A modern version is to e-mail everyone on a list or in an electronic discussion group, although I suspect that very low response rates are likely.

5 Opportunity or convenience samples are common in small-scale research. The sample comprises people who you can get and it is unlikely that they will be truly representative of the population. This is a problem for researchers who want to generalize from the sample to the population. They often tackle it by comparing characteristics of the sample, such as age, gender, race, educational attainments, with the population's characteristics. Where there is a close match the assumption is that the opportunity sample may be regarded as representative. Researchers who will not themselves generalize but who will leave that to readers will also make sample/population comparisons to help readers to make their own judgements.

6 Snowball sampling is a form of opportunity sampling in which one informant is asked to name others who the researcher could approach. Sometimes snowball sampling is used just to recruit informants (Boxes 3.6, 3.7, 4.11, 5.4). At other times informants are asked to name people who would be good informants, because they speak well, have rich experience or hold key positions.

With the snowballing sampling we have moved from sampling as an exercise in locating people who are representative of the population because they are typical to sampling people who are representative in the sense that they are atypically good as informants. One sampling strategy is only better than the other in terms of a particular inquiry and in relation to the sorts of claims that the researcher wishes to make.

Furthermore, there has already been a hint that researchers do not pick one of the sampling methods to the exclusion of all others. Multistage designs are common. In the exploratory stages snowballing may be the strategy of choice, leading to more systematic inquiries when some form

Stage	Sampling strategy	Field inquiry methods	Instruments	Generalizing
Exploratory	Opportunity Convenience Snowballing Key informants	Interview Observation	Lightly structured with open responses	Researchers and readers generalize intuitively on the basis of recognizability and plausibility
Pilot	As above but methods, instruments and samples will be more deliberate (targeted and structured) because things have been learnt from (1) the exploratory work, (2) documentary research, (3) any early literature review			Depending on the sampling strategy and sampling size, researchers may be able to argue that it would be reasonable to treat findings as if they were typical
Depth work or main study	Any strategy is defensible (and all need defending). Methods 2, 4, 5 often chosen, 6 is common	Interview Observation Questionnaire Scales, tests, measures Sorting and ranking etc.	Lightly structured instruments will be mindfully used. More structured ones common	
Estimating the reach: how representative is the story?	Greatest where methods 1, 3, 4 can be used	Survey	Highly structured – they give the greatest reach	In addition to intuitive generalizing, researchers may want to claim that survey findings are representative of the population

Figure 5.1   *Elements in a multistage research design*

of stratified or site sampling would be preferred. After that, researchers might try to see how their conclusions look to a wider audience and do a survey by traditional or electronic means, using opportunity, systematic or random samples. Thus sampling moves from small samples of atypical informants through moderate samples that are more formally typical of the population to larger samples with some claim to be representative. At the same time it is likely that the research instruments will change from the initial lightly structured open-ended ones to more structured ones with some fixed-response items that call for some quantitative data analysis techniques. This is shown in Figure 5.1.

Remember two things. Response rates are usually low (Chapter 4) and those who respond are not typical.

Sampling and Generalizing

It is possible to classify research studies in many ways: whether they rely on quantitative or qualitative methods; in terms of where they can be located on the scale that runs from positivist realist to interpretive idealist;

by labelling them as 'neutral', feminist, critical or Marxian; or as case studies, longitudinal studies, phenomenographic inquires, action research, evaluations, quasi- experimental or whatever. Alternatively, they could be differentiated according to the researchers' positions on generalizability, which is necessarily intermingled with their positions on the other issues listed in the previous sentence. So, researchers who want to assert that their findings should be trusted to be representative of the pattern in the population will be using random samples. Their stance will be close to positivism, with its emphasis on control and reliability, which usually take the form of highly structured instruments requiring the research subjects to make fixed responses. Control, reliability and random samples would be less important if the investigators were happy to make other sorts of claim.

Suppose that instead of trying to identify the factors that people report as sources of stress in family life (which might be done through a positivist-looking survey and which might be feasible as a small-scale study), researchers wanted to understand how stress operated in families. Behavioural psychologists could say that this could be done by using structured observation schedules to see which behaviours preceded stressful incidents and to describe the behaviours that occurred in those incidents. Other researchers might say that this provides a limited form of understanding and that semi-structured interviews would be better, especially if they could be done soon after stressful events (and best of all if the researchers had also observed or recorded the events, probably in a semi-structured way). There are plenty of ways of elaborating on this base design by using sorting, mapping, dissociative techniques, measurement instruments, scales, questionnaires and so on, but whatever the refinements, five things are obvious:

1   It will be hard enough to get informants (snowballing and opportunity sampling are likely to be needed) and very hard to get ones willing to be observed in stressful situations. Samples are therefore likely to be limited in size and unrepresentative.
2   Each informant will take up far more researcher time than would be the case with survey research. This further limits sample size.
3   Stress operates in many ways at many times in many situations. No matter how large the sample of people, researchers will be limited in their sample of stress types and situations, for practical, ethical and cost reasons. The sample of stress incidents is unlikely to be very representative of all the stress incidents that can be envisaged.
4   In order to get rich accounts from informants, the researchers will craft the interviews to achieve the greatest rapport with them. Each interview will be different, and the differences will be amplified because the interviews will tend to concentrate upon spontaneous understanding.
5   Data analysis cannot be reliable in the same way as tallying up the answers on a fixed-response questionnaire used in a survey (see Chapter 8).

So, these researchers should not claim that the understandings they construct about the ways stress operates in families should be trusted to be representative of the population at large. They should, however, point out four things:

1   They have made a justifiable, honest and systematic attempt to understand the people and incidents that they could sample.
2   Human life has marked regularities, even though context-specific features shape them. These regularities make it reasonable to assume that the research findings are *in some ways* representative of stress in families. Unless there is good reason to suspect that the sample is odd in some way, it is plausible to say that these findings provide some fair understanding of family stress.
3   When these findings cohere with others, then it is all the more reasonable to see them as representative of family stress incidents. A lack of coherence means that further research might be needed in order (a) to develop an account that would bring all the findings together in a coherent account or (b) to give further reason for doubting the representativeness of existing research.
4   Readers will generalize by reflecting on the match between the findings and their own conceptions of family stress. This may lead to (a) the findings being assimilated into existing understandings, (b) some findings being assimilated, others ignored, and (c) some or all existing ideas being accommodated [changed] to the findings. As acts of sense-making, each of these three responses is also an act of generalization.

So, assuming that readers, as sensemakers, will generalize, how can researchers doing this sort of non-positivist work influence these generalizations? How might they suggest that readers would be well advised to prefer the researchers' understanding of family stress to any others? The four points above imply that researchers do so (1) by making a case for believing that the findings may or may not be a fair picture of family stress in general and (2) by showing that their research practice has been disciplined and offers a reasonable way of getting information that allows claims to be plausibly made.

   So, a key question to ask at the design stage is about the sorts of claims that you will want to make. It is a difference between saying:

1   This is a good representation of the wider world (positivist research).
2   This is plausible as an impression of the wider world (interpretive or hermeneutic research).
3   This is a slice of life: think about it. It also might mean that we need to rethink some assumptions (case studies, $n = 1$ designs, microstudies, many evaluation studies, action research).
4   Here is one way of playing language games (post-structuralist narratives).

Two further points need to be introduced. One is that claimsmaking is done with an audience in mind, so questions must be asked about the research audience. Much small-scale research is done by students as part of their degree work, which means that their prime audience is whoever is going to grade their work. Their supervisors should make it pretty clear what counts as legitimate research in the context of a bachelor's, master's or doctoral degree in that subject and in that department. If in doubt, students should ask. In some cases it will be apparent that good research is work that conforms to one model: here it is action research, there it is experimental work, elsewhere it is ethnographic. In such cases, further discussion of audience becomes redundant: the research design is fixed by a conventional definition of legitimate research and the sorts of claims that can be made also follow from it. For example, if the aim is to say something that academics should take seriously as a statement that is generalizable to social phenomena at large, then highly structured methods should be chosen that make it reasonable to get large samples, preferably drawn at random. Readers will also be expecting a full, up-to-date review of the literature and a clear indication of how the sorts of claims you hope to make will contribute to the understandings that are supported by existing work and theory.

For many small-scale researchers, doing case studies, evaluations, co-operative inquiry and action research, the main audience is people in the place where the study was done. They will tend to want something useful, which can cause problems if there is also a supervisor to be satisfied by a dissertation with academic credibility. Three implications are:

- The researcher will not be able to make strong claims that the study has any particular significance for other sites, let alone for theory and practice in general. It would be perfectly fair, though, to point to resonances between the case and what the literature, professionals and the researcher's own experience say about theory and practice in general and claim that this study might inform thinking about them.
- Having two audiences probably means that the study will be more demanding than if the investigator was just doing a contract research job for a practitioner audience in one site. When a supervisor also needs to be satisfied, researchers have to take the literature seriously and connect the research activity firmly to it. There is, though, a strong view that it would be poor practice to do *any* evaluation, case study or action research without having a good grasp of the academic literature. In this view, the extra work comes from having to make sure that the research satisfies the participants who, ethically speaking, ought to have the chance to learn from the research.
- The problem of two audiences is most acute when it comes to report writing (Chapter 9). A common approach is to write participants a concise paper summarizing the principal findings in plain English. A formal report is also written for the academic audience and includes

the report to participants as an appendix. Claims should be appropriate: helping people in one site to see their practices, thoughts or beliefs with a research-informed gaze is a worthwhile academic achievement *in its own right.*

The second idea to introduce is that even small-scale researchers often choose more than one method from the palette and combine methods that yield numbers with those that do not. It follows that they may be able to make a combination of the four types of claim described above. That is treated more fully in the next section.

Multi-method Design

Some researchers act as if the more methods used, data sources tapped, theories invoked and investigators involved, the more accurate the research findings. This maximizing strategy is often called 'triangulation'. It is easy to see how triangulation could give greater certainty and just as easy to be dubious about it. If social phenomena are coloured by context, if chameleon-like they change, if observers legitimately see differently, then triangulation should produce more complex accounts and it is likely that there will be disagreements. In the words of Huberman and Miles, 'In the disorderly world of empirical research, independent measures never converge fully' (1994: 438). Far from producing greater certainty, triangulation will frequently produce greater uncertainty.

There are two versions of this disquiet. One concentrates on what researchers should do when faced with diversity, asking what principles they ought to use to arrive at an interpretation. In this version the main fear is that researchers may semi-consciously discount inconvenient findings, which raises the question about why triangulation was considered in the first place if the multiple findings that result are to be treated as an inconvenience to be tidied away.

The second version says that some methods are incommensurable, just as oil and water do not mix. Data obtained with methods that rest on very different views of the social world cannot be blended together because positivism, on the one hand, and hermeneutics, on the other, produce accounts stemming from fundamentally different ontologies and epistemologies. In this version, it is simply misguided, for example, to start counting mentions of certain sorts of beliefs in transcripts of lightly structured interviews in an ethnographic inquiry. It is equally bad practice to let survey interviewers help respondents to give authentic answers. Pragmatists occupying the middle ground will borrow insights from both positions according to the problems on which they are working.

Both versions imply that the term 'triangulation' is best avoided and that it is better to talk about multi-method inquiries using mixed data sources. Multiple substantive theories should be used, remembering that realism and anti-realism are not compatible positions. In some studies it is important to have more than one researcher in order to get a better fix on what appears to be happening, and in others a second or third researcher helps to identify the complex, multi-layered and convoluted features of the research situation. This reworking of 'triangulation' does not discourage investigators with a positivist disposition from using multi-method approaches to try and get more valid and reliable conclusions, but it also clearly indicates that multi-strand research designs may be chosen because they complicate rather than because they converge.

Besides, disparate methods are used in many studies without any discomfort, mainly because one set of methods is a prelude to the other. For example, q-sort, Likert scales and attitude measurement all produce numerical data that are processed statistically in studies that are intended to be 'scientific'. Yet it was seen in Chapter 4 that lightly structured inquiries using open-ended questions are often used to get raw material from which the scales and measures are constructed. Qualitative inquiries often produce interpretations that researchers then check against a wider sample by using survey methods. In both cases there are no problems about the potential incommensurability of methods because the researchers are perfectly clear about how different methods contribute to the overall research strategy and about which set of methods is the dominant set within it. Box 5.1 summarizes a study in which the validity of a self-report questionnaire was judged in terms of how well it captured the tone of informants' responses to semi-structured interviews.

This still leaves open questions about how researchers can deal with findings that cannot be neatly lined up to point in the same direction. Table 5.2 lists some inquiry methods that could be used in a study of morale and work performance and shows how they might produce a complicated set of findings. This is not a warning against multi-method design but an echo of the theme that the quality of thinking takes precedence over methods and data capture. So, when trying to make sense of the seven sets of findings in Table 5.2, investigators should remember that they will be shaped by five methodological factors:

- The difference between receptive and spontaneous understanding (see Chapter 3 and Box 3.1) helps make sense of the findings produced by method 1.
- Quite small variations in task design and wording make a difference to responses because things that are formally or logically the same are not psychologically the same: they are understood differently. Unless good piloting has taken place, it is not clear how far responses to any of the seven methods will be quirky.
- Unless the same subjects were involved in all seven studies, sampling differences might be behind some of the variations, especially if sample sizes were modest.

Table 5.2 *Multiple methods, diverse findings*

Method	Findings
1 Rating scale. Respondents rate the impact of 10 factors on their effectiveness in the workplace	Morale is rated third with a mean score of 5.8 (on a seven-point scale)
2 A semi-structured questionnaire about the workplace includes a question asking informants to name factors that contribute to their effectiveness	A few people mention morale and some other remarks seem to be about morale. However, morale is nothing like the third most common theme
3 Lightly structured interviews about workplace effectiveness always have something in them about what makes informants more or less effective	When interviewers ask directly about morale, there is widespread agreement that it affects workplace effectiveness. It is seldom spontaneously mentioned
4 A field experiment gave respondents a task designed to test their persistence and correlated the time they spent on it before giving up with their scores on a job morale scale	Those with higher morale persisted longer ($P < 0.5$) but this difference was no longer significant when those who had poor health (who tended to be more 'down' anyway) were taken out of the analysis
5 A survey asked informants to keep a diary of (1) what they did at work and (2) how long they worked for	There was no difference between those with high and low morale on (2). There was a difference on (1) but it was not statistically significant ($p = 0.61$)
6 A structured observation schedule was used to study people in their workplace	Observation suggested that data in study 5 are trustworthy
7 Absence rates were calculated for each employee for the past three years. It was also predicted that those leaving during the six-month study would have the lowest morale	High- and low-morale employees had different absence rates but this was because low-morale employees were more likely to have chronic medical conditions. Most of the few people who left during the study had high morale

Box 5.1 Mixed methods: using interviews to validate a questionnaire (Paterson and Britten, 2000)

'Self-completed quality of life questionnaires allow patients a say in measuring the outcome of their care, but do they allow patients to measure the outcomes which are important to them? Several studies have illustrated how patients and their doctors differ in assessing treatment benefits' (27).

The Measure Your Own Medical Outcome Profile (MYMOP) had been developed to allow patients to report weekly on the impact of medical treatment on two symptoms that they nominate. This study explored the possibility that MYMOP, like any research instrument, might provide data that were short on validity because they failed to capture adequately patients' experience of disease.

Twenty of 176 people who had used MYMOP as clients of complementary medicine practitioners participated in semi-structured interviews lasting between 30 and 60 minutes. Interview transcripts were coded and analysed independently by two people. Analysis identified the treatment benefits

continued

that patients reported, particularly with regard to symptom reduction, reduction in medication and changes to their patterns of activity.

MYMOP was found to have captured well the changes that 13 informants described in the interviews and to have partly captured the experiences of another three. It had been inadequate for four informants. These results were presented to the complementary medicine practitioners treating these 20 informants, and they were asked to comment on them.

A new form of MYMOP was developed as a result. Although it makes it easier for patients to give feedback about, for example, whether they want to cut their medication levels, it is still regarded as insufficiently sensitive to the impact of treatment on patients' feelings that they are supported, or on the extent to which they feel in control and able to cope. These are themes that matter to informants and MYMOP, to be valid, should be more sensitive to them. Further work is projected.

- Some of the methods, notably 2 and 3, require investigators to make a lot of inferences when analysing the raw responses. Differences of interpretation are greater when analysis has a high inferential load (Chapter 8).
- What researchers expect to be simple associations can turn out to be more complex. Methods 4 and 7 indicate that bad health is a cause of low morale and reduced work effectiveness, so it is unwise to take low morale itself as a cause of reduced work effectiveness. Method 5 suggests that those with low morale *may* do different tasks at work but there is no way of knowing whether these tasks are the result of these subjects being less effective ('put them where they'll do least harm') or the cause of it (boring tasks lead to low morale and poor performance).

While these methodological explanations offer a good way of understanding some of the disparities there are other ways of integrating these apparently contradictory findings. For example, it might be that low morale does not significantly affect workplace effectiveness in stable organizations doing routine work. However, it does affect retention and it is a drag on performance for organizations trying to do complex work in fast-changing environments: it erodes creativity and initiative. Further work would be needed to investigate whether this story really is a robust way of relating morale and effectiveness.

Costs of Complexity

Boxes 5.2–5.4 contain three real examples of the use of more than one method. Although all three show different methods converging, it has been argued things do not always turn out like that. Apart from difficulties that can arise when complex designs produce contradictory data there needs to be a 'reality check' to make sure that a complex design is a doable design. Chapter 7 says that there is no point in choosing methods if it will be too hard to capture the data and if it is likely that more data will

Box 5.2 Mixed methods: the termination of an established needle exchange programme (Broadhead et al., 1999)

Needle exchanges for intravenous drug users have been shown to reduce public health hazards and social problems associated with multiple needle use, although these programmes have been criticized on moral grounds because they appear to undermine legal prohibitions on drug taking.

This study, which was better funded and more extensive than small-scale studies would usually be, was based on data collected in the three years before the needle exchange programme in Windham, Connecticut was closed by the force of 'home town common sense'. Opponents of the scheme argued that closure would discourage drug taking and help clean up the community.

As a part of an outreach health education programme interview data had been collected while the needle exchange was operating from 322 programme clients about how many times they used needles before discarding them. Interviews with 105 drug users after the exchange was closed led to the following estimates for the mean number of times syringes were used before disposal: (1) 5.56 based on the initial interviews done when the exchange had operated; (2) 7.68 after its closure; (3) 8.18 three months later. These figures depended on users' reports of their own behaviour and might be misleading. Fieldworkers also counted the amount of drug-related rubbish, such as needle wrappers and dope bags, at four outdoor sites where drug taking took place. There was no fall-off in the amount of rubbish after the closure of the centre. This contradicted the view that closing the exchange would reduce drug taking. Furthermore, the police, public works and AIDS workers' records of finds of discarded syringes actually showed an increase in the number of discarded syringes found by town officials. The authors comment that 'basing this research both on constructionist [interviews] and objectivist [records of drug-related rubbish] approaches generated an analysis that empirically documents the real-world consequences of a successful claims making campaign [to close the exchange]. This documentation also ironically disproves many of the major claims asserted by the exchange's opponents' (49).

Interviews with people working on the programme, and with civic figures and others in the community, helped to identify the episodes that had been critical in increasing opposition to the programme; the processes by which the opposition had been mobilized; and the political errors made by people employed in the programme. The researchers concluded by making suggestions about the ways in which other programmes might try to protect themselves from closure in a hostile national political climate dominated by the rhetoric of the 'war on drugs'.

Box 5.3 Mixed methods: interviews and newspaper analysis (Ten Eyck, 1999)

The paper begins with a common way of establishing the significance of the inquiry: 'The sociology of food has enjoyed an increasing popularity over the past few years ... and one neglected aspect of this field, at least in terms of sociology, has been food safety' (426).

continued

The research question was how key actors controlled the construction of the food safety debate and press reporting of it. Unstructured interviews were done, either face-to-face or by phone, that focused on the issue of technological advances, especially genetic modification, and food safety. Six reporters were interviewed on a Florida newspaper and six on a Louisiana paper, along with 40 other stakeholders, such as representatives for various interest groups. The Florida paper contained 119 articles on food safety issues for the period 1987–96, the Louisiana paper 34. On the basis of the interviews with this range of informants and a review of the press coverage (triangulation of data sources), Ten Eyck concluded that the reporters saw the issue as a public interest story to be presented in terms of people and views, rather than in terms of information to be disseminated so as to help people decide on an important public issue.

Box 5.4 Mixed methods: literature, interviews and the need for more beside (Scourfield and Dobash, 1999)

Male domestic violence is identified as an area of public concern and the increased use of violence reduction programmes was noted. It was also observed that disputes about the roots of male violence – whether they lay in patterns of bad behaviour learned in a patriarchal society or in a crisis of masculinity – were associated with different views on how to reduce it.

A review of the literature was complemented by 25 telephone interviews with case workers in agencies providing male domestic violence programmes. 'Snowballing' methods were used to identify informants. On the basis of the analysis of the literature as amplified by the interviews, the authors argue (1) that further work is needed to triangulate this picture with observations and more substantial programme evaluations (which would themselves be multi-method studies); (2) that this work should look for differences between programmes where men are required to attend by the courts and those catering for volunteers, and between those using psychodynamic approaches and others. This study indicates that a substantial investigation of these programmes would have to be sensitive to a range of underlying theories and treatment approaches and to use a mix of methods.

---

be created than can be analysed. It may seem like a good idea to use three methods but it is necessary to check that there are the resources to get data from each method and to analyse all the data in suitable ways (see Chapter 8).

Costs quickly curb complexity. Small-scale work is usually unfunded or low-budget research and, as a result, it is often done by a lone researcher. Friends and colleagues might be persuaded to volunteer to help but there are usually questions to be asked about their expertise and limits to what can be expected of their goodwill. Attempts to use multiple methods may also founder because, for example, people who might be willing to be involved in a study if it means ticking some boxes on a questionnaire are not prepared to be interviewed, do some psychometric tests, fill in a second, personal questionnaire, and be observed. Small-scale researchers usually settle for the least complex design consistent with retaining a good chance of being able to make the sorts of claims they hope to make in response to their research questions. For those committed to complex views of social practices this is deeply corrosive, since every act of simplification (for example, having to look only at people's beliefs as shown on a fixed-response questionnaire) denies the diversity that is the central feature of their world view. Some are fortunate enough to participate in research networks in which people working on small studies share their ideas and findings and consequently create impressions of complexity at the network level, rather than in each individual study. In this way the network also becomes a site for exploring different theoretical positions, something which is not always easy in small-scale studies because it can cost too much time and money to design in the refinements needed to give purchase on more than one line of interpretation. A creative use of this approach has been made by Smyth and colleagues (2000) who have collectively explored schools as learning organizations by linking a series of half-a-dozen small-scale case studies, each done by one investigator, each of whom appears to have been doing a study as a doctoral candidate. Although it is not always possible to make small-scale studies as complex as they ought to be, some redress can be had when it is possible to locate small-scale work within a network of inquiry.

Quality

Seale (1999) quite reasonably extends this view of research quality by saying that it is about the complete research process. Without disagreeing with that, here I want to use 'quality' to organize a review of things that have to be seriously considered once research methods have been provisionally settled. For convenience this account is organized around the notions of validity, reliability and ethical practice.

In classic terms research quality is safeguarded by one being satisfied that data are reliable and valid and ethically obtained. Those who reject the assumption that social research is positivist research insist that what matters is not reliability but trustworthiness and transparency; not validity but credibility and appropriateness. So, although books on positivist research may give the impression that quality is achieved by meeting a number of clear validity and reliability criteria, investigators with more complex views of inquiry need more complex views of quality. For them the investigator has to:

- Set out reasons for believing that the design of the study is a fair and honest way of getting a good answer to the research questions.

- Make the methods of inquiry transparent, or clear. In Mason's words 'explain how *you* came to the conclusions that your methods were valid' (1996: 148). Some authorities recommend that you make it possible for others to do an 'audit trail' of the way the research was done so that they could satisfy themselves that it was done honestly and carefully (for example, Erlandson et al., 1993).
- Discuss how the researcher – you – might have contributed to the findings by being more susceptible to certain lines of inquiry and interpretation (in classic research traditions this reflexivity would be no more than a discussion of any ways in which objectivity was compromised by researcher subjectivity).
- Consider alternative ways of understanding the data and explain why they are not the preferred readings.
- Make a case that is specifically tailored to each research project. In this world there is no such thing as an off-the-peg claim to quality. Quality is not established by simply saying that standard procedures were followed and approved methods were used.
- Come clean about whether the design is intended to capture the world as it truly is (a realist view) or to provide some defensible representation of experiences, actions and feelings that will have been partly constructed by the research itself.

Getting to the Heart of the Matter: Validity

In positivist, scientific research the fundamental design question is about the reliability of the research instruments. If they are as reliable as trying to measure a doorway with a piece of elastic, then the whole investigation is discredited. For other researchers validity questions are the most important for two reasons. First, they say that many social phenomena can never be measured – or even described – objectively. If there is a reality for researchers to capture, it is too complex to be pinned down, it is not homogeneous but contexted and changing, and investigators cannot be objective bystanders in the research process. In other words, reliability, in the sense of objectivity, is a chimera, an illusion, which means that it must be a mistake to make it the most important issue in research design. Secondly, they say that reliability can only be had by restricting the research gaze so that the result is a 'reliable' account of something limited, artificial, or both. For example, reliable reading tests may be reliable because they are limited to measuring word recognition, which is a very limited view of reading. The experiment summarized in Box 3.9 produced reliable measures of the relative influence of sounds and symbols in students' reading but only in circumstances that could be described as artificial (to put it mildly). Many interpretive and qualitative researchers put validity first, while post-structuralists might ask how interesting and enjoyable the work is and consider whether it looks beyond established dualities and disrupts assumptions about how things are (and disrupts critiques of those assumptions as well).

This section looks at internal validity, which is one face of validity. External validity is another; I have already written about it but used the alternative term 'generalizability'. The third aspect of validity is to do with the ways in which research data are analysed and meanings are constructed. The concern is that the interpretations really are fair to the data. This is addressed in Chapter 8.

The key internal validity question is, 'Has the research really investigated what we claim that we have investigated?' This may seem too obvious a question to bother with, but it is deceptively hard to answer with 'Yes' because the attempt to design a rigorous but feasible inquiry can push the researchers off course so that they end up investigating something similar to and different from what was intended. For example, researchers might want to know about medical and nursing staff's hygiene practices but have to make do with questionnaire and interview data when only observation could provide satisfactory evidence about what people do rather than about what they say they do. An internal validity prompt sheet is shown in Box 5.5.

Box 5.5. An internal validity prompt sheet

- Use techniques that build rapport, trust and openness and which give informants scope to express the way they see things.
- Use instruments that contain questions drawn from the literature and from pilot work with respondents.
- Ensure that questions, probes and stimuli fully cover the issues raised by the research questions and key aspects are not ignored.
- Don't ask questions that are irrelevant to the research topic – a waste of scarce interview time.
- As far as possible, prompt informants to illustrate, expand and clarify their initial responses, talking in detail and about specifics.
- Use a sample that is fit for the purpose of the research. If the work is preliminary, opportunity samples and snowballing are acceptable but make sure that all relevant points of view are appreciated. Big samples, preferably selected at random, are needed if you want to claim that your findings are likely to hold good for a population.
- Think about the possible effects of research times and settings on the data you collect.
- Take opportunities to investigate in depth (but recognize that informants' time is limited, as is yours).

Many forms of validity have been identified. Seale (1999) mentions catalytic validity, imperial validity, voluptuous validity and transgressive validity, amongst others. The ones that mainly concern researchers are face, content, construct, concurrent and predictive validity.

FACE VALIDITY   Researchers working within a 'scientific' tradition can be rather dismissive of face validity because it is probably impossible to measure it. For other researchers the 'weakness' is a strength, not least because things that can be measured have a tradition, according to interpretive researchers, of not being particularly important. Put crudely, there is a view that if you can measure it, then it isn't it. Precisely because face validity defies measurement it has a better chance, on this view, of being valid than the other forms of validity. Another strength of face validity is that a clear and full case has to be made that an investigation has face validity. Interpretive and qualitative researchers are dispositionally inclined to favour well-made arguments over claims based on a rule that produces a number to indicate how valid a study is. Face validity, then, may be the most important form, although to those working on positivist lines with a predilection for numerical data it is the weakest. It simply means that, at face value, the study seems to be fairly addressing what it claims to address.

CONTENT VALIDITY   Content validity is similar to face validity but rather sharper. It assumes that there is or can be a clear specification of the phenomenon to be researched. So, if the question is about children's science learning, then minimal content validity in English schools would mean that the inquiry was sensitive to children's learning of the material specified by the national curriculum and the norms of achievement laid down for each age range. Again, in a study of school effectiveness, content validity would involve either or both of (1) exploring the goodness of fit between a school's characteristics and practices and those identified in the school effectiveness research, and (2) exploring the goodness of fit with the characteristics and practices identified by the school itself as markers of effectiveness.

CONSTRUCT VALIDITY   This too may be seen as a variation on face and content validity. Let us return to the school effectiveness example. Where content validity might ask whether the research is sensitive to the elements that have been identified as key components of effectiveness, construct validity would be about the way in which the construct itself – effectiveness – is understood in the research. It can be a contentious question to ask. In this case effectiveness is usually operationalized, or understood for the purposes of the inquiry, to mean that learners get better scores in public examinations than would be predicted on the basis of their previous achievement and social class. In other words, effectiveness is taken as added examination value. While this is an understandable operationalization, and while examination performance is certainly important, something has got missed by defining school effectiveness only in terms of exam scores: parents, employers and educationists say that effective schools make a difference to emotional, social, moral and spiritual learning. Consequently, school effectiveness research tends to be short of construct validity because these aspects of effectiveness are insufficiently captured by the majority of research studies.

Many studies are vulnerable to criticism of their construct validity, especially where complex constructs such as happiness, personality, effectiveness or intelligence are involved *and* where there is an intention to measure them reliably. The complexity means that any operationalization is open to objection, while the concern for reliability forces researchers to concentrate on things that are simple enough to be measured by low-inference means. Government measures, SMART objectives and most performance indicators are usually the unfortunate product of mangerialist drives for accountability which spawn reliable measures with low construct validity (SMART: specific, measurable, achievable, realistic, timely).

CONCURRENT VALIDITY   This mainly applies to individual research instruments and involves asking whether the one in question produces results that are concurrent or consistent with other indicators. This means that concurrent validity, unlike face, content and construct validity, cannot be judged before some data have been collected and analysed. A reading test that gave low scores to children who were judged to be good readers by experienced teachers would have questionable concurrent validity. By extension, questions can be asked about inquiries that produce findings that are out of line with other work. Of course, that does not mean that a study lacks concurrent validity – it could be better designed, more thorough or have better construct validity – but it does indicate that there are questions to be asked. The obverse is that if a test does produce findings consistent with those obtained with other measures, then it is quite sensible to ask why the new test was needed in the first place. High concurrent validity may indicate that the researcher needs to defend the instrument or study from criticisms that it is a waste of resources, only telling us what we already knew.

PREDICTIVE VALIDITY   Results have predictive validity if they allow predictions to be made that turn out to have a good fit with what does happen. Again, this is more commonly applied to instruments than to studies and it can only be estimated some time after the instrument has been used. So, the predictive validity of a scale measuring empathy might be judged by comparing it with career choices, the assumption being that people high on empathy will be more likely to have careers that call for good interpersonal skills. But even if the assumption is correct there are problems because social behaviour does not come from one, unmediated cause producing one, unmediated effect. There are lots of factors apart from empathy that account for the jobs people do.

Consider too a case where an instrument has good predictive validity. The A-level examination that 18-year-olds in England sit correlates better with the class of degree that those who enter higher education get than does any other measure. At least two points arise. First, there is the 'So what?' question. It would be surprising if one measure of the ability to write examination answers did not correlate with another. Secondly, the reported correlations vary but a figure of +0.30 is a fair summary, which means that A-level scores account for 9% of the variance in degree class. This level of predictive validity is not impressive yet it is the best predictor that we have for the later degree performance of students at the point of entry to higher education. As with concurrent validity, then, there are questions about the practical value of predictive validity, even though it can be tidily expressed by a somewhat misleading correlation coefficient (square a correlation coefficient to find out what proportion of total variance is accounted for by the correlation).

THREE WAYS OF IMPROVING VALIDITY

- There is a better chance that complexity will be recognized in research that uses multiple methods, multiple sources of information, multiple theories and more than one researcher.
- Piloting is an opportunity to reflect on whether the research design is really getting at what it was intended to do.
- It can be very helpful to check research findings with participants. Some researchers act as if this 'member verification' makes a study valid. Certainly it helps but at best it means that *from their perspective* informants reckoned that the work was or was not a fair depiction. There are other perspectives that might have every bit as much claim to be taken seriously. Member verification assumes that investigators can feed findings back to participants in language they can understand. This is not always so.

Trustworthiness: Reliable Inquiry

Both the inquiry and the data analysis should be trustworthy (data analysis is in Chapter 8).

The notion of reliability comes from positivist science with its long-standing preoccupation that neither the observer nor the apparatus should skew the results. Here, researchers must be objective. In trials of new medicines, for example, neither the patient nor the medical staff, nor the people analysing the data, should know whether a placebo or the drug is being taken. That ensures that they do not unwittingly treat one group differently from the other and contaminate the results through their own subjectivity. Just as researchers should be objective, so too the instruments: they need to measure accurately exactly what they are designed to measure and nothing else. Something of this concern with reliability is seen in the study reported in Boxes 4.1 and 4.2, where the investigators were careful that all participants got exactly the same treatments.

This sort of reliability has had spectacular results in what might be called 'normal science', but scientists also recognize that there are phenomena, most famously in quantum mechanics, where the very act of observation affects what is observed. That has little significance for most work in the natural science, where it is possible and helpful to try and achieve highly reliable results, but it has caught the attention of social scientists who say that it also applies strongly to social research. These researchers say that investigation disturbs the things that are being investigated or even helps to create them. For example, video recording can disturb normal behaviours, while lightly structured interviews about the impact of new technology on feelings of competence may involve the interviewer and informant together exploring something that the informant had not systematically addressed previously. Nor, they add, is it realistic to expect that researchers can be universally objective or neutral when inquiring about things of which they are a part because they are social beings themselves. High reliability may be demanded when the research is about observer-independent phenomena (the commonplace actions of people randomly observed, the behaviour of lobsters under thermal stress, the effect of a philosopher's stone on lead) but is less desirable or less feasible (or both) when observer-dependent phenomena are involved.

Box 5.6 Reliability in survey interviews: guidelines for interviewers (after Arksey and Knight, 1999)

- Look interested.
- Stick to the schedule: read the questions exactly as printed, in that order; read all of them.
- If there are pictures, cue cards or other apparatus, use them as scheduled.
- Try not to signal approval or disapproval of any answer.
- Do repeat the question if asked.
- If the respondent refuses to answer a question, that has to be accepted, and without any signal of irritation.
- Make sure that you understand a response.
- If not, probe in a non-directive manner ('Would you tell me more about that, please?'), if need be repeat (but do not alter) the question.
- If an answer is not adequate (it is an answer to a different question), thank the respondent for the answer and repeat the original question ('Thank you. And could you tell me ...').
- Do not answer for the respondent, explain the question, or give any other new information, unless the schedule allows it.

Although some doubt that reliability is a useful concept in social inquiries, there are many more who think that its principles are worth following as safeguards against rampant subjectivity and 'anything goes' practices. Positivists try to minimize sources of contamination from their work. For example, interviewer reliability might be enhanced by measures such as those described in Box 5.6 and scales, grids, tests and sorting procedures would be developed to have known qualities and provide dependable numerical data (see Chapter 4). But while these routines might produce 'objective' data they often fail, say their critics, to reflect the complexity of human life. Objective data, they argue, tend to be artificial and to give information about those things that can be objectively measured. Anything else, no matter how significant, gets ignored. This can be illustrated by returning to the example of school effectiveness. The data used to judge school effectiveness are exam results. They are quite reliable but that objectivity has been purchased by questioning students only on those aspects of the subjects that can be reliably graded. In every subject students' skill at designing, managing and completing semi-independent inquiries goes unmeasured by examinations, even though it is a part of the curriculum. The exams are equally insensitive to other widely valued qualities, skills and achievements.

Books on research methods used to say that reliability was the fundamental requirement for good research because nothing measured subjectively and with defective instruments could be valid. Agreed, the more reliable an instrument or study the better, *provided that*:

- Reliability is not achieved by narrowing the inquiry so that construct and content validity are jeopardized.
- Reliability is not achieved by restricting the inquiry to highly controlled circumstances that have little relation to normal social practices (unless a good claim is made to justify it in a particular case).
- It is recognized that the concept of reliability assumes that there are fixed realities that *can* be objectively depicted and understood.

Many small-scale researchers who are neither positivists not post-structuralists share reliability's concern that inquiry should be careful and honest but they do not buy into the erosion of validity and the realist position that go with its raw concept form. They ask:

- Is the research substantial, in the sense of being a serious investigation that is as thorough as could be expected in the circumstances and which combines fieldwork with a good grasp of the literature?
- Have the researchers considered how their lives and views have contributed to the ways in which they designed the study, collected the data and analysed them? In other words, have they been reflexive about the interplay between themselves, the data and the conclusions? The study summarized in Box 3.3 is an example of reflexive practice.
- Are inquiry methods, sampling and data analysis explained so that readers can understand what was done, why and why these decisions were fair responses in the research setting? In other words, are the methods clear or transparent?
- Are alternative research designs and interpretations discussed and are reasons given for discounting them? In other words, is the reasoning transparent?

- Does this *feel* like an honest attempt to investigate, something that is trustworthy, even if I'm doubtful about the findings and have a hunch that a different study would find something quite at variance with this one?

This view of reliability parallels the view that face validity is far more important in some forms of social research than predictive and concurrent validity, even though they can be more precisely defined and estimated. Those who need to have figures to show that a research instrument is reliable will be interested in the following.

REPEATED MEASURES   The more measures there are of something then, generally, the more reliable the findings. A paper instrument that contains many items intended to tap the same construct will often be more reliable than one with fewer; repeated observations of workplace performance give more reliable estimates than a one-off observation; and if two instruments produce similar findings, the results are taken to be more reliable than those coming from one instrument alone. One implication is that reliability is costly because simple, one-shot measures tend to have lower reliabilities than can be achieved through repeated observations and extensive testing.

An important exception is where researchers do manage to develop a short form of a complex instrument that can be shown to get very similar findings to those produced by the full version. Similarly, research may establish that only three observations of performance are needed to be fairly confident about someone's competence. Notice, though, that these more economical measures emerge from work that has had to take the belt-and-braces approach to reliability by using long instruments on many occasions, perhaps in conjunction with other measures.

TEST-RETEST RELIABILITY   The instrument is used and then used again, usually with the same respondents. The two scores are correlated. A good instrument is defined as one that has a high test–retest correlation. That does assume that the instrument is measuring something that is fundamentally stable, which is not always a wise assumption to make in social research: attitudes, for example, can be pretty volatile.

SPLIT-HALF RELIABILITY   Responses to half of the questions or items on a draft instrument are correlated with responses to the other half. If the instrument is homogeneous, with every item getting at the same construct, there should be a high correlation between the scores for the two halves. The procedures used to construct rating scales (see Chapter 4) may also be used to make sure that the instrument has known properties. Problems arise when an instrument is structured so that some items must come after others, or when it is not designed to be homogeneous, or when each item has a distinct and unique purpose.

PILOTING Piloting may not show that an instrument or design is reliable but it helps to identify problems. For example, piloting a service satisfaction scale might produce an unexpected pattern of responses. If these were followed up by interviews with respondents it could emerge that they were interpreting the instrument in ways that the investigators had not anticipated. Again, if a scale contains three questions that are formally similar in that they all appear to ask the same thing but one gets answered quite differently to the others, then there is an obvious reliability problem.

INTER-OBSERVER RELIABILITY This is also an issue in data analysis and is covered in Chapter 8 as well. It is about estimating the degree to which different researchers agree. For example, several researchers could watch a video of a counselling session and code it up using a structured observation schedule. It would be easy to show how far their codings converge. Anyone whose codings appeared to be erratic could be retrained. Similar principles could be used to make sure that different researchers making lightly structured observations were reliably sensitive to the same events. Of course, this assumes that there is a 'master discourse', a way of coding the data that is better than the alternatives.

SUPERVISION Telephone interviewers' work is routinely monitored to make sure that they follow the script. Those who do not are retrained or returned to the job market.

Ethical Practice

Research should cause no harm to research subjects, whether directly or indirectly. In North America investigators routinely expect to have to get the approval of an ethics committee before doing any research with human subjects, including analysing student records, doing surveys, interviewing, testing or observing. Less exacting requirements may apply in your workplace.

Research subjects or others with authority to do so should give their informed consent to participating in the study and to the data collected being used in the ways that the researcher describes to them. It is increasingly common for written consent to be sought and many researchers include a clause asking informants to waive their copyright over what they say, although a lot more don't bother. In some places interviewers, for example, are required to file a consent and copyright form for each interview as evidence that they really did the interview rather than faked it.

Researchers must promise that subjects' identities and those of the sites in which the research is done will remain confidential. Be aware that it is very easy to identify people and sites inadvertently. It usually happens when the researcher gives contextual details that allow insiders to deduce who is being studied. If it allows them to attribute derogatory remarks to individuals, this can get very unpleasant. Inadvertent disclosure is most common in interpretive, qualitative research, simply because quantitative researchers usually deal in large samples and many sites and give few details that allow respondents' identity to be inferred. In all cases legislation about data protection must be observed. In Britain the Data Protection Registrar's guidelines apply: <http://www.dataprotection. gov.uk/dprhome.htm/>.

Recognize that research subjects and sites can be damaged by the way research findings and reports are used. For example, research on a minority group may show that they differ from mainstream culture in unattractive ways. If the report gets picked up by the media and sensationalized the group can be damaged by the research, even though nothing was further from the researcher's mind. Even small-scale research can be mis-reported in damaging ways.

Lastly, some investigators say that it is not ethical to engage in research without intending to make a beneficial difference to things. Although action researchers and critical theorists are committed to change, and co-operative or feminist inquiries are often change-centred, these are not the only groups believing that researchers have a moral duty to improve situations when it is within their power to do so.

For more information consult the statements produced by professional bodies such as The American Psychological Association <http://www. apa.org/ethics/code.html>, The American Sociological Association <http://www.asanet.org/members/ecoderev.html> and the British Sociological Association <http://www.britsoc.org.uk/>. Chapter 7 adds to this note on ethical issues.

6

Complexity

This chapter is something of an interlude in the remorseless patter of advice about methods and design because it is not about how to do inquiries but about what those inquiries might find. The argument is that in many ways social phenomena are complex, dynamic and indeterminate. The reason for saying it is to encourage small-scale researchers to recognize that even if they do not share anti-realist or post-structuralist views they are still likely to find themselves with information that is untidy and equivocal. New researchers often worry about whether their research will 'get it right'. This chapter extends the treatment of ontology and epistemology in Chapter 2 by suggesting that even realists, faced with the complexity of human thought, feeling and behaviour, are likely to experience doubts about the 'rightness' of an answer and uncertainty about what a 'right' answer might look like. It is placed before the chapter on doing research as a signal that what inquirers find is likely to be messy, uncertain, contingent and changing. The message is just as important for analysing data (Chapter 8), for writing (Chapters 9 and 1) and for choosing and orchestrating inquiry methods (Chapters 3–5).

The first five chapters have shown that there are more complex alternatives to common-sense assumptions about what exists (ontology) and how we may know about it (epistemology). They have drawn the conclusion that research can have many purposes and serve many audiences. For these reasons, researchers use any methods that they can present as fit for the purpose. This is a far more complex view of research than the common-sense version of it as 'scientific' inquiry that uses the right methods in rigorous ways so as to expose essential truths. It is also less elitist because it means that research can legitimately be a small-scale activity open to anyone who is prepared to put sensemaking at the heart of systematic inquiry. This glimpse of complexity is included in a book on inquiry methods because researchers who expect their work to reveal the neat patterns of common-sense 'science' are likely to be disconcerted by what they find. This chapter is a resource for thinking about what you may find, a possible aid to sensemaking and claimsmaking. The first section presents some key ideas about complexity. The second relates them to the ways in which organizations can be understood, and the third extends them to people. The argument throughout is that research findings are often messy and that mess need not be treated as evidence of poor design, inadequate methods and sloppy techniques. 'Mess' can be a valid representation of complexity. Small-scale researchers, like others, need not feel disconsolate if their findings lack the neatness that common sense expects of research.

The idea of complexity is best treated as a metaphor because it means rather different things to different people. Complexity has been rather promiscuously identified with quantum mechanics, intuitive understanding, ecosystems, shamanism, Mandlebrot sets, Taoism and the weather. In some sense they may be similar but it seems prudent to remember that the face differences look greater. Just as Hacking (1999) has carefully explored different meanings and uses of the carry-all term 'social constructionism', so too there is a need for an appraisal of the ways in which the several natural science notions of complexity might – and might not – be helpful in the social sciences. Thrift has argued that the decision to treat complexity theory as a metaphor is not a problem: 'I would argue that metaphors are at their most powerful when they are at their most diffuse: then their breadth of meaning allows many meanings to be enlivened by them' (1999: 36). That is my view. My position is that if systems comprising inanimate matter are often complex, then it is all the more plausible that human systems will also be complex or messy. That needs some qualification because it rather depends on the levels of analysis that are used, the depth of understanding sought and whether prediction is required. Human systems may be tolerably predictable on a large scale and in the long run. But while macro-economists act as if forecasting were possible, historians tend to be suspicious of views of the past that make sweeping generalizations about the life-cycles of civilizations or about ages of revolutions and are downright sceptical of the idea that the future is in any sense predictable. Historians notwithstanding, there are many social scientists who act as if the behaviours of large numbers of people can be captured in the language of probabilities. Yet even if it were legitimate to describe some aspects of human life in terms of probabilities and to assume that the free wills of many people over extended times cancel one another out and leave stable patterns in their wake, that is a far less plausible approach to understanding the interstices of thought, feeling and action on smaller scales.

So, this chapter's emphasis on the messiness and complexity of social research findings excludes those social science inquiries that identify aspects of human life that can, according to practitioners, be fairly predictably summarized by means of objective observations, pure research instruments, sufficient care and good statistical analyses. My suggestion is that the language of complexity fits well with other approaches to social science and that they are the ones most used by small-scale researchers. Bryne (1998) provides a more sustained exploration of the potential that the concept of complexity has for understanding in social sciences, although it is not the last word on the subject.

The Significance of Complexity

Newtonian science assumed that the universe is determinate and integrable, which means that if you know the exact state of a system you can use scientific laws to predict fully its state at any future time and, by implication, each point in the transition from now to then. Such laws formed the basis of classical mechanics, which allowed the motions of planets to be predicted and the effects of heat on enclosed volumes of gases to be understood. Although there were problems in natural science that continued to defy neat, classical solutions, the determinist explanation was that they were too complicated for existing techniques to cope with and/or that there were hidden variables at work. These problems were treated as pragmatic problems, not as signs that the determinist view was a poor fit with reality. More recently natural scientists have acknowledged that although there are problems that may yield to more computational power or to the identification of missing variables,

> Our data-gathering abilities can never be sufficiently extensive to know all there is to know about a complex system ... For one thing, in a complex system there is no clear distinction between one 'part' of it and another, which makes getting 'all' the information impossible. (Briggs and Peat, 1999: 170)

In fact, most problems will not be resolved by brute force because the determinist assumption itself is wrong and complexity is normal. Determinism and the integrable phenomena of classical mechanics are exceptions (Cohen and Stewart, 1995; Cushing, 1998).

Complex systems are not simply complicated (if they were, then brute force would eventually provide answers). They are indeterminate and non-linear. They are indeterminate in the sense that if we know exactly the state of a complex system now we cannot (1) predict exactly how it will be at a future time and (2) describe accurately each point in the transition from now to then. This is usually illustrated with reference to quantum mechanics, which is about the indeterminate behaviour of subatomic phenomena. Light may behave like a wave or as a particle but until an observation is made it is not known which will characterize a particular photon on that occasion, although the behaviour of photons collectively can be summarized with a very high degree of accuracy in the language of mathematical probability. What cannot be predicted is the trajectory and behaviour of any one photon observation. The system is indeterminate because although accurate estimates can be made of the probable behaviour of ensembles of photons, the behaviour of a photon is indeterminate. Rather like people.

Complex or indeterminate systems, whose behaviour can only be described at the system level and in terms of probabilities, are non-linear. The explanation is that there are resonances between particles (or people) that are not predictable at the individual level. Their effects are cumulative, so that 'When we start at a point P_0 in phase space, we can no longer predict with certainty its position P_t after time period t. In short, the initial point P_0 leads to many possible points – P_1, P_2, P_3 – with well-defined possibilities' (Prigogine, 1997: 38). So, relatively small changes, especially early on and before attractors are at work and cycles have become established, can produce dramatically different and unpredictable outcomes. These systems are initially very sensitive to contingencies; in human systems, contingencies include the individuals, resources, context and specifics. Consequently, 'their past is co-responsible for their present behaviour' (Cilliers, 1998: 4). This helps to explain why innovations are always changed when they are transferred from one site to another. The ways in which the innovation develops are highly sensitive to the contingencies of the new site in which they are started up, which means that an innovation that is exported to 10 sites will morph into 10 shapes, each reflecting different start-up conditions. In the same vein, Gould argues that:

> Humans are not the end result of predictable evolutionary progress, but rather a fortuitous cosmic afterthought, a tiny little twig on the enormously arborescent bush of life which, if replanted from seed, would almost surely not grow this twig again, or perhaps any twig with any property which we call consciousness.

It is this thinking that underlies a common piece of advice about innovating in complex systems, namely to get in place the ingredients for success and to encourage people to follow the sorts of process that have been successful elsewhere. The things to avoid are trying to specify the outcomes to be attained (after all, this is an indeterminate system) or trying to regulate the process of innovation (Fullan, 1999; Lewin and Regine, 1999). But note too that the innovation, no matter how shrewdly it is introduced, is liable to be steamrollered by the established cycle of behaviour and its powerful attractors.

When complex systems have settled into a pattern of operation it can be very hard to shift them away from it. Strong attractors emerge in stable systems, attractors that make them resistant to change. In Stacey's words,

> an attractor is a pattern of behaviour into which a system ultimately settles in the absence of outside disturbances … We might say that an attractor is a potential state of behaviour, a disposition, or an archetype that is in the process of being realised through the specific experience of a system. (1996: 55)

Notice that attractors are not 'things' in the system. They describe the system's tendency to settle into cycles that get repeated. So, even when changes seem to be shifting the established pattern, the pattern may become fuzzy for a while but is likely to re-establish itself. In determinate systems the pattern is neat and can be exactly summarized and perhaps depicted with one line on the computer screen, but in complex systems the pattern is like the rhythm of a healthy human heart, which

> *isn't* quite regular. It exhibits a strangeness that involves endless chaotic variations, microjolts, and tiny variations within each heartbeat ... a healthy organism ... [is] jiggling, moving, shifting, filled with positive feedback loops that push the system into new directions and negative feedback loops that keep processes from flying off into merely random oblivion. (Briggs and Peat, 1999: 65–7)

This means that the pattern itself is a wobbly one which, if plotted, shows a lot of overlapping pathways that together form a recognizable, rather messy shape. 'In nature, it seems,' said the developmental psychologist van Geert, 'the shortest line between two points is the wiggle' (1994: 153).

The strength of attractors obviously cannot mean that complex systems are impervious to change. They are dynamic systems, which means that they are always changing but they seldom get transformed. For example, the ecological balance between two species is always changing – at its simplest an increase of predators means a decrease in prey (which then leads to a decrease in predators, then to an increase in prey ...) – but they are quantitative changes around the attractors, changes in the balance within the system, not to the system itself. System changes are exceptional and stability is normal, always recognizing that stability means that there are lots of bumps and twitches that get reined in by the attractors. If complexity theory is understood to imply that attractors tend to keep systems moving around familiar routes, an implication is that most studies of the impact of innovation should find that impact is slight or short-lived. Consider, for example, the strong similarities between classrooms in recent times (at the end of the 1980s) and in 1900 (Cuban, 1991). It also follows that it usually takes time before it is clear whether the system really has changed or whether what appears to be a change is explicable as just part of the normal variations between one cycle and the next. Furthermore, historians are accustomed to the idea that what one person will take to be a fundamental change or a time of transition, another will take as an indicator of essential continuity. Was sixteenth century Europe medieval or modern? In my view, both and more. This thinking about the social world implies that there is a need for descriptive studies (see Chapter 1) and that research that reports that innovations have not made (much of a) difference should be reported and valued because in a world of complexity, that is the way things mainly are.

In the context of the fossil record of life on Earth, Gould has argued 'that stasis should be an expected and interesting norm (not an embarrassing failure to detect change)' (1996a: 128). Yet complex systems can become sensitive enough to be changed. They can come to the edge of chaos when changes can be set off by small contingencies that would normally be obliterated by the attractors. This is a catastrophic view of transformation in which a small change (lowering the temperature of water from 33 °F to 32 °F) produces a catastrophic or phase change (still water becomes ice). For Gould the fossil record is one of punctuated equilibrium, a few short periods of massive change punctuating the operation of stable cycles or stasis. Van Geert (1994) argues that human cognitive development involves passing through up to four stable stages, each of which spans several years with jumps (phase changes, catastrophes or state changes) marking the transition from one stage to another. Small-scale changes happen all the time without changing the basic character of a developmental stage. By definition there are no more than three phase changes between birth and adulthood, each depending on the accumulation of hundreds of small changes over a long period. Interestingly, he extends his remark about the wiggle being normal in nature by suggesting that these normal oscillations in performance are accompanied by a larger-than-usual drop in performance just before a phase change. In this sense a marked fall-off in performance could be a cause for celebration, a sign that things are about to get much better. This is a good example of the way in which complexity thinking runs counter to common sense.

The final feature of complexity is that it is not imposed on the system but is the outcome of resonances and other interactions between parts of the system which are all acting on the basis of simple rules applied in their own local settings. The parts neither have nor need to have a view of the purpose or workings of the system as a whole: complexity still arises as a result of self-organization through the local application of simple rules. The system of food supply for London is truly complex but it is achieved by millions of shoppers making simple decisions according to a few rules and with only limited local knowledge. Complexity is an emergent property that arises out of those rules. An emergent property is a characteristic of a system that cannot be accounted for just by describing the sum of its parts. For example, life is an emergent property of body parts. Families are complex systems with emergent properties that do not come from any one family member or any subset of family members. The emergent property of a family comes from all of them and from nothing less. At the same time this complexity and its emergent properties arise from each family member using fairly simple rules in their interactions. Notice that complexity comes from each part of the system acting on the basis of simple rules applied to its own local setting. The parts do not need to have a view of the purpose or workings of the system as a whole in order for complexity to arise, which helps to explain why it can be so hard to change systems from the top down. Complexity is a bottom-up achievement produced by individuals using simple rules to deal with local, pragmatic situations.

Consider an academic department in a university. Assume that each faculty member follows three rules. They do not have to share the same rules and it is likely that the rules that best describe their behaviours are not ones they would volunteer, or even acknowledge. A researcher may have concluded that the rules that one faculty member appears to use are 'avoid more work; look important; protect my research activity'. Another has 'my teaching comes first; avoid being shown up as a researcher; respond only to here-and-now things'. And so on. With a set of simple rules like this a researcher could see how people speak in favour of change but unwittingly or surreptitiously thwart it. Argyris (1993) presents an analysis of these 'organizational defences' which contains a simple set of rules to counter the complex, emergent phenomenon of people not doing things that they say they value. My guess is that his counter-rules will seldom be powerful enough to trigger the phase change that would block people's reliance on their three rules of engagement. This would be because beliefs might have changed but all the other elements in the pattern of interactions that create complexity would not have changed and would inexorably erode the new thinking. But if people were coming together for the first time, or if a system were teetering on the edge of chaos, his counter-rules might just be enough to break the attractors' pull and start something unusual happening.

If complexity and chaos theories can describe the indeterminate states that natural scientists explore, then there is all the more reason to assume that they are appropriate to the human world in which people make decisions about how they think it best to act. Atoms are fungibles, which means that to the scientist one atom of gold will do as well as any other. I have suggested that in some social research people can be treated as fungibles, as when large random samples are taken for social surveys. Researchers and their methods of inquiry can also be treated as fungibles when stringent actions have been taken to secure high levels of observer and instrument reliability. There is still a place for a classical, determinist science of inanimate matter because, quite pragmatically, there are integrable phenomena on which it works well and because it gives predictions of other phenomena which are accurate enough for the purpose in hand. So too with social science. A complexity view does not mean that there is no place for positivist inquiries, generalizations and rational policy-making. It does mean that there need to be pragmatic decisions about when these classical approaches to social phenomena are likely to provide information that is fit for the purpose in hand. Just as, in natural science, determinist phenomena that can yield to classical approaches are fewer than those to which complexity applies, so too in social science.

Implications for small-scale researchers, who are likely to do inquiries where the personal, the specific and the particular loom large, are:

1   If your work is positivist, realize that you are assuming that the phenomena you are studying can be treated determinately and that you should not cry 'complexity' if your data are not as neat as you had hoped.

2   Appeals to complexity are not allowed as excuses for not thinking hard enough. If your research is to be of interest to others, you will need to

help them to see things that they might learn from it. That will not be achieved by presenting them with thick slices of life as though they are inherently valuable. Complexity calls for *more* attention to sense-making, for *more* considerate claimsmaking and for *more* mindfulness.

3   You may not be able to sum up what you found, concluded and claim in simple terms. In other words, point 2 is a tough one to accept.

4   Be pragmatic. Do your best, explain why it is your best, make an honest appraisal of what the information you create might mean and to whom. In principle simple, or determinate, systems can be neatly summarized but complex ones cannot, which means that researchers can do no better than offer honest accounts and interpretations of the systems as they saw them and understood them.

5   Take contingency seriously. What you create in your research has a history that helps to explain it and to explain why it is not identical to similar cases.

6   A study of the parts can only do so much to explain the whole because whole complex systems have emergent properties that have grown through the contingent operation of all of the parts. So, informants may tell you the rules that they think they use and they might appear to use them but the system's behaviours lie in the repeated interactions of all the rules and contingencies.

7   Expect what you study, whether it is people, organizations, behaviours or beliefs, to be dynamic. That just means that they will change, not that they will appear to 'improve' from any given point of view.

8   Don't expect to be able to innovate (after all, if things could easily be improved, they probably would have been) and don't expect to be able to create change in any predictable way. Of course, expectations can turn out to be delightfully wrong.

Complexity and Organizations

There are three simplifying tendencies in organizational research and theory. One reifies organizations by treating them as distinct things. A second tries to explain their behaviours as though they were rational beings following one clear goal, such as profit maximization. A third accepts that all organizations exist in wider environments but still tends to analyse things as if organizations could choose to buck the trends, assuming, for example, that a malign English government is responsible for difficulties in higher education even though most English-speaking countries are having similar problems and responding in similar ways.

Complex views of organizations reject the independent, rational beings model and are more likely to use neural nets as a metaphor (Cilliers, 1998). This connectionist metaphor sees organizations as sets of dynamic relationships between people, tasks, rules, materials and symbols, much as the mind is understood as a neural net, a dynamic set of connections between billions of neurons. On this view it is as hard to say exactly what the organization is as it is to explain what consciousness is: both comprise a set of changing relationships which are not very well captured by the flow charts or maps that purport to describe how either is organized and operates. In fact, it may not be easy to define what is in the organization or mind and what is outside because each is inextricably a part of the wider world of signs, people, practices, objects, tasks and meanings. This is indicated by Figure 6.1 which gives one view of the connections that make up an activity system (a human system for carrying out an activity). It suggests that the boundaries of any one activity system are fuzzy, not least because people simultaneously belong to many activity systems. Checkland (1981) pointed out that one of the biggest problems in thinking about human systems is defining what the system is: what it is for, who is in it, how it works and why, for example. Different definitions of what appears to be the same system lead to very different accounts of problems and possible solutions. There are alternatives to seeing organizations as aggregations of activity systems. Some sociologists prefer actor network theory, which is about the ways in which people and material objects are brought together in networks to achieve shared meanings and purposes (Arksey, 1998; Miettinen, 1999). Many others are attracted by the idea of communities of practice, which provides a way of thinking about how workgroups organize themselves as they define, do and change collections of activities (Wenger, 1998).

Yet, although this connectionist view of organizations means that they cannot be properly understood without understanding their environments, it does not follow that they respond in a determinate – predictable – manner to environmental changes. Part of the reason is because if they are seen as constellations of practice (Wenger, 1998) or shifting sets of activity systems or coalitions of actor networks, then it follows that there is no single, simple decision-making process. Even if the organization's formal goals are compatible with each other (which is not necessarily the case), the goals that emerge out of the actual workings of networks, communities and systems will often be different. So,

> Complexity theory questions whether long term intended action is possible. It points out that the way things unfold is inherently unknowable to the human mind, emerging through spontaneous self-organisation originating from some distant detail, rather than advanced planning. The most that we can do is manage what is local. (Flood, 1999: 90)

Two themes, power and knowledge, help to illuminate this complex view of organizations. When people saw organizations as monolithic bureaucracies, like the armies of the Second World War, then power was seen as something that the chairman (sic) had and that flowed downwards through the system. Sometimes it met resistance and the good manager either fired resisters, by-passed them, or won them over. There are times

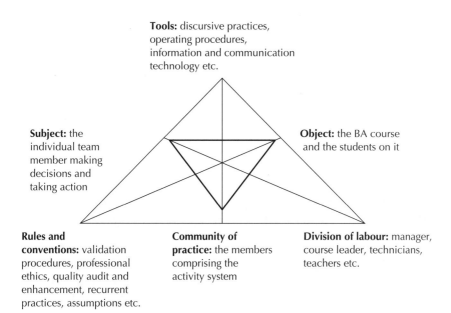

Tools: discursive practices, operating procedures, information and communication technology etc.

Subject: the individual team member making decisions and taking action

Object: the BA course and the students on it

Rules and conventions: validation procedures, professional ethics, quality audit and enhancement, recurrent practices, assumptions etc.

Community of practice: the members comprising the activity system

Division of labour: manager, course leader, technicians, teachers etc.

Figure 6.1   *A degree programme represented as an activity system (Trowler and Knight, 2000: 31)*

when it is still useful to look at organizational workings in this way but most social scientists will need to recognize that while power may be used to induce people to do something, it can also inhibit them from acting and affect what they would consider or imagine doing. Following Foucault (1975) there is a tendency to see power as something in the capillaries of social interaction, always there, always moving. It is insidiously pervasive, operating by affecting what we are able to think, as well as what we are likely to think and what we are likely to find acceptable. A complex view of organizations would draw attention to the ways in which the constructions of workplace culture establish and perpetuate power relationships. Whatever the professed goals of the organization, the way in which power seeps through everything affects what is possible and attracts social practices to established dynamics. Furthermore, if there are senses in which power is distributed through the organization, then people are likely to experience a 'receding locus of control' – to find that even leaders say that other people, groups or factors have the ability to make a difference but they do not.

Knowledge is seen in similar ways, as something that is ever-changing, as is power, and distributed through a system. It does not reside in any one place or person, nor does it take any one form; indeed, the formal, propositional 'book' knowledge that easily gets mistaken for knowledge itself is the least important form of knowledge for many purposes (Nonaka and Takauchi, 1995; Wenger, 1998; Claxton, 1998; Tomlinson, 1999).

Blackler (1995), for example, recognizes that some knowledge, which he describes as 'embrained', is of this propositional type and that it is often explicitly encoded in books, manuals and programs. There is also embodied knowledge (a tacit, 'knowhow' knowledge that is tied to doing); encultured knowledge (knowledge that is carried by the language and beliefs that saturate interactions); and embedded knowledge (which is expressed in the very relationships between people). So much of this knowledge flows through what people do and how they connect with each other in daily practices that Blackler suggests that it is better to think of knowing than of knowledge, because 'knowledge' does not really capture the flowing and changing features that he identifies. Goleman (1998) adds that knowing is emotional and not just rational. There is much more to be said but this is sufficient to make it clear that these complex views of knowing in organizations show why traditional approaches to organizational improvement that concentrate on embrained and encoded knowledge have limited chances of success – because embodied, encultured, embedded and emotional knowing are important, get left untouched, and pull the dynamics back into the established patterns. Worse, they are hard to change.

Organizations may also be insensitive to environmental change because they fail to see the change or misunderstand it. Even then they may not agree how to act and, since knowledge and power are distributed through the organization, the decision to act may lead to change without change – to ripples but no big waves. In other words, the effects of a change in the environment on any organization are indeterminate: neither the outcome, nor the route taken to get to that outcome, can be predicted on the basis of what is known about the organization in the first place and there are frequently problems in agreeing what count as 'the organization' and 'the first place'.

This complexity view of organizations suggests that there are many ways of understanding them and that different ways will lead to different understandings and to different ideas about organizational improvement. Morgan (1997) develops this theme in his book *Images of Organization*, while Hunt (1991) makes a similar point about leadership and Easterby-Smith (1997) does the same for organizational learning. In each case the message is that different ways of understanding complex phenomena, such as organization, leadership and learning, are legitimate *and* lead to quite different understandings with quite different implications. Just as this means that there is a variety of defensible approaches to organizational research, so too the information that is collected can be appreciated through a variety of lenses. It is likely that the research design will have made it best to look through one or two lenses but researchers need to realize that complexity views of organization mean that the same information can be read in multiple ways.

It also implies that researchers should have some humility in making suggestions for action. When indeterminacy is rife it is not evident what effects any action will have. Of course, research may have shown that a certain range of effects have been identified when similar actions have been taken in similar circumstances in the past. However, in complex systems it is not possible to be sure that similar circumstances are similar enough, or that similar actions are similar enough: indeed, Fullan (1999) has argued that the best move is to concentrate on reproducing the elements of the processes that have led to desirable outcomes elsewhere rather than to try and reproduce the innovation itself. Notice too that neither the research nor Fullan's advice predicts the outcomes, except in terms of probabilities. So, despite years of unremitting government pressure for school improvement, recent English evidence (Gray and colleagues, 1999) is that only about one high school in seven sustains a rate of educational improvement that is above average for more than three years. It also indicates that these successful schools can get started on the improvement trajectory by taking up one of five different innovations and that it does not seem to matter which one they adopt. In complex systems different changes can lead to similar outcomes and changes that look identical can have different outcomes.

Implications for researchers include:

1 No matter how clear the organizational chart, goals, policies or descriptions of how things work, expect to find things that do not fit. This is normal.
2 Naming something as an organization is a major act of interpretation in its own right. So is identifying its boundaries.
3 Recognize that there are organizations (activity systems, communities of practice, networks) within organizations. Expect them to be distinctive rather than miniatures of the whole; they may be subversive, not supportive.
4 Power and knowledge are distributed through the organization. Although some networks may be more powerful or more knowledgeable than others, do not expect to find a real seat of power or a fount of knowledge. But you might be surprised.
5 Indeterminacy means never being certain about what causes what; in fact the notion of cause, as it is usually understood, is not a very useful one. Things happen because of the interplay of contingent connections in the network of relationships.
6 Your results and conclusions – sensemaking and claimsmaking – will be simplifications of complexity. Other simplifications are possible and might be better.
7 Simple models that emphasize the formal, rational, rule-based and goal-directed aspects of organizations are arguably not very good for most purposes. They involve making abstractions that are far removed from the reality of complexity.
8 Dichotomies, as between cognition/emotion, female/male, powerful/ weak, limit thinking because they obscure the complex position that

it is the relationship between the things that are polarized that is important. Pure opposites seldom exist but relationships between the idea of the opposites do.

9   Recommendations for change and innovations that are based upon this simplicity may appear to be common sense but are likely to be inappropriate.

10 Recommendations for change and innovations that are based upon complexity concentrate on making a difference to the networks of relationships and contingencies without being sure about what the outcomes will be. (They are based on a view of what is possible and of what is most conducive to it.)

Complex People

Careful social science research has used, amongst others, experiments, surveys, observations, attitude scales and dissociative techniques to develop a body of knowledge about patterns of human thinking and acting. Inquiries that might broadly be described as positivist have established plenty of general propositions about topics as diverse as human perception; learning and reasoning; differences between (Western) male and female minds, preferences, attitudes and aspirations; relations between 'ingroups' and 'outgroups'; altruistic behaviour; the impact of strong emotions (usually fear) on cognition and behaviour; associations between the ways in which we explain successes and failures and life success; and so on. Although the findings of this sort of research are often widely reported, it is not always appreciated that they usually take the form of statements about the frequency with which different reactions, thoughts, emotions, attitudes or behaviours are likely to be found in large numbers of people with similar characteristics to the research subjects. Although it is easy to assume otherwise, generalizations about people are indeterminate in that sense that they do not allow us to predict the behaviour of any given person in any particular situation. The best that can be had is a prediction that if there is a good match between what a small-scale researcher is considering and the conditions that gave rise to an apparently relevant generalization, then there is a good probability that the small-scale researcher will get findings in line with the generalization. The point of restating ideas developed in Chapters 2 and 5 is twofold.

First, small-scale researchers should anticipate that what they find might not match too neatly with generalizations offered by large-scale research. This is partly because large-scale research smooths out individual variations and produces a photofit picture that fairly describes the composite average but disguises the complexities that have been blended together to make it (van Geert, 1994). The main reason, though, is that small-scale researchers tend to work with small numbers of informants, although some do surveys that ask a large number of respondents a few things. The smaller the number involved in a study, the greater the chance that normal random variations in the sample will skew the outcomes away from the pattern established on the basis of a much larger sample where individual quirks tend to cancel one another out. Besides, small-scale researchers often have to make do with the samples they can get and are not always able to reject informants who do not quite match the criteria used in selecting samples for the large-scale research that established the benchmarks.

The second and more important point is that generalizing research has often depended on the tacit assumption that people are more simple than they are. The remainder of this section draws attention to views of human complexity that stand in opposition to the simplifying tendencies of positivist research. The intention is to reassure small-scale researchers that it is reasonable to collect information that resists generalization and to offer explanations of it that are provisional and couched in terms of the specifics of the informants, the situation and the dynamics. Small-scale researchers who study people close up are likely to get messy findings because people, as complex beings, produce messy information that may be very resistant to generalized interpretation.

The observation that 'People think that stories are shaped by people. In fact, it's the other way around' (Pratchett, 1992: 8) captures something of a constructionist view that identity, beliefs and behaviours are situationally sensitive. From the researcher's point of view a complication is that an outsider cannot know how a situation is understood, or what the intention is behind an action. One person's failure is another's success; I feel rebuked by what the line manager said to us but you noticed nothing; she gives children plenty of advice on doing a task because that is part of her professionalism but he gives none because his professionalism tells him that children need to learn to be autonomous. Another example: I take a thinking problem and write two stories that should both raise the problem in exactly the same way. The two versions are logically similar and I expect them to get the same responses, but in piloting I find that the stories are psychologically different because I get two different patterns of response from the informants. Differences in the ways in which people perceive things that are supposed to be the same dog attempts to describe what developing children can and cannot do: on one measure children appear to be competent but on another, which is supposed to be identical in all important respects, they appear to be incompetent. The point is that thinking and doing are situationally specific *and* that they are specific to the situations *as constructed by the people participating in our inquiry*. At the very least this means that it is disputable whether the information that researchers collect tells them about the thing they are trying to explore, about the situation, or about the situation as the participants understood it (which includes the research tasks or questions).

Just as some classical research treated situational influences as contaminants to be disinfected out of the study of people, so too it could assume that people are essentially stable beings, in the sense that intelligence, values, personality and habits do not change. For example, IQ has been depicted as a general and stable mental attribute which pervades human action. However, it has become accepted that IQ is a measure of one form of mental ability which is partly affected by the environment and which can certainly be developed or coached. Furthermore, there are considerable variations amongst the life successes of people of similar intelligence and it seems as if 'practical intelligence', which involves expertise and social skill, may be more important than IQ (see Sternberg, 1997; Resnick, 1999). In other words, IQ is not as stable as has been supposed, it is not as important a measure of potential as had been assumed, and what does look important – practical intelligence – is the result of good social learning. Nor do people think consistently. For example, people are more likely to attribute their bad behaviour to the pressure of mitigating circumstances but to conclude that others doing similar things are acting out of malice. In the same way our failures are easily attributed to malign chance but our successes are frequently explained by a 'clever person working hard' script. Dweck (1999) adds that bright people who believe that intelligence is something that you have or do not have are less persistent in the face of difficulties than bright people who believe intelligence is also about being mindful and working hard. There is no doubt that there are regularities in the ways in which a person thinks and acts, especially in situations that they take to be similar, but there is also no doubt that people are not as stable as some researchers presume, nor do they act as uniformly across situations as others imply.

Note also van Geert's (1994) observation that human things wiggle. What you measure now should be different from what you can measure later. Whether the difference is enough to worry about is a matter for expert judgement in specific cases.

One reason is because although psychological research has been attracted to cognition, people are influenced by emotions and processes that are below the threshold of consciousness (Claxton, 1998). What they say or do is likely to be situationally rational – to make good sense to them in the light of matters as they perceive and feel them – but this is not the calculating-machine sort of rationality that seems to infuse some social science generalizations. It is well established that what people say and what they do diverge, which is not so much the result of people 'faking good' as of the operation of two different forms of thinking: espoused logic (what we say) and logic-in-use (our practical, in-action reasoning) (Schön, 1983). Espoused logic draws on embrained and encoded knowing while logic-in-use brings in the other forms. However, we may not be aware of the impact of embodied, embedded or encultured knowing and we are likely to find it hard to put these forms of knowing into words. When what people do and what they say do not fit too closely together there is a temptation to blame them (they lied) or the research (wrong methods, too small a sample). An alternative is to recognize human complexity and accept that there will be differences between what people tell us and the largely tacit knowings, emotions and unconscious forces that affect what they do more than what they say.

So, while it may be useful to use terms such as motivation, self-esteem or self-identity, there is a risk that the shorthand can be treated as if it describes real, fixed attributes that predictably affect human deeds and words. Harré criticized such thinking and

> tried to show that self-esteem [for example] is not a standing property of a person causing certain kinds of answers to questions and certain kinds of behavioural manifestations, related to the degree of strength of the alleged attribute. Rather, like all such attributes, it is a property of the flow of personal action, context dependent and jointly produced. (1998: 145)

Weick offered a similar interpretation of identity, arguing that:

> Identities are constructed out of the process of interaction. To shift among inter-actions is to shift among definitions of self ... depending on who I am, my defi-nition of what is 'out there' will also change ... Once I know who I am, then I know what is out there. (1995: 20)

For Harré it was not just that personal 'traits' are more changeable and socially situated than many psychologists recognized but also that the very notion of self is misleading. He referred to self 1, the 'sense of self occupying one and only one standpoint from which to perceive and act upon the environment'; self 2, 'the totality of attributes of a person, including that person's beliefs about him or herself'; and self 3, the sort of person we are taken to be by others' (1998: 3). It is easy to see that selves 2 and 3 can take more than one labile form.

At this point, with the deconstruction of self, post-structuralist thinking has come to the fore but it is not necessary to accept it in order to appre-ciate that small-scale researchers can quite reasonably expect people's words and behaviours to be more complex, less determinate and harder to summarize than they might have expected. Evans claimed that

> Despite considerable psychoanalytic (and indeed empirical) evidence to the contrary, the social expectation – increasingly enforced by the culture and the demands of the labour market – is that we are a 'knowable' person, a person with a coherent emotional *curriculum vitae*. For many individuals the demands of being this kind of stable, never-changing self are impossible. Nevertheless, what auto/biography often tends to endorse is the view that the 'real' person can be identified. (1999: 23)

Gordon (1997: 405) talks of 'complex personhood', a concept that takes seriously the fact that people get tired, forget, are beset by contradictions, get things wrong, can be caring and altruistic, might be lazy, might harm each other, and so on.

Implications for researchers include:

1 Expect to find that people's feelings, words and actions are more complex and less predictable than you anticipated.
2 Do not be surprised if your findings do not square with findings from other studies. The difference may be because your research is sloppy but it could also be because your research is valid, sensitive and scrupulous.
3 What people say and what they do are related, but do not expect words to match deeds. Different forms of knowing are involved in telling and doing.
4 Simple models of people and their doings that emphasize rational, general and goal-directed features have their place but are also likely to be misleading, especially when trying to understand individuals and small groups in specific settings.
5 Persons and their selves have enduring attributes but this does not mean that they are unchanging, or that the relationships between selves are constant, or that they are impervious to situational and social variations. Consistency and inconsistency are two manifestations of this dynamic.
6 Dichotomies, as between cognition/emotion, female/male, powerful/ weak, limit thinking about individuals as well as about organizations.

Unlike determinate laws in natural science, generalizations (which are a form of simplification) about the human world are fuzzy approximations about the ways in which we believe that people in general tend to behave in circumstances of certain sorts. The small-scale researcher who anticipates reaching neat conclusions may not have appreciated this. That is not to say that it is impossible to simplify things by making sense of them: if that were the case, then research findings would always be complete narratives of everything discovered, which would be impossible. Sense-making and simplifying go together but they involve discarding some complexity. This chapter has alerted small-scale researchers to that and gone some way to alert them to the common reality of messy research data. Sometimes mess, noise or complexity come from poor research but often they are authentic traces of the way that social things are.

7

Doing It

This chapter contains three sections. The first insists that inquiries seldom turn out as planned, although the more experienced the researchers, the more realistic their designs and the better the match between plans and practice. The second reviews ways of capturing data, and the third is about exploring sensitive or distressing issues. Two other important aspects of research practice – personal safety and the dynamics of face-to-face work – have been covered in Chapter 3.

Being Pragmatic

Research reports tend to give a serene and orderly picture of the research process, implying that it follows a clean sequence from choice of topic through literature review to research questions; thence to design, doing, analysis and reporting. It also implies that a good design plays out smoothly in the fieldwork, which is the prelude to data analysis and discussion. That does happen, especially with captive audiences and highly structured instruments and in much documentary work. Others, especially those working within hermeneutic and *verstehen* traditions, find that thinking, doing, analysing and writing seep into each other, while low response rates, unexpected responses and difficulties of access conspire to subvert the research as it had been planned. They experience inquiry as a non-linear, complex process teetering on the edge of chaos, even toppling into disarray. Too many small-scale researchers start without being sufficiently alert to what can go wrong. Novices can be so wrapped up in their own work that they never ask why anyone should be willing to participate and they imagine that organizations will give them access, that people will talk to them and trust them, that practices can be reorganized so that they can do field experiments and that questionnaires will be eagerly completed and swiftly returned. Expert researchers are more pragmatic and allow for access difficulties and low response rates and know how they might adapt their plans if need be. Good design should have screened out silliness but designs still collapse in the face of malign circumstances. Something is usually salvageable if the researchers settle for making their claims less confidently than they had hoped. Data collection remains a time of uncertainty and improvisation. Recognize that what happens will frequently differ from what you intended: one of the greatest attributes a researcher can have is the ability to improvise and make interesting claims even when participation rates are plummeting. So, when you read research reports be mildly sceptical of those that make it seem that the research went to plan. Nine common difficulties and some pragmatic responses are listed in Box 7.1.

Box 7.1 Pragmatic responses to nine common mishaps

Mishap	Possible response
1 Participants withdraw	Good designs have redundancy built in so that the loss of some potential participants is not critical. In other cases investigators have thought about possible substitutes. Lastly, many small-scale studies are exploratory and are based on ideas about research where sample size is not crucial. Here the price of withdrawal may be that claims have to be made more diffidently. In some cases, one or two research questions may have to be abandoned
2 Data collection delays	Again, experienced researchers know that it's a bonus if delays don't happen. Others find that delays threaten deadlines for analysis and reporting. Two coping strategies are (a) seriously consider doing without the delayed data, (b) analyse the delayed data very selectively, focusing on the main claims you hope to make and the key research questions
3 Response rates too low	(a) If you know who has not responded you can make a personal appeal, explaining why you would appreciate a response (NB: never use insistent language; informants are doing you a favour); (b) with e-mail and web inquiries try posting a message saying that you have x replies, hope to get y and that you will post a summary of responses as soon as you get them; (c) consider extending your target group
4 An intervention is compromised	It can be very serious for experimenters if they find that a variable that should have been controlled hasn't been. Often the only thing to do is redesignate work to date as an exploratory study and try again. Shortfalls with other interventions, such as those in action research projects, may be less serious because it is seldom obvious that the shortfall will be critical. However potential claims will have to be reconsidered
5 Data lost	This should not happen if you make back-ups and keep them in a different place from your computer. Files that are too large to go on a floppy can be stored on your website

continued

6 Partners not pulling their weight	Experienced researchers work with people who they know will pull their weight and deliver on time. They try to distribute tasks so as to use partners' strengths and avoid their weaknesses. Novice researchers working in groups need to be open about their ways of working and ask for tasks suited to them. If things come unstuck, see your supervisor or sponsor and together explore what can be salvaged: an individual report may be the way forward
7 The null hypothesis is retained	This means that an intervention that was intended to make a difference hasn't. In quantitative research this might mean that $p = 0.061$ where the rules say that only $p < 0.05$ counts. With near misses like these, consider ignoring the convention and making the claim that the difference should be taken seriously as something worth exploring with a larger sample. In other cases recognize that the fact that the intervention didn't work is interesting: Chapter 6 suggested that the idea that changes can be made easily is a naïve one
8 Your computer or web connection crashes	Sometimes I think that every student doing a small-scale study uses a computer programmed to crash the day before the report is due in. Anticipate the problem and know what you will do if it happens
9 A new article anticipates your findings	Good. You are amongst the first who is able to engage with this new line of thinking

Data Capture

Earlier chapters have insisted that research methods need to be fit for research purposes and that those purposes ought to be consistent with the investigator's views about the relationship between research and what exists. A complementary theme is that similar care should be taken in choosing ways of recording what happens. Although it is important not to record too little, it is easy to use more extensive and sophisticated methods of data capture than are called for by the research purposes. That means using 10 open-response questions when the research purpose is only to see how many people will agree to those 10 propositions. Conversely, make video recordings if the investigator takes seriously the evidence that body language is as important in communication as is verbal language, although this ideal is likely to take second place to a realization that, even if the equipment can be provided and used unobtrusively, full analysis of the video recordings will not be possible because it is harder, slower and costlier than analysis of audiotape, which is itself an expensive hobby.

So, a major reason for not doing those semi-structured interviews that can add so much to most studies is that the costs of data capture look prohibitive. Most researchers would expect to make audiotapes of interviews, acting on the basis that:

> committing verbal exchanges to paper seems to result in their immediate dete-rioration: context, empathy, and other emotional dynamics are often lost or diminished, and the language seems impoverished, incoherent, and ultimately embarrassing for those who have cause to read back over their contributions (including the interviewer/researcher!). (Poland, 1995: 299)

Stereo cassette recorders are quite affordable, although a professional quality model with microphones of comparable quality ought to cost hundreds of pounds or dollars. It is good practice to use one cassette per interview, to use good quality C90 tape (C120 breaks too easily), to make at least one copy of each tape and to keep another as a master for reference purposes. Mini-disk recorders are better in every way but because the technology is new there are problems finding people to transcribe disks. What makes recording seem impossibly expensive is the belief that the interviews will need to be analysed in detail, which will require typed-up word-for-word transcripts. Estimates vary of how long it takes to transcribe an hour of tape, although the figure of seven hours is often mentioned. Add to that the time needed to check the transcript and to make the corrections that are always necessary, and two things are obvious. Small-scale researchers do not usually have the money to pay someone else to do the transcription, nor do they have the time to transcribe their own interviews. There are two possible exceptions to that assertion. Those who are proficient as typists could cope and could simultaneously bene-fit because the transcription process will help them to be much clearer about ways of analysing the data. Secondly, ever-improving voice dicta-tion software makes it feasible for investigators to play back interviews and simultaneously dictate them, bit by bit, into a word-processing file. Dragon's *Simply Speaking* and IBM's *ViaVoice* are the two most versatile programs at the time of writing. Experience with less sophisticated soft-ware was that about four hours listening and dictating would be enough to get a decent transcription of an interview lasting an hour. This is still a big drain on the researcher's time although it should make analysis eas-ier. The high cost of capture can be cut by changing your assumptions about data analysis. For example, if you decide to analyse fieldnotes and not full transcripts then costs plummet. On the other hand, analysing body language means costing-in video recording equipment and plenty of analysis time. Table 7.1 sets out some of the ramifications.

Your intention may be to make bold claims that are based on a variety of methods and sources but it can be subverted by the twin costs of data capture and data analysis. Many investigators become frustrated because they failed to anticipate these costs which emerged when the work was in progress and appeared to threaten the whole inquiry. Their main fault was to think of research design as a process of putting together a good mix of methods of inquiry without asking hard questions about how they

Table 7.1 Data capture methods and costs

Method of data capture	Information complexity	Costs of data capture	Examples of use
Fixed-response questionnaires, interviews, observation schedules, tests etc.: (a) Respondent or researcher ticks an answer, which is manually coded into a database (b) Optical mark reader used to read responses directly into a database (c) Direct data entry: respondent or researcher keys responses directly into an electronic database	Low. Fixed-response questionnaires can be very informative because they should be precisely targeted on something important. They tend to be limited in scope and to contain easily handled information	Low response rates jack up costs because more people need to be contacted in the first place and reminders may have to be sent. The cost matters less with electronic inquiries but response rates seem to be very low: (a) low financial and time costs; high risk of transcription errors (b) cheap, fast and very reliable once the equipment has been purchased (c) electronic questionnaires are the cheapest of all	These questionnaires are a good way of extending the 'reach' of more intensive interviews. Suppose long interviews suggest that a particular pattern or theme may be significant. If a suitable fixed-response questionnaire can be developed then the significance of the theme or pattern can be explored on a larger scale than would have been possible with interviews
On-the-spot note-making. The researcher makes written notes during an interview or observation. Alternatively, notes are dictated onto audiotape or into a word-recognition computer program (Similar ideas apply to sketches, diagrams, charts etc.)	Complexity can vary greatly. Dictation or fast writing can produce pages of narrative. Alternatively, researchers who are very focused in their inquiry may produce very concise notes that are nevertheless highly informative	Researcher time is a major cost The cheapest way of capturing data without using fixed-response schedules, especially if speech recognition software can be used to get on-the-spot notes directly into electronic text	Ideal for the exploratory stages of research when it's important to get a sense of 'the big picture' Written notes may be the only data capture method available in ethnographic fieldwork situations where it is not desirable to be seen to be making records A relatively cheap way of exploring the robustness of interpretations reached through more expensive means

(Continued)

Table 7.1 (Continued)

Method of data capture	Information complexity	Costs of data capture	Examples of use
Still images using disposable film cameras; conventional cameras up to professional standards (those with telephoto lenses are best); digital cameras (ease of data manipulation on computer but more limited functions than conventional professional cameras).	Medium. Although still photographs have a high information density, a roll of film is less complex than a video or audio record of the same event or site	Fairly low. Digital cameras with a capacity of at least two megapixels (the minimum) are more expensive than equivalent film cameras Photography may be unacceptably intrusive, imposing a time cost in acclimatizing research subjects to the camera	Giving informants a disposable camera and asking them to photograph key moments, places, people, signs etc. Supplementing interviews about work, for example, with photos of workplaces
Audio tape recordings. Tape recordings are the most common. A stereo Walkman or clone with a socket for a stereo microphone is good enough for most purposes. A professional portable recorder and separate throat microphones is an excellent investment. Mini-disk recorders have great potential but the lack of machines designed for disk transcription limits it	High to very high	Equipment costs can be high. Then costs depend on the way the tapes are translated. Choose from: (a) on-the-spot notes made, and tape archived for reference purposes only; cheap (b) tape played, and headline themes and quotations noted (c) tape played, and a fairly full summary made with some quotations (d) notes, as above, plus full transcript of key passages (e) full transcript (and there are different levels of transcription fidelity)	Full transcription may seem to be best research practice but for many purposes it is a waste of money and time. With a large number of interviews it may be wise to transcribe the first ones in full and then to rely mainly upon methods (c) and (b), especially if it is possible to involve others in judging the goodness of fit between the notes and the original Methods (a)–(c) are most common where (1) time and money are short, (2) researchers are fairly certain about what they are looking for. Methods (d) and (e) are needed when (1) discourse or semantic analysis will be used, (2) fresh theory is to be grounded on close study of the data

(Continued)

Table 7.1 (Continued)

Method of data capture	Information complexity	Costs of data capture	Examples of use
Video tape recording. Although concealed cameras and unobtrusive webcams are sometimes used, video recording usually involves conventional video cameras A camera operator gives great flexibility. A fixed camera only captures what comes into its cone of vision, a serious limitation	Very high	With video tape, costs are multiplied because the richness of the record makes it possible to analyse so many information streams – sound, setting and body language being the main ones. A common coping strategy is to use method (c), above, and identify key moments or to take random clips and analyse them intensively, often with the help of structured observation schedules.	Video tapes are, of course, the main data sources when the research questions call for information about the non-linguistic aspects of interactions and inter-personal communication.

would cope with the flood of data. Shrewd research design involves thinking about the sorts of data analysis that will be needed to sustain the claims that have been envisaged: hence it means thinking about how research information is to be captured. Box 7.2 contains some advice on data capture practices to complement this summary of the importance of thinking about data capture when designing a small-scale study.

Box 7.2 Collecting data

This assumes that you have negotiated access to your research sites, that participants know what is involved in the study and that you have informed consent for it.

- Fieldwork arrangements come unglued. Have an idea what you will do if an interview has to be squashed into 15 minutes, if filming is unexpectedly banned, or if what you observe is not what you had expected to see.
- Ballpoint pens do not write in the wet, or on damp paper. Pencils do.
- As soon as you get them, number all paper questionnaires, tests, tapes and the like and update the index that tells you what the numbers or codes denote.
- Batteries fail. Carry spares, including spares for the microphones.
- Mains power supplies can be inaccessible and/or in use. If you need mains power, carry extension leads and socket doublers.
- Two tape recorders are better than one. Using two also saves time making back-up tapes.
- Use the best equipment you can afford. Too many interview transcripts are littered with {unintelligible} and {inaudible}. If audio recording, use clip-on or throat microphones with extension leads. Remember to switch them on. With photography, remember that disposable cameras have poor lenses and dull flash capabilities.
- Recording equipment can influence behaviour. Three strategies are: (1) be upfront about the equipment and hope that openness reduces its impact (if you explain why you are taking notes, informants will often be less distracted by it); (2) use the smallest, least conspicuous recording devices available and hope they hardly get noticed; (3) hope that people will forget about the equipment (especially in long interviews, repeated observations and longitudinal studies).
- Privacy. In interviews, a lack of privacy will affect (1) the questions it is fair to ask, (2) participants' responses. It can jeopardize the ethical integrity of the work.
- Two researchers are better than one. One does, the other watches and thinks. It improves data analysis.
- Make labelled copies of all notes, tapes and files. Immediately.
- Before sending tapes and questionnaires for processing, make sure that all means of identification have been removed, apart from the code you use to match records with the identities of the informants.
- Give transcribers precise instructions on how you want the transcription done.
- Check transcripts and datafiles. There will be errors. Since you best understand the research questions and purposes, only you can decide how serious the errors are and whether to spend much time correcting them.

Disclosure and Harm

Much social research asks questions that people who can be bothered to answer do not find particularly intrusive, but there is also a great deal of research into sensitive issues – bereavement, terminal illness, sexuality, criminality, disability, child abuse and so on. Researchers with these interests have the twin problem of acting ethically by ensuring that their inquiries will not harm participants while also encouraging them to disclose fully their thoughts or to act in front of the researcher as they would in private. This is not just about causing harm by compromising informants' safety or freedom. It is also about harming them by resurrecting distressing memories or by exploiting them with flattery so as to get disclosure without any commitment to give them something back.

Researchers should also know that they themselves may be harmed by researching some topics. Research into crime may involve physical risk (see Chapter 3), while other topics, such as illness, can be distressing. Finding out more about hurt, misery and terror can corrode the spirit. Small-scale researchers need to talk through the dangers with friends, colleagues and supervisors and go into their inquiries knowing how best to deal with likely threats to their equilibrium. With inquiries that are going to be distressing is it important to make sure that there are people to talk to after interviewing. Friends are fine for some studies and trained counsellors should be available for others.

These problems are usually less virulent with survey research because the questions are less penetrating and face-to-face contact between researcher and respondent is less usual. Yet even in survey research, sensitive issues appear to inhibit disclosure. Consider, for example, the newspaper report of a 1993 survey of 1509 people who were asked about their top sources of pleasure. The top 13 were: (1) drinking tea and coffee, (2) reading, (3) holidays, (4) watching TV, (5) family and children, (6) entertaining friends, (7) listening to the radio, (8) going out for a meal, (9) shopping, (10) having visitors or visiting others, (11) going out for a drink, (12) having an alcoholic drink, (13) sex. Similarly, market research suggested that a million people a year would visit a national museum of weapons and armour if it were sited in Leeds, England. In 1999 the museum had 200,000 visitors. A newspaper commented that people tell researchers that they would visit such a museum and ignore the voice that says they would really prefer to go to the movies.

The discussion of sampling in Chapter 5 has already indicated that it is difficult to get participation, let alone disclosure, although the dissociative techniques mentioned in Chapter 4 encourage people who do participate to be less concerned to 'fake good'. But, as I said in Chapter 3, researchers who want to hear real stories, to see real behaviours and to ask real people questions about both thinking and doing cannot use those techniques. They need to build relationships of trust, which involves:

1 Getting potential participants' informed consent by telling them clearly what the research is about.
2 Explaining why they are interested in exploring something that is normally private and why it is valuable.
3 Promising confidentiality and anonymity.
4 Where this is both possible and ethical, inviting potential participants to reassure themselves by talking to other people who have participated.
5 Doing the inquiry in places where participants feel safe. In interview studies it is usually important to find private space.
6 Being a good listener and observer. Good interviewers know that that is nothing like being a good interrogator: humility is needed.
7 Being ready to disclose information about similar experiences they have had. For example, it helps that I can talk with teachers about how *we* have felt when *we* have taught classes that have been more intent on larking than on learning.
8 Being able to empathize, which means being able to show informants that they understand and maybe sympathize too.
9 Not persisting if informants signal that they do not wish to go further.
10 Where it is feasible, inviting participants to edit transcripts, to add to them as well as to remove sections that, on reflection, they do not wish to be used.
11 Blending in. There are things that researchers cannot affect (their age) and things that they can (clothing).
12 Becoming an insider. This is not always possible but participant researchers can establish their claim to be trustworthy through becoming close to the people they want to study. On the other hand, Hughes (1996) tells of a participant researcher studying police in Amsterdam who only found at the end of the study that he had missed all the evidence of police corruption.

Some would also say that you can only get real trust by being or becoming accepted as an insider. Box 7.3 contains a critique.

Box 7.3 A critique of insider research (after Hammersley, 1993)

Hammersley's paper considers the claim that educational research, like most social research, is too detached from what should be its main concern, which is classroom practice in this case. One way of reconnecting research to practice would be to encourage practitioners to become their own researchers and to value their work highly on the grounds that they, as insider participants, have different and better knowledge and better access than outsiders. His objection is that 'In my view ... the epistemological position ... that knowledge comes from contact with reality – is unsound' (217). The development of his critique is shown in the following table.

Continued

Claim for superiority of insider participant inquiry	Response
1 Teachers have better access to their intentions, motives, thoughts and feelings than researchers	'People can be wrong even about their intentions and motives' (218); they may mislead themselves
2 Insiders have privileged insights from their close knowledge of setting	These insights may be limited, 'superficial or distorted' (218). They may also involve unrecognized misconceptualizations
3 Insider relationships are a special and important source of information	'[The] relationships available to the practitioner will exclude as well as include, and may not be what is necessary for research purposes' (218–19)
4 As key actors, practitioners can test theoretical ideas in a way outsiders cannot	'What is required to test theoretical ideas may well conflict with what is needed for good practice' (219)

Novice researchers quickly spot that they will need to get access to research sites and they become aware of just how difficult it can be to persuade the gatekeepers – managers, committees, directors – to let them in and to let them have a free hand in collecting the information they need. They are less prepared to find that the formal right of access is meaningless unless they can realize it by establishing their trustworthiness so that people on the ground are willing to begin to open up. Access needs to be negotiated and then created by honestly using strategies such as the dozen above. It goes without saying that strict notions of objectivity are not compatible with those 12 strategies. Developing relations of trust means that the researcher's interaction with each participant can be different and that the inquiry can take different shapes in different research settings.

Disclosure and grief sometimes go together. Although it can be cathartic for the participant it is not necessarily so and the researcher must be ready to stop and become more human and consoling. Sometimes you say, 'I'm sorry this is upsetting you. I didn't want that to happen. Would you like to stop?' and the answer is, 'No, I'll be alright ... go on.' Go slowly. Give the participant plenty of room to sob, stop or take a break. Most researchers will try to appreciate the other's grief but to stay apart from it, although others say that if you're moved, show it. So too with anger, although this emotion needs handling with a different kind of care because it can become dangerous and frightening. Almost always the researcher needs to stay apart from the anger and be a calming influence. Things can go badly wrong if researcher and participant groom each other's rage.

Disclosure can – and often does – evoke pity and some people will have agreed to participate because they hope that somehow the researcher will rescue them. Researchers who have the interpersonal qualities to encourage people to open up are also those most likely to be moved and to feel that they *should* help. The standard advice is that general help can be offered by putting participants in touch with people whose job it is to help (in many cases social workers), suggesting courses of action (contact a helpline), providing information (on state benefits), and telling stories about what others in similar situations have done. Experienced researchers carry with them information leaflets and lists of contacts to give to participants. The standard advice is also not to become personally involved, partly because it can be dangerous (some participants are disturbing people) and also because there are limits to what a lone person without the right expertise can do – and can do without disrupting the official help systems. Researchers should not be case workers. But it is advice that does not apply very well to the situation of participant and action researchers and it is also ignored by others who feel that researchers have an ethical duty to give as well as to take.

to look at *school* effectiveness is not only a subjective one, but a disputable one too. Better units of analysis might be departments (Sammons et al., 1997) or individual teachers (Gray et al., 1999). When we want to know how old people are cared for in their homes, then social work clients may be the units of analysis but it could be care homes or social services departments as purchasers of care.

Decisions about units of coding are decisions about how to interpret different data sources. Suppose that a study of domiciliary care of the aged produced interview transcripts, documentary records of care delivery, measures of the physical condition of elderly people's homes, and questionnaires completed by their friends and families. In the interviews we have a choice of possible units of coding, which might be each distinct judgement about the adequacy of provision or suggestion for improvement, or each paragraph, each sentence or whatever. The units of coding the physical condition of people's homes would clearly need to be quite different (see Box 4.8 for an example of how units of coding can be combined to get measures at the level of each home, which was the unit of analysis). In the sense that data analysis depends on decisions about data capture, the units of analysis, the units of coding and the level of analysis, then it is not quite the objective process that it might first seem.

However, once those decisions have been made, some data can be analysed objectively. As far as numerical data from fixed-response instruments are concerned, it is hard not to do highly reliable analyses, thanks to computer software that cuts out calculation errors. There is still choice though, and 'hard' numbers represent the outcomes of a series of not-objective decisions. One of the least obvious decisions is the one that leads the researcher to follow conventional assumptions about the appropriateness of numbers in social science. Michell (1997) argues that in psychology data are often coded and analysed in numerical terms when the assumption that they are numerical data is questionable. He claimed that numbers which really do nothing more than describe preferences (which is what the numbers on a Likert scale, for example, do) are often wrongly treated as if they represent continuous phenomena like temperature or distance, which are measured on interval (or ratio) scales. Cliff commented that: 'we are left with few if any psychologically defined variables that have well-assured interval-scale status' (1996: 7). He explains in some detail why tests devised for continuous data (ratio and interval quality) will tend to mislead if they are applied to categorical data, which are measured on ordinal and nominal scales. In fact, researchers frequently use statistical techniques that assume the data to be of interval quality or better, when the data are at best of ordinal quality. (See Box 8.1 for an explanation of interval and ordinal data quality.) Assuming that the appropriate statistical routines are applied, there are still judgements to be made. Gould (1996b) has argued that the statistical technique of factor analysis, which is designed to identify underlying factors in sets of numerical data, will produce factors, regardless of whether they have much useful correspondence with reality. Researchers not only have to judge whether they are a fair fit with social phenomena but also have a choice of how many factors they want to include and what they want to name them. Boyatzis (1998) shows that the same evidence of agreement between two data coders leads to different numerical claims about the level of inter-observer reliability depending on which calculation techniques are used. (On page 189 he advises on which calculation method to choose in different circumstances.)

Box 8.1 Statistical techniques and four qualities of data

Numbers are widely used in the social sciences but they do not always refer to the same sorts of things. This matters because analytical techniques that are designed for one type of data – ordinal data, for example – are less trustworthy or inappropriate for other levels. The most widely (ab)used tests assume that data are at least of interval quantity.

- Female = 1; male = 2. Here numbers are simply being used as abbreviations for non-numerical categories. It would make no sense to do calculations with these numbers, although it would be very easy for a computer to identify all the males in the sample and to say how many of them there were. These data are of *nominal* quality.
- Majid 68% (grade B); Soile 62% (grade B); Brad 59% (grade C); Rachel 34% (grade E). These marks are of ordinal quality because they contain information about the order in which these people can be ranked but they say nothing else. Notice that the ordering can be more or less fine grained: in this case the numbers are more discriminating than the letter grades. Notice also that we cannot say that Majid's work is twice as good as Rachel's, or that it 15% better than Brad's. We know that it is considerably better than Rachel's but we cannot describe that difference in objective terms. That does not stop people analysing grades and exam results with computer programs designed for interval quality data.
- Soile 100.1 °F; Brad 99.0 °F; Rachel 98.4 °F; Majid 98.2 °F. Not only do these figures describe an order but they are also on an equal-interval scale. Whereas we cannot be sure that the difference between a test mark of 95% and 100% is the same as that between 30% and 35%, we do know that *interval* data are on a continuous scale such that the difference between 100°F and 110°F is the same as that between 90°F and 100°F.
- Brad 93 kg; Majid 85 kg, Soile 62 kg; Rachel 59 kg. *Ratio* quality data have all the features of interval data *and* we can say that there is a real sense in which Soile is two-thirds of Brad's weight. A volcanic explosion index of 6.00 is 10 times as big as one of 5.00. Ratio scales have a true zero, defined as a complete absence.

Note that although these distinctions are based on common practice, Flood (1999) attributes the same logical properties to ratio and interval quality data and Cliff (1996) considers that there are problems in treating length and time as ratio quality data and temperature as interval quality data.

When it comes to qualitative data, a big difficulty is deciding on what counts as a judgement or suggestion and on how to record it. If in the middle of an interview a respondent says, 'I don't know why the government doesn't spend more money on our social services', is that a suggestion for service improvement? If something similar is said later in the interview, does this mean that two suggestions have been made, or that one suggestion has been made insistently? And is it a more important suggestion than 'Well, I'd make sure that they made regular visits at set times, instead of just looking in when they're passing', which was said just once? Later in this chapter it will be shown that good coding definitions, indicators and contra-indicators provide answers to these queries and so analysis can be done fairly consistently. Nevertheless, the basis of that consistent coding of qualitative data is not an objective one. It should be plausible and defensible but it will not be objective. It is harmful if researchers are confused about this because the assumption that analysis can be objective effectively locks their imagination within tunnel vision and they can fail to appreciate that other ways of reading the data are possible. It is also harmful for readers who might be misled into believing that the analysis tells the only valid story about the research questions, when it will really be telling one, more or less plausible story.

The third general point about data analysis is that it is continuous. It begins with the research design and data capture and it continues as repeated thinking about meanings that might be identified in the data. It is an all-pervasive musing about the likely units of coding, possible coding categories, definitions and indicators; and a persistent reflection on what the categories, patterns and stories might mean, both in terms of the research questions and in terms of understandings that had not been envisaged when the research was designed. This is usually more pronounced with qualitative than with quantitative data, but in both cases the underlying point – that data analysis is not something that happens only, or even mainly, after all the data collection is done – is something that novice researchers can miss.

Numbers and Data Analysis

Small-scale research can generate large amounts of numerical data when fixed-response questionnaires, surveys, scales or tests are completed by large numbers of people who key their responses directly into the database or whose responses are read with Optical Mark Reader technology. Open-ended questions and qualitative inquiries in general can also provide numerical data of nominal and ordinal quality. Data on respondents' age, sex, class, race, job etc. are often coded up as nominal data so that it is easy to do computer searches to identify all the 50-year-old female manual workers and look at their data alongside those from the 50-year-old male manual workers. It is also very common for qualitative researchers to do counts within their data. What, for example, do teachers think makes their job a professional one? Identifying the different ideas they use and tallying them up allows researchers to see whether some subgroups, such as younger teachers, tend to make their case very differently from other subgroups, such as mid-career teachers. So, small-scale researchers may need to know how to handle numbers. That said, although statistical practices in data handling are well established and powerful, statisticians would be the first to insist that procedures must not be allowed to take over and cut the thinking out of data handling.

These techniques are used to summarize data (descriptive statistics) and to look for patterns (inferential statistics). Descriptive statistics are essentially ways of taking the complexity of a few hundred answers to a 10-point questionnaire and getting it into a manageable form. As a matter of course the arithmetical mean and the standard deviation (SD) are calculated to show the central tendency of the data and how the scores are distributed around the mean. So, a mean of 5 and a SD of 1 indicate that two-thirds of the scores are in the range of 4–6 and that they are tightly bunched around the arithmetical average of 5. A mean of 4 and a SD of 3 indicate that scores are lower and that they are quite dispersed, with two-thirds of the scores falling between 1 and 7. Standard deviations are important in descriptive statistics because two sets of data may be quite different, even though they might both have means of 25. In one case they might cluster around the central tendency (mean 25, SD 5) and in the other they are scattered (mean 25, SD 9.17). It helps readers to appreciate these figures if they can be displayed as box-and-whisker plots, charts or graphs, which can be done directly from spreadsheet programs and statistics packages.

It is easy at this point to lose sight of what the means, standard deviations and charts show. The temptation to exploit the potential of numbers needs to be resisted unless the data really are of the right sorts. For example, when we asked teachers about the professional nature of their work and tallied the ideas they used, we got a pattern that showed that they put a lot of emphasis on conscientiousness and on the special knowledge they needed to do the job. We could say how many times one idea was used and compare that with how frequently others were used. We could have explored whether women used different ideas than men, older teachers than younger ones, maths teachers than technology teachers, and so on. We could have put the data into the computer and got figures to several decimal places that described relationships and the probabilities that those relationships could have been just chance occurrences. (This is misleadingly called statistical significance. It only indicates when something is unlikely to have happened by chance.) That would have been a mistake, since our judgements of how often an idea was volunteered were exactly that: they were careful *judgements* of how often someone *volunteered* an idea (in Chapter 3 this was called 'spontaneous understanding'). We used the descriptive statistics as interesting indicators. We ignored small differences and only looked seriously at substantial variations. The ideas that were volunteered were put in a rank order and where two ideas were identified a similar, but not equal, number of times, this was treated as a tie in rank order (McCulloch et al., 2000). We rejected the allure of the precision that goes with numbers. Numbers were treated as a way of helping thinking, not as a substitute for it.

Inferential statistics help you to identify patterns of association and to decide whether associations are likely to be happenstance or not. It is important for small-scale researchers to recognize that patterns happen naturally. There are patterns in sets of random numbers. (People who bet in fair games of chance, such as roulette, often mistakenly act on the 'Monte Carlo' principle that if the ball has three times landed in a red hole, then it should land in the black next time. In a fair game with just two choices – red or black – the chance of black coming up on any occasion is 50%. What happened on the previous x occasions makes no difference.) Some of the patterns in numerical data can be found just by looking carefully at them. In a set of 20 questionnaires we could quickly spot that 12 girls have a particular preference but only 8 boys. Other patterns have to be revealed with the help of formal statistical techniques which also calculate the probability that the patterns are just one of those many patterns created by chance alone. Because patterns can be random events, even those that can be identified by inspection have to be formally checked out if you want to make any claims that you have identified a pattern that needs to be taken seriously. There is nothing very special about 12 girls and 8 boys having a preference in a sample of 20. In the same way, if a coin is tossed four times the commonest pattern is two heads, two tails, but there is nothing unusual about three heads and a tail or three tails and a head. There is, though, a lot unusual about a pattern of 300 tails and 100 heads: 3000 tails and 1000 heads is reason to believe that the paranormal has broken through. Notice, though, that the ratio of heads to tails is unchanged in each of the three cases. With a small number of cases 3:1 is an unremarkable ratio, well within the bounds of chance. With thousands of cases a 3:1 tails–heads ratio is highly improbable. This represents the rule that as the number of cases increases, the more that proportionately small differences are unlikely to have happened by chance. With small samples, proportionately large differences between the two groups are necessary before we can assume that imbalances are unlikely to be chance occurrences (that they are statistically significant). With big samples, small imbalances between two groups are unlikely to happen by chance. Most statistical techniques were designed for large samples and creak, even collapse, when numbers get low.

This is not the place to review the many ways there are of exploring and testing patterns, or to show how to do these tests with software such as SPSS, SYSTAT or Minitab, or to describe the ways in which models and predictions can be made and tested. The computer programs have manuals and there is no shortage of books on how to use them and on statistical techniques in general (Kinnear and Gray, 1999; Brace et al., 2000; Fielding and Gilbert, 2000 all advise on statistical analysis aided by SPSS).

For up-to-date information about common statistics packages consult the following websites: SPSS <http://www.spss.com/software/spss/prodlist.htm# base/>, SYSTAT <http://www.spss.com/software/science/systat/> and Minitab <http://www.minitab.com/>. Advisers and supervisors should also be consulted because the books and manuals can be tough for people who find difficulties with the style of mathematical writing and because decisions about the best tests to use are best talked through with experienced researchers. What matters is that small-scale researchers *understand* what statistical testing is about. For example, it is vital to appreciate that just because a pattern can be identified in a small sample, it doesn't mean that there is anything there that is beyond the realms of chance. In such cases, researchers working within a positivist framework ought to test for statistical significance and, if the probabilities of the difference being a chance occurrence turn out to be greater than 5 in 100 (5% or $p > 0.05$), they should either increase the sample and test again (proportionately small differences become more significant as sample sizes increase), or consider dropping the claim that there is a real difference between the two groups. Interpretive researchers might also do the tests but they can be more relaxed about the outcomes. If no significant differences are found ($p > 0.05$) then there is less of a problem because it is unlikely that the researcher was intending to claim that this small study was representative of the world at large. Instead, the standpoint is likely to be that this is a study of one set of people in one situation; that there are differences amongst *these* people; and that it is for the reader to consider how this case speaks to other settings and other groups. In this case the researcher should do what is widely advocated but seldom done, namely report the exact probability of the difference being a chance one: it is worth knowing if the difference has a probability of happening by chance of 6.5% as opposed to 27%.

A second reason why small-scale researchers need a basic understanding of statistical significance is because it can be unimportant. It is easy to assume that something is important because it is statistically significant. Not so. Certainly something that is statistically significant at the level $p < 0.01$ is no chance event (its probability is less than 1%). But the small-scale researcher who administers a short Likert scale to 500 people should not crow at statistically significant findings. For example, a computer program like SPSS is an invitation to look at the association between every pair of variables in a data set. If the Likert scale has 10 items, then it is possible to look at how strongly each variable is associated with nine others. This is usually done by calculating the correlation coefficient. A coefficient of +1.0 means there is perfect correlation: as one variable increases, the other does so at the same rate. A coefficient of -1.0 signifies perfect inverse correlation: as one rises the other decreases at the same rate. Zero means that the two variables are orthogonal, or entirely unrelated. SPSS will do all the correlations in a trice and it will invariably find correlations where $p < 0.05$ and some where $p < 0.01$. With large numbers in the sample, even weak correlations will register as significant at the 5% level. A correlation of + 0.30 will very often be statistically significant but the rule for calculating the amount of variance explained by this coefficient is to square it, which gives a figure of 9% ($0.3 \times 0.3 = 0.09$). Put another way, 91% of the variation in these two measures is *not* accounted for by the relationship between them. A statistically significant correlation tells us something about what is happening but in this case it only describes a small part of it. And coefficients can be less strong than ±0.30 and still be (statistically) significant.

In social research where human thought and behaviour are complex and dynamic it may really be a great achievement to identify something that accounts for 9% of variance, but that is a matter of judgement and the case needs to be made for accepting the judgement. Consider the influence that schools have on children's educational achievements. In the last 20 years politicians around the world have made school improvement the top priority in their attempts to raise educational achievement (whatever that might be – it is surely more than just exam grades). But research consistently finds that school contributes little to educational achievement. Jencks and colleagues concluded that:

> Nearly anything can happen in a place called school ... some ... are run like prisons ... other schools are like [mental] asylums with constant battles to maintain order and no sequential activity that lasts more than a few minutes ... Given this diversity, we did not expect all schools to have precisely the same effects on children's test scores. The differences are, however, surprisingly small. (1972: 89)

Although their estimate that the mean effect of attending the best fifth rather than the worst fifth of all elementary schools is almost certainly no more than 10% and probably no more than 5% has been challenged by subsequent research, even those who put a lot of faith in the school effect concede that the quality of a school accounts for about 10% of the variance in pupil achievement, assuming that like is compared with like. (On average, children who have high grades on entry to a school have high grades when they leave. In order to identify the school effect it is necessary to compare the achievements that similar schools have with similar pupil intakes.) This 10% difference on a level playing field is very significant – statistically. Is it socially significant though? There are three answers to that question, each of which depends on the insight that the 'So what?' question cannot be settled by recourse to a statistical authority. Statistics may identify cases to think about but that does not mean that those cases have much practical importance.

One answer to the question about the practical significance of the finding that the school the children attend contributes about 10% to their educational attainments, *on average*, is that this is interesting but it is unimportant unless we know how to bring schools in general up to the effectiveness of the best. If there is a difference and we are powerless, the finding is not very helpful. In fact researchers are becoming increasingly aware of how difficult it is to improve schools. Some schools may make a relatively large contribution to pupil achievement but it is formidably difficult to extend that to all schools. A second pragmatic response asks whether this size of difference is worth bothering about. What about other things that contribute to educational achievement? The child's socio-economic status (SES) is, on average, the greatest predictor of educational achievement, so that the richer children are the better they are likely to do. It could plausibly be argued, then, that reducing social inequality, which is greater in Britain than in the rest of Western Europe, holds greater promise for better educational standards than does educational research. But, thirdly, school improvement is much cheaper than reducing social inequality, so perhaps the small, relatively cheap gains on offer from school improvement are worth trying to get. The same sorts of thinking can be applied to small- and large-scale research into effectiveness in caring professions and organizations in general. A further example illustrates the ways in which research and statistical analysis tend to raise questions but not answer them.

It is surprisingly hard to establish whether class size is generally related to educational achievement, but the consensus (Bennett, 1998) seems to be that there are sometimes *small* gains as class sizes drop from 30, to 28, to 26. Big gains are only had when class sizes are reduced to about 16, and they are then dependent on teachers adapting their teaching methods to take advantage of new possibilities. This is all very statistically significant, but is it important? For political reasons governments want to see mean class sizes reduced by one or two, although it has little, if any, educational effect and costs an enormous amount. As Bennett says, perhaps the money would make more of a difference were it spent on other ways of improving schooling.

A final point about the meaning of statistics is that a high correlation between two factors does not mean that one causes the other. Any claim that one causes the other needs to be justified and that cannot be done just by showing that there is a correlation. Height correlates with rank in many bureaucracies but one reason for that is that white males tend to be promoted over females and they tend to be taller. Another example shows the dangers of looking for a single cause. Plainly, the more exercise people take, the less fat they tend to become. Important though exercise is, an article in *The Guardian* of 11 May 1999 reported that: 'Some people use up as little as 1067 calories in a day, while others consume a huge 3015 … Some people do indeed benefit enormously [from exercise] – in terms of stronger hearts and muscles, more stamina and so on … but other people show almost no improvement in weight or health, despite exercising five times a week for 20 weeks.' Whatever causes weight loss or gain, it is not exercise alone, despite the general association between exercise and weight.

Interpretive researchers working with small numbers of people can benefit from counting and looking for patterns, although they are rarely able to make strong claims that their findings should hold good for the population as a whole. That is not a problem because their background assumptions are such that they are uninterested in positivist generalizing. Other small-scale researchers will collect numerical data and will quite properly analyse them with the aid of more or less powerful statistical techniques. The theme of this section is that this business of looking for patterns and establishing their statistical significance is no substitute for good thinking about what the patterns mean and what claims might be fairly based upon them. Research, even when aided by statistical techniques, is thinking.

Analysing Qualitative Data

Data analysis is treated here as a two-stage process, although that is just a convenient fiction because it begins when you start to think about the inquiry and finishes when you let go of the whole topic. In fact,

> The analysis of the data gathered in a naturalistic inquiry begins the first day the researcher arrives at the setting. The collection and analysis of the data obtained go hand-in-hand as theories and themes emerge during the study. (Erlandson et al., 1993: 109)

In the interests of simplicity, though, analysis is treated as (1) indexing or coding the data and (2) developing and reflecting on interpretations of the data. Coding involves 'tagging' or marking the units of coding so that similar themes, ideas, examples, or cases are put in the same categories, and so that any counter-examples are also identified and indexed for later attention. The business of interpreting permeates the whole research activity but it is done more reflectively when the researcher goes carefully through the different categories of data and the counter-examples looking for the simplest stories, hypotheses or judgements that make defensible sense of the whole set.

Qualitative data are easier to categorize and make sense of if you know what you are looking for, and easier still if the research was designed explicitly to look for that and that alone. The obvious danger is that when qualitative data are looked at in order to test a theory, or with precise research questions in mind, it is easy to see only what is obviously relevant to those perspectives and to miss indications that things might be rather different than the perspectives imply. For example, when the research questions are about the effects of change, it is easy to tally up instances and to count the frequency of different effects and to miss the evidence of continuity. Similarly, the theory that an occupation, such as social work, can be classified as a profession by establishing how far it possesses certain traits will send the investigator off on a trait hunt at the risk of missing evidence that this view of professions is at least problematic, at worst bankrupt. This is where triangulation, discussed in Chapter 6, can be very helpful, especially in the shape of triangulation of theory and triangulation of researchers. Seven ways to guard against tunnel vision when analysing qualitative data are:

- Early in the data analysis process, raise your awareness of theories, positions or views that could be brought to bear. For example, be alert to the possibilities that, rather than things deteriorating, they are simply changing or that in some respects they are improving; that the effects of change are unevenly distributed according to people's gender, child care responsibilities and self-theories; and that people, such as your research subjects, can usually find things to criticize, for problems are always to be found and morale always seems to be declining. Alternatively, remember theories and positions that were rejected at the literature review stage and reappraise them against a sample of your data.
- Ask someone else, who might be a friend who knows little about your research purposes, to examine some of the data and talk with you about the ways in which they saw it. As the conversation develops you might explain in plain language how you were looking at the data and the ideas you were developing and ask how far this seems to be a fair way of going about things.
- If you are reviewing data in a cross-sectional way by looking at slices of the data from each respondent so as to build up a picture about, for example, the emotional costs of caring for a disabled partner or child, try the alternative approach of analysing on a case-by-case basis. Conversely, do some cross-sectional analysis in order to see things afresh if you have been analysing case-by-case.
- More formally, other people who are skilled in the discipline and know the general topic should appraise your indexing or coding system and how you are applying it. (A coding system is the categories you put the data into and the rules you use to identify what should go in which category: it is discussed more fully below.) They should check the set of categories you will use in your analysis against a sample of research data in order to see whether the categories look to be comprehensive (covering virtually all of the relevant material) and usable. Secondly, other people should use your categories to analyse a sample of the data and your responses should be compared with theirs. It is traditional to calculate inter-rater reliability to show how close your judgements are to theirs (Boyatzis, 1998). Differences between coders should prompt reflection on how your emerging interpretation of the data might be modified or better presented or on ways in which your analysis might be improved.
- Limit tunnel vision by looking for counter-examples. If analysis is driven by a theory, it can be useful to imagine what would count as evidence against the theory and then look out for it. Consider having one code for counter-examples and discordant evidence and put in it

anything that does not quite fit the theory. Mason (1996) describes this as creating 'bags' containing resources to think about later.

- Stop. Assuming that you have written down the rules for coding the data, take a break and come back to analysis in a couple of weeks' time. In that time the codes will become strange and the experience of using them often shows the points at which your categories creak.
- Pace the analysis. Tunnel vision comes easily when you are immersed in coding, especially if fills days in which there are too few breaks and too little variety so that tiredness half-heartedly competes with boredom.

There is a world of difference between analysing 100 responses to an open-ended questionnaire containing three prompts and inviting written responses of a third of a page each, and dealing with 50 hours of video-tape or 200 transcripts of hour-long, semi-structured interviews. In general, complex data analysis will take a path like that indicated in Figure 8.1, although when data are relatively straightforward, as in the case of writ-ten responses to a few open-ended questions about a rather unproblem-atic matter, then there is no great problem with deciding on the categories to use in the analysis. Figure 8.2 illustrates something of the range of demands in qualitative data analysis and four hypothetical examples are used to give a better sense of what might be involved in a small-scale study. It is assumed throughout that the investigator is not engaged in latent analysis, where the intention is to find meanings that are hidden well below the surface, following the example of the interpretation of dreams in Jungian or Freudian psychoanalysis.

Case A is represented by a researcher who has a set of 87 responses to a one-page questionnaire comprising three questions and space for written response. Almost all of the informants have answered on one side of the questionnaire and many of them have given their answers in bullet point and note form. Sixty-three have responded to the invitation to add their names and addresses so that they can be contacted. If this questionnaire had been distributed by e-mail, then all of the informants could be con-tacted subsequently. A set of coding categories was easy to establish (see example D for an explanation of how this is done) and to apply. The data and categories are so straightforward that it was easy to calculate inter-rater reliability for a sample of 30 questionnaires using the formula (number of times rater 1 and rater 2 agreed) ÷ [1/2 (number of ratings made by rater 1 + number of ratings made by rater 2)]. A problem was that some responses were unclear. In most of those cases it was possible to contact the informant and get clarification. There was also a danger that the researcher would misinterpret the data because they were so skimpy. To reduce this risk the researcher's analysis was crisply summarized in plain English and sent out to the 63 informants who had identified themselves. They were invited to say whether this account resonated with them and to comment on it.

Case B involved the analysis of 26 videotapes showing trainee dental surgeons conducting treatment sessions. The task of analysis was relatively

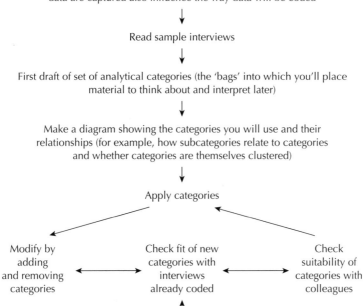

Figure 8.1 *Qualitative data analysis: creating and applying coding categories*

straightforward, despite the volume and apparent complexity of data, (1) because the researchers were interested in dentist–client communication at the beginning of the session and (2) because they were concentrating on the dentists' body language in order to test the hypothesis that those who were better at interpersonal relations (as measured by body language) had more satisfied clients (measured by a post-treatment client satisfaction questionnaire). The researchers had taken from the literature a body language observation schedule and learned how to apply it rapidly and with high levels of reliability to the first four minutes of each video. They produced a table showing the frequency of body language 'moves' and then did statistical analysis to explore the relationship with client satisfaction. Had they been using a more complex – and arguably more authentic – measure of dentist–client communication and sampled more than just the first four minutes then the analytical task would have been huge.

In case C, the researcher had an archive of 30 audiotaped interviews to deal with. Immediately after each 30 minute interview she had jotted down a summary of the key points, as she saw them. These notes had been extended into two-page summaries after she had listened to each recording,

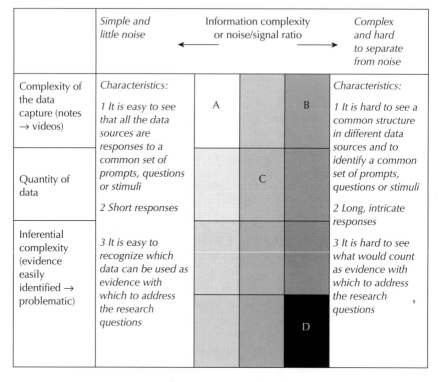

	Simple and little noise	Information complexity or noise/signal ratio ← →	Complex and hard to separate from noise
Complexity of the data capture (notes → videos)	Characteristics: 1 It is easy to see that all the data sources are responses to a common set of prompts, questions or stimuli 2 Short responses 3 It is easy to recognize which data can be used as evidence with which to address the research questions	A B C D	Characteristics: 1 It is hard to see a common structure in different data sources and to identify a common set of prompts, questions or stimuli 2 Long, intricate responses 3 It is hard to see what would count as evidence with which to address the research questions
Quantity of data			
Inferential complexity (evidence easily identified → problematic)			

Figure 8.2   *Variations in the complexity of qualitative data analysis*

and all the summaries had been updated to use the same headings and key words. The hardest part was developing a set of categories with which to code the summaries (see case D, p. 189). The data were already quite well organized, which made it easier to establish inter-rater reliability on a sample of six sets of notes, and it was feasible to code it manually by marking the notes in different colours and with different signs and then cutting the notes up and bundling the cuttings together in different folders.

Interpretation of qualitative data generally involves making sense of these files of clippings (or their electronic equivalents) by looking for themes that are broadly consistent with everything in the file and that make sense in terms of the literature and research questions. In practice this often involves putting the emerging interpretations alongside evidence that has been collected by other means and from other sources. It is a continuing, sensemaking toing and froing between the data, the categories, the emerging stories or theories, and the literature. In case C the advantage of coding from notes rather than transcripts carried through into the work of interpretation, which was easier because the material was more concise and better structured than transcripts would have been, which means that cross-referencing could be done manually.

Interpretation is also easier to do when the researcher is essentially testing an existing theory or trying to supplement or supplant other research findings. This is because the research purpose makes it pretty clear how the data are first to be interpreted: they will be interpreted in terms of the positions set out in the literature review. In this sense, the literature review does much to determine how difficult it will be to code and interpret the data. The hard business is when an inquiry is exploratory, complex or concerned to get to grips with the specific, contexted and distinctive features of a case, event or situation. There, sense has to be made from the ground up and the literature review cannot be so useful as a template for interpretation. Building an interpretation from the data up, rather than reading the data to test interpretations or findings, is frequently referred to as building grounded theory and is widely discussed in the literature (for example Strauss and Corbin, 1990). It is an extremely attractive approach to interpretive researchers whose intellectual position is that realities are socially constructed fluxes that have features which are person- and context-specific. If that is the case, it follows that each case, situation, group of events or set of beliefs needs its own story, interpretation or theory. But,

> There is no formula to aid the researcher in interpretation of qualitative research data ... amongst the most essential [qualities is] to be able to stand back from the problem to get a new perspective; work with contradictions; explore new relationships; turn the problem around, perhaps even upside down; understand basic motivations and apply them; see behind rationalizations; ask and try to answer the question 'what is the meaning of this?' (Mostyn, 1985: 140)

One parallel is with a sculptor at work, as in this story carried by *The Guardian* (30 October 1999):

> For a sculptor, there is tenderness to be found in the hardest of materials. 'Portland stone is so pure and so old – 135 million years old – that when you open it up you feel as if you are revealing something already present. I remember once working on the head of a woman, and I heard myself saying quite loudly, "We'll get you out of here soon."'
>
> Last week Mike Chapman delivered a baby from a block of Portland stone ... The baby is just emerging from the stone, or perhaps sinking back into it, like water. It has a detailed umbilical cord running back into the block in which it lies.

Some interpretive researchers would not be happy with the implication that there is just one baby or, indeed, any babies at all in the block of stone. That aside, like sculpture, this is hard work, especially if a substantial number of transcripts or notes is involved. In the words of an academic researcher, 'The whole process took 2½ years. I was disappointed in the final product and my eyebrows turned white during the interviewing. I was actually under a level of stress that I never want to experience again' (van Buskirk, 1997: 60). In case C the researcher was able to get new perspectives, explore, turn things around etc., because the data were eminently manageable. Thirty 10-page transcripts would have been a different matter.

Huberman and Miles (1994) offer a set of tactics for generating meanings from the information that has been collected. This list is the based upon those suggestions.

- Look for patterns and themes (this, of course, begins when you start thinking about the study and pervades the data capture phases).
- Begin sensemaking early, trying to develop stories that draw themes together, offer explanations, give you a feeling of understanding. Good quality literature reviews should help here.
- Early on, try imagining clusters of themes, concepts and cases.
- Explore metaphors as ways of drawing the data together: for example, the metaphor of the change agent as a *bricoleur* (artisan or craftsman) who improves things by tinkering provides a powerful metaphor for understanding change processes in many organizations.
- Try counting to see whether something is as common (or as rare) as it seems.
- Compare and contrast to see whether categories are distinctive.
- If appropriate, group, cluster or relate themes, cases, explanations. If you have quantitative data, statistical packages can help.
- Try unclustering. Often the hard thing is to find just a few big themes, concepts or patterns to summarize sprawling data, so it seems perverse to suggest trying to split them up. However, trying to split clusters is a good way of testing whether you are satisfied that the cluster (theme or pattern) does stand up and helps to identify subgroups, sub-concepts and subthemes.
- Keep thinking about the suitability of the categories as you use them: be prepared to revise definitions, examples and counter-examples.
- Explore relationships between variables by trying to identify stories that might link some or all of them.
- Look for mediators and moderators. A mediator is an intervening variable. So, where $X{\rightarrow}Y{\rightarrow}Z$, Y is a mediator: X causes Y causes Z. However, where the pathway from X to Z is more complex and several variables have some, shifting influences, then Y_1, Y_2 and Y_3 are all moderators (Petrosino, 2000).
- Check whether your analysis can be put together in a story that holds together, that is plausible to you, and that can be related to the picture you drew in the literature review.

With interpretations somehow coaxed from the block of data, checks are needed, not so much to ensure that the interpretation is right but to see if it is plausible and to explore whether it can be extended thanks to other people's insights. In case C the notes obviously involved discarding so much of the information generated in the interviews that when clarifications were needed, whether for coding or interpretation purposes, it was necessary to check back to the original tape recordings and sometimes transcribe a section in full. The other checks on tunnel vision should also be considered.

Case D involved coding and making sense of 50 transcripts of long interviews, which puts it outside the range of most small-scale studies, simply because the transcription costs could be in the region of £4000. It is included, though, to develop this account of coding and managing data, and hence of making interpretations. A small-scale researcher could face an even more demanding analytical task than this one if confronted with a pile of videotapes that could not be dealt with by means of sampling or the use of an observation schedule, as in case B; or if photographs had also been taken of the informants in their homes and needed to be brought into the analysis; or if the transcripts were to be subject to discourse analysis (see Boxes 4.11 and 4.12) and sampling was not considered as a way of reducing the bulk to be processed.

In case D, the aim was to develop grounded theory from a series of interviews exploring the extent to which aged social services clients had experienced some form of rationing of provision. In order to avoid assuming what was to be investigated, namely that social and health care provision *were* being rationed, the researcher had to avoid leading the informants to talk about rationing and, for the same reason, chose not to use Klein and colleagues' (1996) categories of rationing in the analysis of the interview data. Instead, the experiences of social and health care had to be interpreted from the ground up. The process of category development had already started in the literature review, formation of research questions and data collection, when ideas about themes had developed. A more systematic approach involved reading through five transcripts and, using distinct ideas as the units of coding, making a list of possible categories for informants' talk organized around the six main interview prompts. The rough list was added to the ideas developed during the research and light sorting was done to merge some categories into one another. The investigator then identified categories that logically could have existed but which had not already been inferred from the sample of transcripts, and checked the five transcripts for data that could be coded into those categories. This was to confirm that the original set was likely to be complete and to see whether new coding categories needed to be added.

A working set of categories was used to code up another five transcripts. There were four things to do at this stage:

1   To see if the categories covered everything that mattered: if not, revisions were tried and new categories added and tested.
2   To look for opportunities to reduce the number of categories used to code conversations around each interview prompt to a manageable number. Boyatzis (1998) recommends 7 ± 2.
3   To begin a definition of each category that was sufficiently clear for another researcher to use it to code the same material. This provides a reference point which will be valuable some months later when the

meaning of the category has become partly forgotten. It is also necessary if inter-observer reliability is to be established to show that the system is comprehensive, usable and trustworthy.

4   To give further coding guidance in the form of some examples of speech that would fit a coding definition and some samples of borderline cases that would be excluded from it. Again, this helps the researcher to be consistent and makes it easier to show others how the analysis has been done.

While this early work can be done manually, the full analysis of so much complex data is best done on computer, which can act as a sophisticated filing system for different types of textual data, storing cross-references, and allowing patterns to be explored, searches to be done and emerging interpretations to be tested. The main limitation is that the data need to be in electronic form, so interviews and notes have to be typed up, which may be beyond the resources of small-scale researchers. A popular program has been NUD*IST 4, although it is less flexible than its successor NVivo and its rival Atlas-ti (which also has powerful image-handling facilities). Others include Ethnograph <http://www.qualisresearch. com/> and HyperRESEARCH <http://www.researchware.com/>. This is not the place to go into detail on how to use these programs, not least because a program available to some researchers, such as Atlas-ti, will not be available to others who have to make do with NUD*IST 4. Richards (1999) describes the NVivo package and Gahan and Hannibal (1998) do the same for NUD*IST 4. Bryman (2001) has a chapter on the use of NVivo. The Atlas-ti home page is http://www.atlasti.de and both NUD*IST and NVivo can be explored at <http://www.qsr-software.co.uk/software>.

Three issues may arise if you use qualitative data handling software:

1   The software does a good job of keeping track of the codings and then retrieving all the data that have been coded into a certain category. (It also allows you to give a unit more than one code to show that more than one thing is significant about it.) The danger is that when data segments are retrieved and offered up for inspection, they are separated from the context in which they make the best sense. This violates the core assumptions of researchers who value context and specificities. Researchers who have different stances see no great problem here.
2   Mason (1996) goes further and suggests that the programs make it easy to start treating categories as variables by using the software to search for patterns of association between categories, rather like a quantitative researcher using correlation to identify patterns in numerical data. If the study was designed with this sort of analysis in mind, then there are no problems here, only advantages. But it could be misleading in this study of care provision for elderly people, where the research methods are such that it would be unwise to say that the

gender of the informant was associated with the level of care they thought they had received. What might be said is that an analysis of the responses (which has unknown reliability) from the people who were interviewed (and they were not a sufficient or a random sample of the elderly population with care needs) indicates that females more often *volunteered* certain comments about the level of care than did men. It is easy to overdo the warning about treating coding categories as variables to be compared and manipulated because doing it is a part of exploring the meanings of the data. The danger lies in not recognizing that the quality of the data is such that patterns identified in this way are things to think about and explore, not secure conclusions about unproblematic meanings and relationships between variables.

3   You can no longer code in the bath. This point is not as frivolous as it appears. Coding on paper with coloured highlighters, slips of paper and a set of signs is something that can be done in odd spaces in all sorts of places, including out of doors on a fine day. That way of coding spreads the work out and can make it more palatable than having to switch on the machine, load the program and work in an office (except for the rich researchers with a laptop computer with a large, sharp screen – essential in this work – and long battery life). The old ways can be less tiring, less boring and more human.

The seven suggestions for limiting tunnel vision given earlier were kept in mind when coding the transcripts in case D, which meant that the researcher could be confident that the analysis was as trustworthy, defensible, plausible and reliable as could be expected by anyone. The interpretations developed in the ways described in case C, the only difference being that checking them out was a lot more complex because of the volume of data involved. This is where NUD*IST 4 was valuable.

Beginning with Chapter 2, it has repeatedly been said that the sorts of claims that it is reasonable to make on the basis of an inquiry depend on the researchers' position on some general issues and then on the research design. It also depends on the way the data are analysed, which is not, of course, independent of the design. Irrespective of whether readers of the research report are invited to consider the implications for their own thinking and practices, or whether they are told that the results indicate that your findings have a high probability of applying to the target population, the credibility of the claims you make about the significance of the study depend, in part, on showing that the data analysis has been careful and trustworthy enough. To researchers working in the positivist tradition, it is necessary to demonstrate that analysis has been valid (coding the data in defensible ways and using appropriate statistical techniques) and reliable (that the figures you have produced are the same as those that any other person would get using the same methods on the same data). One implication for the way that the study is reported, which is the theme

9

Writing, Disseminating and Influencing

Public Writing

Chapter 1 recommended private writing as an aid to sensemaking and claimsmaking, as well as for its usefulness as a store of paragraphs that can be parachuted into a final report. Those reports can be for participants, practitioners or academics and each audience has its own expectations. This section begins with writing for academics and then identifies some differences with writing for other audiences.

Reporting need not be tantamount to writing. There are electronic doctoral theses where clicking on an interview extract activates speech clips from the interview, and hypertext links can be used for photographs and video too. Here the technology brings the reader closer to the research and, it seems, reduces the mediating role of the author, which has been a recurrent concern for some commentators on social research. Richardson (1990: 26) considers that 'writing is an ethical "authority" problem', explaining that authors do not mirror social realities but use authorial power to stage them and make meanings. New technologies may allow 'readers' to hear and see research participants but it is still the researcher-as-author who selects the clips, locates them in webs of meaning and makes claims about their significance. This unease with authorial power is often associated with suspicions that it tends to perpetuate the commonplace ways of thinking, seeing and feeling that reproduce discrimination and disempower 'others', such as women and minorities. A response to this crisis of representation has been to explore ways of bringing participants' voices to the fore by, for example, (1) giving more space to the stories they tell in their words, (2) enriching our knowledge of their worlds through photographs, artefacts, art works, vignettes, (3) including participants' responses to drafts and the final report in the report itself, and (4) arranging reports as sets of hypertext pages which readers explore without being confined by the author's chapter structure. None of these strategies entirely removes the authorial voice and the third can be unrealistic where participants have little taste for reading and the researcher is writing for academics, while the fourth can be plain tiresome. Furthermore, these strategies imply that there is some form of truth to be captured, whereas for some post-structuralists there is none and the real crisis is that representations tend to privilege some readings where there ought to be multiple questions and understandings. Others, though, see these strategies as licences to amass sprawling and self-indulgent descriptions that are free of meaning or claims. They make for lazy writing in the sense that authors only have to reproduce what they have collected and they lead to strenuous reading because readers have to work hard to make sense of the reportage and to deduce the claims it might be standing for. In most academic communities this would lead to low marks because the conventions reward displays of analytical, synthetic and critical thinking, and they may be hard to detect in post-structuralist texts.

Nevertheless, as was seen in Boxes 1.1 and 3.1, some researchers are becoming adventurous reporters. This is most common with small-scale research because it is more likely to be qualitative and the crisis of representation is primarily a crisis that has been recognized by qualitative researchers. There are now more people who will use fiction, poetry, photographs, art and other creative work, performances, presentations, collages, posters and narrative in their reporting. These writers expect to be reflexive, to consider how their lives, experiences and beliefs might colour their representations and then share it with their readers. In such communities of practice it is quite normal for people to write in the first person, to enjoy the words they use and to write with passion. As ever, though, researchers need a sense of audience and if yours will be academics who think not wearing a skirt or tie a lesser sin than using 'I', then act accordingly.

When research has been approached as a matter of sensemaking and claimsmaking then the task of reporting should not be too intimidating. You should have a fairly good idea of what you want to say, the literature review gives you something to build upon, and data analysis should have consolidated your thinking. Your private writing (Chapter 1) provides an archive of material for cutting and pasting and it should have dispelled the gloomy belief that you will be unable to write, a common problem for writers (Brande, 1934/1983). Yet however thoughtful you have been, writing will expose gaps in your thinking, as Sternberg explains:

> I have often thought that I knew what I wanted to say, only to find that when the time came to say it, I was unable to. The reason for this, I think, is that in thinking about a topic, we often allow ourselves conceptual gaps that we hardly know exist. When we attempt to communicate our thoughts, however, these gaps become obvious. (1993: 5)

Sharples (1999) suggests that public writing is best understood as design, by which he means that it is about creatively meeting expectations while operating under constraints such as the time available, the facilities you have and the research information itself. Three major processes are involved: planning, composing and revision. Each is a mindful process and each impinges on the others. He identifies different approaches to planning, recognizes that the evidence about which works best – drawing concept maps, doing a rough outline, listing the main points to cover – is ambiguous, and suggests 'that the main benefit of planning is that it prolongs writing time' (1999: 87). I am not entirely persuaded because some of the research on children's learning questions the idea that working longer means doing better. It is easy to imagine someone spending a lot of time planning how to organize sets of notes and then writing a report which carefully summarized those notes without developing a point of view, argument or claim. I encourage people to plan by making connected outlines. Box 9.1 illustrates this by describing the section headings that are commonly used in research reports and indicating how they can be connected to each other. Using this as a guide would involve jotting points to make under each of the headings (the main ideas, information and arguments) and then writing out in full the first and last paragraphs for each section. Introductory paragraphs to each section will look back and say something on the lines of, 'So, it has been established that ... The question then arises of ... This section provides a response by ... '. Concluding paragraphs will be similar but will summarize the argument more fully and preview what is to come. This forces the writer to be clear about how the information and ideas are going to be *used*. It is also prudent to do a check to see whether the main claims at the end of the report pervade the report – whether the writing will sweep the reader to the conclusions or whether they are likely to emerge as a surprise. In Sternberg's words, 'Your paper should be guided by your ideas and your point of view. Facts are presented in service of ideas: to help elucidate, support, or rewrite these ideas' (1993: 8).

Box 9.1 Planning a report: a connected outline

Section 1: Introduction   This is often short. It should explain what the problem is, make claims about its significance and set out your conclusions. It should connect to the arguments you develop in Sections 5 and 6. When you plan, highlight (literally) these connections.

Section 2a: Literature review   As was said in Chapter 1, this needs to be so connected to the rest of the report that if it were to be accidentally missed out, the incomplete report would barely make sense. It is *the* place for making claims about the inquiry's significance by explaining why you have chosen to concentrate on the research questions you identify in this section. It is also a bridge into Section 3 in which the choice of research methods will be fully explained. What you say in this section should provide a chorus that runs through the closing sections. It can take 20–25% of a report for an academic readership, although confident, clear-thinking writers can manage with much less.

Section 2b: Background   The literature review may provide all the background you need but ethnographies, case studies, evaluations and action research demand you provide a good description of the research setting. The danger is including swathes of information that really are not needed in order to understand what is being investigated or claimed.

continued

Revieweverything you plan to include in this section by asking why it needs to be there. Aspects that are important for your interpretations and claims need to be prominent and they do not need to be swamped by clutter. Remove it.

Section 3: Research design   In order to show that the methods used were the best of all those that might have been used, this section must be strongly connected to Section 2, and so to Section 1 as well. You need to show how the choice of research methods, the choice of instruments and their questions, and the choice of standpoints and forms are fit for the purpose of exploring your research questions, given the work that has already been done. Give details of the development and piloting of research instruments; attend to sampling, generalizability, reliability and validity issues and the like; account for your plans for data analysis. Finally, consider the strength of the design overall, if need be indicating how more time or resources would have allowed for improvements. Allow up to 20% of the report for this important section.

Section 4: Results   Say what you found. Some writers like to interweave reporting the results and commenting upon them, in which case this section will be combined with the next, and the two of them reorganized into several shorter sections, each addressing a key theme in the data, describing what was found and commenting upon it. Others, especially those working within a positivist tradition, just present the data, perhaps using the end-of-section summary to indicate the themes that will be pursued in the Discussion. Where the results are presented without commentary, give no more than 30% of the report over to them.

Section 5: Discussion   This section often does more than any other to determine how well a report is received. It *must* be connected to Section 2. It needs to appraise the results and their meaning, mainly in terms of the themes raised in the literature review, making it quite clear how these results confirm or change thinking about the problem or issue. It is here that the argument is fully developed and it is here that the claim to having found things of interest is laid. It can take about 20% of the report.

Section 6: Conclusion (and recommendations)   This is often a very hard section to write because the conclusions should already be clear and restating them makes a dull ending. But this is a good place to speculate on the significance of these conclusions: for example, what are their implications, whether for views of the field, for research methods, or for practice? This section would be mainly about connecting your small-scale research with far larger issues. At the same time it may be short, amounting to some 5% of the length.

Appendices   Appendices are not always included within the length limit, so they can be handy for students working to strict word limits. They are an ideal place to put research instruments, some of the data and a limited number of other images and documents of importance. Number them as Appendix 3.1, 4.2 etc. (the first appendix for Section 3, which might be a list of q-sort prompts, and the second appendix for Section 4, which might be a particularly interesting transcript). That said, keep them to the minimum. Too many can suggest that you lack the power to select what is really important.

References   Find out if there is a style that you are expected to use, or choose one from an appropriate journal or book, and *then stick to it*.

People compose in their own ways and there is no 'one size fits all' formula for composing text beyond saying that the more productive academics write regularly (Boice, 1992). Sharples (1999) describes a fivefold classification of writing styles:

- *The watercolourist* works from broad headings then starts at the beginning and keeps going until the text has been composed. Revisions tend to be few and often done on screen.
- *The architect* makes a detailed plan. The writing is often sequential, although some start with the easiest part. Revisions are mainly on printout and are mainly concerned with individual sentences.
- *Bricklayers* concentrate on producing good paragraphs and sections but not necessarily in sequence and not by following any one planning strategy. As you would expect, their revisions often involve rearranging their paragraphs, which means making a lot of use of printouts.
- *Sketchers* work from rough plans which get revised as work progresses. They may compose sequentially or they may move around from the middle to the end to the beginning. Revision takes place while composing as well as when full drafts are available. A priority is making sure that the writing clearly says what the author means it to say.
- *The oil painter* tends to jot down ideas and then organize them into a rough plan centred on broad headings. The writing is seldom sequential and revision, usually based on printouts, concentrates on getting the sequence right and ensuring that meanings are clear.

I use all five approaches and suspect that most people do not depend upon any one of them. I suggest that the value of this list is that it may reassure novice writers that there is no correct way of composing while also alerting them to alternatives to their preferred style, which can be particularly useful for anyone whose usual way of writing is not getting results and who is looking around for ideas about other ways to try. Two qualifications should be added. First, I am assuming that whatever approach writers use, they are concentrating on connecting the parts to the overall claims they want to make so that their writing is not a mechanical activity centred on lining up short summaries of information from books and articles and data from research inquiries. Secondly, the different revision strategies are not all equally good. It is important that sentences are clear and grammatical and it is nice if they also read well. It is vital, though, that the overall structure brings out the intended meanings and claims. Assuming that you write reasonable English, then revision should be about checking that connections are made and that readers are left in no doubt what you are driving at and why: about structural features, not about the surface. This means that revision is a tough process because many writers are only accustomed to making sentence-level changes. When it comes to revising for meanings and structure it helps to put some distance between you, the writer and the drafts because otherwise you are liable subconsciously to read into the draft the meanings you intended, even though others would find them hard to infer. Distance helps you to read your texts through others' eyes. Well-organized writers are able to put drafts aside for a couple of weeks or longer before revising them. Others get distance by asking intelligent friends to read drafts and talk about the key ideas and claims, as they saw them. Whatever causes difficulty or is misunderstood needs attention. My view is that the sooner other people see drafts the better and that it is a serious waste of time to concentrate on polishing the surface features of a draft before sharing it; the time to polish the prose is when other people's reactions have been used to get the structure and meanings right.

When reports are for practitioners and others whose main interest is not in academic debates, then the writing style will need to be somewhat different. For example:

1   A one- or two-page executive summary tells the busy person what the report says. The report starts strongly and immediately connects with the readers' concerns.
2   The report concentrates on implications for policy and practice. Contributions to academic theorizing and debates are played down or cut out.
3   Academic references are few and purposeful. They are mainly used to give authority to recommendations and claims.
4   Headings, subheadings, bullet point lists and boxed summaries are frequently used.
5   Research findings, whether presented as quotations, tables or charts, are never left to stand on their own. Readers are told what you want them to signify.
6   Writers avoid discriminatory prose (so a manager is only 'he' if this refers to a male individual and it is not assumed that secretaries are female).
7   The prose style is that of newspaper leader columns. In some cases the tabloid press should be the model, although it is more usual to make the broadsheets the benchmark.
8   Attention is paid to making the layout attractive, so there is plenty of white space between paragraphs and in generous margins. Double spacing, which is expected in theses and dissertations, is not used: it looks nasty and is hard to read.

I would like to be more contentious and say that, with some modifications, these points can also be used to define good academic writing (see also Becker, 1986 and Sternberg, 1993). The second point would need changing to recognize that academic audiences tend to value contributions to theory and debate over recommendations for practice, although that is by no means always the case. Those of us who read a lot of academic writing might wish that the eighth point routinely applied but local practices often insist on double-spaced drabness. The third point might need to be relaxed but there is a lot to be said for anything that discourages people from referring to works they have not read or from contriving references to barely significant works they have. Points 1, 4, 5 and 6 need no change.

The seventh point should become a mantra for students everywhere. They often believe that if they are to write well it behoves them to use Latinate words, jargon, complex sentences, the passive voice and orotund phrases such as late nineteenth century stylists might have crafted. Trying to write in this 'high style' ruins the flow of their prose, blocks its sense and makes it unreadable. The aim of writing is to communicate. Newspapers are in the business of communicating through print. Check their manuals of house style (I refer to the *Guardian* <http://www. guardianunlimited.co.uk/styleguide>). However, one point of newspaper style needs to be changed for academic audiences. Good journalists, writing for a general readership, avoid the jargon that academics will use. Let me explain that I am not going to recommend the awesomely baffling language that some social science writers use but I do say that academic writing uses technical terms as a natural and proper way of engaging in complex and sophisticated debates. I understand jargon to be technical language that is inappropriately used, either because good everyday terms already exist or because the terms make no sense to the audience. So, if a term is jargon only when it is used inappropriately, it follows that terms which would be jargon when writing for a general audience are not jargon when used for a specialized audience. Academic writing involves using 'jargon', which only becomes objectionable when technical terms are not needed or they baffle and irritate the audience. Good writing, then, demands a good sense of audience.

Disseminating

Small-scale research has as much right to be disseminated as any other research, although the general presumption that findings should be disseminated needs to be challenged on the grounds that the production of knowledge far outstrips anybody's ability to consume it. I find it hard to stay abreast of British research in my specialist area of education (I have little sense of what is being written across the whole field) and I only have an awareness of what is published overseas in English in my specialism, not a detailed knowledge of it. Electronic searches produce reading lists that make me wistful for the days when Oxford University's library catalogue was a set of large volumes containing typewritten slips that were pasted in as new books were acquired. The international pressure on academics to publish has led to a proliferation of profitable academic journals, academic conferences have multiplied, and web publication has compounded matters with the result that just about anything can get published in some form.

I take dissemination to mean making something available to a wider audience than your academic supervisors or examiners. In this sense action research and evaluations have dissemination built in, although disseminating their findings more widely means connecting them to audiences other than those who were originally engaged with the work. It is evident, then, that dissemination should be easier if the whole research process, from formulating research questions to writing the report, centred on claimsmaking about the connections between your specific project and the wider interests of practitioner and academic communities. This increases the chances of getting your work past gatekeepers such as publishers, journal editors and conference organizers (but be aware that some conference committees accept everything because that maximizes the number of paying delegates). You can avoid gatekeepers entirely by putting your papers on your own website and then e-mailing various associations and interest groups to invite subscribers to visit your site and read your work. However, if you want to use refereed academic journals for disseminating ideas from your small-scale research there are conventions to follow.

Richardson (1990) describes how she created an account of her interview-based study of 65 single women who were in long-term relationships with married men that was accepted by the high-status *American Sociological Review*. Qualitative studies such as hers are liable to be seen as inferior to survey and quasi-experimental work and to be treated, at best, as interesting exploratory work, not worthy of publication in high-status journals such as *ASR*. She describes at some length how she positioned her work as a contribution to ideas that Simmel (a classic authority in sociology) had about the significance of secrets in social relationships, taking considerable care to pitch the writing so that the specific study of single women made claims to be dealing with a set of concepts that (1) are significant in sociology and (2) extend into many areas of sociological thought. What she did was to argue that her study was significant for sociologists in general because it contributes to an understanding of a form of symbolic interaction that pervades society but which has not been much studied. I am reporting her story to repeat the point that getting heard means telling potential readers how this writing engages with issues or concepts that are of general significance and what it says about them that is fresh. Blaxter et al. (1998) make the same point, saying that journal editors need to see that people will be interested by an account of what is often a context-bound and quite limited inquiry. Sternberg (1993) concurs and insists that although researchers can be in love with the information they have collected, what matters is how it is used.

Dissemination is about laying claim to the attention of particular audiences, which means that each article should be written with a particular journal in mind so that it makes claims that resonate with the interests of that particular community of practice. The same goes for conference presentations and book proposals. In all cases editors will expect that you follow their standard instructions to authors or presenters, although you can expect them to be tolerant of imperfect English from people who do not have it as their first language (the kindest editors tidy it up at the copy editing stage, although it is gruelling work).

Once submitted, articles that conform to publication guidelines are normally sent to two or three referees. It usually takes a couple of months before you get their comments, although it is far too common for authors to have to wait a lot longer. Their comments will (1) always identify what appear to them to be faults, (2) sometimes suggest ways of improving the draft, and (3) usually say that the paper should not be published as it stands. In a sense this is like having friends and colleagues comment on your emerging ideas, and referees' comments can often be welcomed as genuine contributions to improving the quality of your thinking. Three problems are:

1 The paper is rejected outright. You could still use the comments as you write a completely new paper for another journal.
2 There are comments with which you disagree. You do not have to accept them but you are strongly advised to recognize that they identify points in your article that are contentious or poorly explained. Revise accordingly.
3 There are too many comments and some contradict others. Ask the editor for advice.

Getting a paper published in an academic journal is good for people trying to build an academic or professional career but it can be like shouting into a gale for all the impact most articles have. It is far more common for a paper to be read by fewer than half-a-dozen people than for it to be widely read and cited. Other dissemination possibilities include the following.

PRACTITIONER JOURNALS These can be good places for reports of small-scale research. They tend to appear frequently, have larger audiences than academic journals and need interesting copy. They prefer short, clear, practice-focused, human interest and topical pieces. Good pictures help sell your paper. Readers are likely to be preoccupied with the 'So what?' question, and this must not only be answered (preferably in the first paragraph) but also answered in terms of the practical implications of your research.

CONFERENCE PRESENTATION Performance skills are very important. Gelb (1988) is excellent on doing presentations. Give participants a paper to take away, or to direct them to your website for it, but don't make your presentation a reading of your paper. Instead, make up six or so overhead projector slides, each containing about six points. Talk about them. Make sure that your claims and their connection to the audience are unmissable: tell the audience what those points will be, make the points and then tell them that you've told them. Allow time for questions. The best presentations include activities that involve the audience; they also gobble up time. Many conference presentations are heard by a handful of people and even if nice words are said to you later over coffee, few presentations are remembered six weeks later. They can be valuable as a way of rehearsing what you want to say in a paper.

LISTS AND WEBSITES   Keep electronic postings to lists and bulletin boards short because people are paying for connection time to download your message. Confine your message to a sharp summary of your main points electronically and finish with the URL for your website on which you have placed the complete article and anything else you want to disseminate. If you want to get people to browse your site then it needs to be quick and easy to use. I refer to the website design advice at <http://www.useit.com/alertbox/>, although some other authorities disagree with its 'keep it simple, make it fast' advice.

BOOKS AND E-BOOKS   Print runs for academic books are normally in the hundreds, which means that books will not reach large audiences, will seldom make your reputation, and certainly will not make you rich. Electronic publishing means that you could publish a book yourself (see 'lists and websites', above) but what I have in mind is an established publisher charging libraries and other readers for accessing your work. Publishers need to be sure that they can expect sales that will recoup the expense of handling your work, so you will have to convince them that there is a market prepared to pay to read about your small-scale research. It's not impossible to do it but it means telling a very good story about the significance of one small study for thinking, practice and policy in general. Even doctoral theses are unattractive to publishing houses and any that evoke interest will have to be substantially rewritten (see Arksey, 1998 for an example of a book based on a PhD dissertation). Most publishers supply guidelines on making a proposal.

Two other approaches to dissemination may have better chances of making an impact than the more conventional ones. One colleague has a goal of telling one new person a day about her work-in-progress. As a member of many electronic interest groups she sees many messages a day and aims to be recognized as someone who is an active respondent to inquiries, ideas and suggestions, telling people about her work in the process. (Cutting edge ideas are held back until she has secured publication for them in higher-status formats.) Not only does this make dissemination something that is going on from the very beginning of a study, it also enriches her work because people from all over the world make suggestions, add references and raise points that need more thought. This, I must stress, is an ideal that guides her, not a target that she fanatically pursues.

Another way of disseminating small-scale research findings is to take action to work them through into practice, by trialling new techniques, routines, heuristics, benchmarks or practices. This is not very feasible for many students but it is attractive to practitioners who are often well placed to change practice and tell others about the advantages of the changes that stemmed from their small-scale work.

Dissemination is not difficult. What is difficult is getting your disseminated work noticed – having an impact. This is not a problem that is confined to small-scale researchers because although part of the difficulty is that academic communities are experiencing information overload, much of it comes down to naïve expectations of the impact research can and should have on policy and practice.

The Influences of Social Research

Common sense says that research ought to benefit practice, and if it does not then it is pointless. Chapter 2 identified action research and evaluations as forms of research that are very much concerned with practice and said that both feminist and critical research standpoints had strong interests in challenging discrimination and exploitation. It also implied that most social research can be associated with pragmatist ontologies and epistemologies, which means that it is not disconnected from the everyday world because it denies that reality and truth can be known. In addition, it has been said that research methods have to be fit for a purpose and that they have to be flexible enough to be used in complex, changing and unpredictable situations: they have to be sensitive to social worlds and not imposed upon them. Finally, it has been said that researchers can benefit from working closely with informants and participants and that research reports might be written for them. In these ways it has been implied that research and practice can be intertwined, although that is not a straight endorsement of the common-sense position for two reasons. One is that research involves satisfying human curiosity and curiosity cannot be confined to practical issues. There is a case for treating research as an aesthetic activity rather than as a practical one, although it will not be developed here. Secondly, even if research and practice are intertwined it does not follow that research must benefit practice rather than being parasitical upon it.

It is often said that social research does not contribute enough to the improvement of social practices and, more strongly, that it is essentially a carping activity that delights in cataloguing practitioners' deficiencies and in rubbishing official policies. One response of the British government has been to take more control of social research activity by inviting competitive bids to carry out research on government-directed themes and by favouring tenders that promised SMART outcomes (specific, measurable, achievable, realistic, timely). Another has been to promote the notion of evidence-based practice, exemplified by the National Institute for Clinical Excellence (NICE), which systematically appraises research evidence to provide practice benchmarks for the health sector. A third response has been to endorse critiques of research quality (Tooley, 1998),

	Conceptual research	Near practice research	Pragmatic research
Research concern is with the particular and contingent	Conceptual, 'pure' or 'theoretical' studies are usually about abstractions, such as 'structuration', that are several removes from practice. The differences within this category are mainly ones of scale: for example, between trying to develop a better theory of the relationship between the development of a global, market-led economy and theorizing about the relationship between economic change and satisfaction at work in an industry. Influence on practice will tend to be indirect (although monetarist economic theories, for instance, had great influence in the 1980s). They influence practice by contributing to better thinking. Maxim: there's nothing as practical as a good theory	This is research directly into social practices – into health, wealth, education etc. – but it is more about understanding them better than directly changing them. Researchers may later use their findings for improvement purposes but they often expect practitioners to discover, understand and apply the knowledge they produce, perhaps with the help of translators and information brokers, such as NICE	Action research projects, evaluations and single-site field or quasi-experiments which aim, in the first instance to improve local practice. They may influence wider practice especially if striking results or conclusions are vividly and widely reported (for example, how a troubleshooter turned a deathwish business, school, hospital etc. around)
The researcher intends to make strong generalizing claims		With small-scale studies the researchers and the practitioners are often the same people. In larger-scale, generalizing projects there is often a gulf between the producers of research findings and the practitioner consumers	Large-scale studies of best practice. They should feed fairly directly into policy and practice but they rarely produce straightforward findings (because reality tends to be complex) and it may be neither politically wise nor affordable to act on them (see Bennett, 1998 for example)

Figure 9.1   *Research purposes and influences on practice*

to concentrate research in more prestigious centres and to favour large-scale projects that are intended to provide more reliable information (Hillage et al., 1998). Certainly, as Table 9.1 indicates, policy-makers and practitioners have plenty of criticisms which, taken together, imply that social research has limited influence because cliques of slipshod or self-grooming academics amuse themselves at the taxpayers' expense without a scintilla of social concern. Some responses to this 'monstering' (a tabloid press term for vilification) are in the right-hand column. However, talking about 'research' as though it were a homogeneous activity hinders attempts to understand the influence that researchers might have. Figure 9.1 offers a more complex picture, distinguishing between generalizing research based on positivism and studies that are usually on a smaller scale and sceptical of positivism's grand narratives (contingent and particularist inquiries). Fifty years ago the picture would have been simpler because the dominant metaphysics were realist and the belief was that the right methods used on a large enough scale would produce robust accounts of a uniform reality or, possibly, of a limited set of different experiences of it. Data capture and analysis were labour-intensive and secretaries were needed to type out the report. Research was a costly activity restricted to elites who had mastered its special methods. Post-structuralist thinking has destroyed consensus about what research is, what count as fit subjects for research, what can be valued as knowledge and who can do it. This popularization of research has been made possible by cheap, portable tape recorders, word-processing software, photocopiers, the internet and statistical software, all in conjunction with the international growth of higher education systems employing millions of people who compete with each other on the basis of their research publications. As Table 9.1 implies, many of the criticisms of current social research make sense from the standpoint of the pre-democratic elite but they are incoherent as analyses of a world in which research is systematic inquiry, open to anyone using any methods that are fit for the purpose and having whatever significance readers choose to give it. However, describing research as a family of activities, rather than as a single practice, is only a prelude to considering the influence research may have.

Some research is obviously intended to have immediate practical impact but much is not, as Figure 9.1 suggests. Furthermore, although researchers can be considerate in reporting and disseminating their findings, their practical impact can be limited because the systems in which practitioners work are not very sensitive to research findings: these systems are not good at noticing and understanding them and as systems they are not easily changed. Governments are also selective users of research, with Hughes, a criminologist, considering that 'We have a long history of political neglect of research-based policy recommendations' (1996: 79), all the more so when research suggests very different ways of doing things. This is not intended as a way of shifting blame for research's limited impact from researchers onto others. It is intended to suggest that there is

Table 9.1   *(Continued)*

Criticism	Response
Research findings are insensitive to policy-makers' situations and may be plain counter-intuitive: for example, saying that prison 'doesn't work'	Yes. But it might be better to criticize the policy-makers who spend millions on reducing class size and on performance-related pay for teachers even though there is compelling research evidence that neither is likely to contribute much – if anything – to raising educational standards. And prisons don't work. There are better investments

considerable inertia in social practices that makes them hard to change and, some would say, impossible to change according to plan (see Chapter 6; Fullan, 1999; Lewin and Regine, 1999). So, even if research influences other people's ideas, it is still far removed from making a difference to what they do. 'Change without change' is common. 'Change with change' means not just that individuals need to adopt new (research-based) ideas but also that the activity system or community of practice needs to change. That is not something that researchers can do. Change is a systemic pheno-menon and intentional change needs systems thinking.

Box 9.2 Ways of improving the chances that your work will have an impact on practice

These suggestions all assume that you are not telling people trivial or famil-iar things and that you explain clearly how people may benefit from know-ing about your small-scale study.

1   Do research that is close to practice and will affect it – action research, evaluation, field experiments to improve practice. It is most likely to affect the practices of those it touches.
2   Use the internet to tell people about your work while it is in progress.
3   Network and publicize yourself in any other ways you can. Students should ask their supervisors about academic conferences where they could do a poster session or contribute to a symposium.
4   Get your findings into the academic journals. It's rather like putting a message in a bottle and tossing it into the sea, but if it's not done, then your work is guaranteed to be unknown.
5   Consider presenting your findings in a style and form that are accessible to practitioners. Refer to earlier advice about writing for practitioners.
6   Consider writing up your findings in a style and form that are accessible to policy-makers and other 'gatekeepers'. If you can influence policy, at some level and in some way, you can have more influence on practice, albeit indirect influence, than you would by any other means. Write in the same style as you would use for practitioners.
7   Think systemically and strategically. Try and identify the hurdles that are obstructing your messages and minimizing their effects on practice.

continued

Think of up to half-a-dozen simple, doable strategies to get round the baffles. Act accordingly.

8   Disseminate practice guides. Your headline might be, 'Do you want to achieve [insert the name of the main idea you have for changing practice]?' Follow it with a list of three, four, five or six steps to take and then give direct, practical explanations of them. Ask others you meet or talk to on the net to distribute the guides.

9   Look for opportunities to contribute to or influence initial and continuing practitioner education. What about a summary of the meaning your work has for practice that is directed to students in initial training? What about contacting course tutors? What about professional bodies, which usually have education subcommittees?

10 Educational researchers might do best to think about producing texts and other learning materials for children, embedding the research findings within them.

11 Confident researchers might try to sell their services as consultants. The research message goes with the consultation. This is easiest for those who also have quite a lot of work experience in the field.

12 Contribute to and comment on state and national benchmarking exercises or commissions producing best practice guidelines.

Seen like this, it is easier to understand why so much social research is unappreciated by practitioners. Box 9.2 contains 12 suggestions for improving the chances that your work will have an impact. Even where you have followed the first six, there is still a fairly slim chance of having any impact on practice. There would have to be considerable changes to social systems for research to have more impact and not only would those changes from closed to open systems be hard to achieve, but they also run counter to governments' continuing attraction to micro-management.

There is no reason why small-scale research cannot have a considerable impact on thinking and social practices, for the size of a study does not determine the meanings readers can attribute to it and prevent them from generalizing from it. However, like most social research, its influence is, at best, indirect and, at worst, non-existent. Like all social researchers, small-scale investigators can act in ways such as those listed in Box 9.2 to improve the odds that their work will be influential, but there is no guarantee that they will work. Until there are better linkages between the systems of practice and the work of researchers, then research will continue to have uncertain and often marginal influences on social practices.

So, what are the consolations of small-scale research? If it is done in order to get an academic award, then it has the instrumental value of securing a qualification. If it is done by practitioners trying to improve their thinking and practices (and perhaps the thought and practices of those they work with as well), then the reward lies in the improvements that follow. Academics doing small-scale work may value it because it supplies materials for their teaching but are they more likely to expect to get an academic article from it. But, unless the work is done solely in order to comply with expectations or requirements – for extrinsic reasons – there are also personal rewards available. People who have enjoyed doing research report benefits such as:

1   The pleasure of working with informants and participants. It is quite common for researchers to feel that some participants have become friends.
2   Being intellectually stimulated.
3   Becoming proficient with research techniques.
4   Learning more about professional practices.
5   Developing professionally as a result of points 2 and 3.
6   Feeling empowered because they have moved from being a consumer of other people's assertions to becoming a producer of knowledge.
7   The experience of autonomy, of owning a substantial piece of work which has required self-management and self-motivation.
8   And, in some cases, the glow of making a positive difference to other people's lives or work.

Understood like this, it may be said that small-scale research is unlikely to make much difference to the world but it has enormous power to change the individual researcher. Arguably, those effects on the small scale of the self are the greatest of all. Seen from the outside the self is truly small scale. But looking from the inside out, the self makes everything else small scale.

10

Reflecting

The two sections in this chapter comprise hints and prompts that encapsulate themes that have run through this book and which encourage you to reflect on how you work and what makes for a good research project.

Hints for Hard-pressed Researchers

Almost all researchers are hard-pressed but small-scale researchers may feel particularly hard done by because they are often novices who are isolated from other people who, like them, are wrestling with similar problems and feeling just as much a dithering fraud. I suggest that you pick two of these hints and concentrate on them for up to a month. Then add another two for another few weeks, and so on. Don't try to use all 20 at once.

1   The clearer you are about what you want to do and the claims you hope to make, the easier it is. Of course, being clear about a study that is too ambitious means you are still going to be hard-pressed.
2   Find out what your audience will welcome and try to give it to them.
3   Keep records. It saves time later. They only need to be as full as you need them to be.
4   Network, especially electronically. It takes time, yes, but you can also get a lot of help and advice this way. On the internet, everyone can appear equal, so you can set status fears aside.
5   Find up-to-date papers, discussions on the web. Be disciplined, though, because you can end up using browsing as a reason not to do something more important.
6   If you've never developed routines for 'gutting' papers and books – for getting the main points fast – do so now. Begin by aiming to summarize papers in the literature review in under an hour. Then reduce that time again. Important papers obviously get as long as they're worth.
7   Edwards and Talbot (1994) advise researchers to be selfish. One thing that means to me is protecting your research space and time from other demands. Be assertive and say 'No'. Another is deciding that this

study will be the best that can be done in the circumstances, without wrecking your relationships or well-being. Be selfish and design a study that you can be happy doing.

8   Write your research questions boldly on a large piece of paper and post them above your desk. Each week use one of them as a screen-saver on your computer. Learn to ask how what you are doing now is *really* helping you to answer them.

9   Check that the methods and instruments that you envisage using in your inquiry don't have the reputation of being time monsters. By all means use lightly structured interviews but appreciate that the tran-scription and analysis costs (time and money) can be enormous.

10   What would be lost if you did a smaller-scale study than the one you first thought of? What could be gained? Remember $n = 1$ studies are permissible.

11   Expect to have to make a lot of effort but recognize that the most important effort is that used to improve your thinking – sensemak-ing and claimsmaking. Everything else is only done to provide mate-rials for those two, central activities.

12   If you want to do collaborative research, spend time making sure that you will not be saddled with 'easy riders' or people who fail to deliver on time.

13   Write something as often as possible.

14   Don't spend a lot of time getting your grammar and expression right until you are sure that what you're writing *is* going to be in a report. It's easy to waste time polishing writing that will get junked later.

15   Get feedback on your writing early and often.

16   If you are a slow typist, don't type. It may be possible to do a hand-written report or to use voice-dictation software.

17   Ask.

18   Identify your inefficient habits. Some of them do have useful, hidden psychological functions, so begin by choosing one which you are pretty sure is dispensable and try and lose it.

19   When and where do you work best? Is it possible to aim to do the most demanding work at peak times and in good places and work that takes perseverance more than thought at other times?

20   Most people work best in short bursts (perhaps 20 minutes, often no longer than an hour) with a short break or changes of routine in between.

A Quality Check

The following set of prompts for reviewing reports of research studies is used as an aid to thought by undergraduates who are becoming 'research literate' and learning to evaluate research publications. You will detect positivist assumptions behind some of the prompts, but they are reasonably appropriate because most research papers seem to have positivist or pragmatist foundations. Bearing that in mind, my suggestion is that if you are satisfied that what you plan to do (or what you have done or written) allows you to respond to these prompts without feeling shifty, then you have a sustainable small-scale study.

1   Who is the audience? Is the style of the report appropriate?
2   Why is the research significant and worth attention? Crudely put, why should anyone read it?
3   Does the summary of the research literature clearly identify issues that need further attention?
4   Is it clear what the research questions were?
5   What are the ontological and epistemological assumptions on which the study is based? Does it have a particular standpoint, such as critical theory? Does the research fit an established form, such as case study research?
6   In the light of your response to point 5, consider whether the research methods are fit for the audience and purpose (prompts 1–4).
7   Does the study appear to be ethically sound?
8   Are the instruments fit for the purpose?
9   What evidence is there that this is a systematic, honest and careful study? Some researchers would prefer to ask what the evidence is that it is reliable and valid.
10 Are you satisfied that the study is such that it is reasonable to accept the report's conclusions and claims? You could see this as a sampling issue, a question about depth of study, about the breadth of inquiry, or about all three.
11 Was data analysis rigorous and careful, irrespective of the methods used? Were statistics used appropriately? (Did qualitative researchers count and report numbers when it was reasonable to do so? Did quantitative researchers use the best tests? Were you baffled by vague reporting or bemused by unexplained statistics?)
12 All data analysis can be criticized and with qualitative data many alternative interpretations could be sustained. Does the report say something about them, identifying limitations to the analysis and explaining why alternatives are not convincing?
13 Findings: is it clear what's new, significant or useful? Have the research questions been answered *or* has the report gone as far as could reasonably be expected?

References

Argyris, C. (1993) *Knowledge for Action: a Guide to Overcoming Barriers to Organizational Change*. San Francisco, CA: Jossey-Bass.

Arksey, H. (1998) *RSI and the Experts: the Construction of Medical Knowledge*. London: Taylor and Francis.

Arksey, H. and Knight, P.T. (1999) *Interviewing for Social Scientists*. London: Sage.

Atkinson, P. and Hammersley, M. (1994) Ethnography and participant observation, in N.K. Denzin and Y.S. Lincoln (eds) *Handbook of Qualitative Research*. London: Sage, 248–61.

Audi, R. (1998) *Epistemology: a Contemporary Introduction to the Theory of Knowledge*. London: Routledge.

Balloch, S., Pahl, J. and McLean, J. (1998) Working in the social services: job satisfaction, stress and violence, *British Journal of Social Work*, 28(3), 329–56.

Balloch, S., McLean, J. and Fisher, M. (1999) *Social Services: Working under Pressure*. Bristol: the Policy Press.

Baruch, Y. (1999) Response rates in academic studies – a comparative analysis, *Human Relations*, 52(4), 421–38.

Baum, S. (1999) Self-reported drink driving and deterrence, *The Australian and New Zealand Journal of Criminology*, 32(3), 247–61.

Becker, H. (1974) Photography and sociology, *Studies in the Anthropology of Visual Communication*, 1(1), 3–26.

Becker, H. (1986) *Writing for Social Scientists*. Chicago: University of Chicago Press.

Bennett, N. (1998) Annotation: class size and the quality of educational outcomes, *Journal of Child Psychology and Psychiatry*, 39(6), 797–804.

Bhaskar, R. (1986) *Scientific Realism and Human Emancipation*. London: Verso.

Black, P. and Wiliam, D. (1998) Assessment and classroom learning, *Assessment in Education*, 5(1), 7–74.

Blackler, F. (1995) Knowledge, knowledge work and organizations: an overview and analysis, *Organization Studies*, 16(6), 1021–46.

Blaxter, L., Hughes, C. and Tight, M. (1998) *The Academic Career Handbook*. Buckingham: Open University Press.

Block, J. (1978) *The Q-sort Method in Personality Assessment and Psychiatric Research*, 2nd edn. Palo Alto, CA: Consulting Psychologists.

Boice, R. (1992) *The New Faculty Member: Supporting and Fostering Professional Development*. San Francisco, CA: Jossey-Bass.

Borowsky, R., Owen, W. and Fonos, N. (1999) Reading speech and hearing print, *Canadian Journal of Experimental Psychology*, 53(4), 294–305.

Boyatzis, R.E. (1998) *Transforming Qualitative Information*. Thousand Oaks, CA: Sage.

Boyer, E.L. (1990) *Scholarship Reconsidered: Priorities of the Professoriate*. Princeton, NJ: Carnegie Foundation for the Advancement of Learning.

Boyle, M. and Woods, P. (1996) The composite head: coping with changes in the primary headteacher role, *British Educational Research Journal*, 22(5), 549–68.

Brace, N., Kemp, R. and Snelgar, R. (2000) *SPSS for Psychologists: a Guide to Data Analysis Using SPSS for Windows*. London: Macmillan.

Brande, D. (1934/1983) *Becoming a Writer*. London: Macmillan.

Briggs, J. and Peat, F.D. (1999) *Seven Life Lessons of Chaos*. New York: HarperCollins.

Broadhead, R.S., Van Hulst, Y. and Heckathorn, D. (1999) Termination of an established needle exchange: a study of claims and their impact, *Social Problems*, 46(1), 48–66.

Bryant, P. (1986) Developmental psychology – methods of study, in R. Harré and R. Lamb (eds) *The Dictionary of Developmental and Educational Psychology*. Oxford: Blackwell, 64–7.

Bryman, A. (2001) *Social Research Methods*. Oxford: Oxford University Press.

Bryne, B. (1998) *Complexity Theory and Social Science*. London: Routledge.

Buzan, T. (1974) *Use Your Head*. London: BBC Publications.

Campbell, D.T. and Stanley, J.C. (1963) *Experimental and Quasi-experimental Designs for Research*. Boston, MA: Houghton Mifflin.

Checkland, P. (1981) *Systems Thinking, Systems Practice*. Chichester: Wiley.

Checkland, P. and Holwell, S. (1998) Action research: its nature and validity, *Systemic Practice and Action Research*, 11(1), 9–21.

Checkland, P. and Scholes, J. (1990) *Soft Systems Methodology in Action*. Chichester: Wiley.

Cilliers, P. (1998) *Complexity and Postmodernism*. London: Routledge.

Claxton, G. (1998) *Hare Brain, Tortoise Mind*. London: Fourth Estate.

Cleveland, H. (1985) *The Knowledge Executive: Leadership in an Information Society*. New York: Truman Talley.

Cliff, N. (1996) *Ordinal Methods for Behavioral Data Analysis*. Mahwah, NJ: Lawrence Erlbaum.

Coffey, A. and Delamont, S. (2000) *Feminism and the Classroom Teacher*. London: Routledge.

Cohen, J. and Stewart, I. (1995) *The Collapse of Chaos*. London: Penguin.

Cooper, H. (1998) *Synthesizing Research: a Guide for Literature Reviews*, 3rd edn. Thousand Oaks, CA: Sage.

Cox, R.W. (1980) Social forces, states and world orders, *Millennium*, 10(2), 126–55.

Crawford, J., Kippax, S., Onyx, J., Gault, U. and Benton, P. (1992) *Emotion and Gender*. London: Sage.

Cronbach, L.J. et al. (1980) *Toward Reform of Program Evaluation*. San Francisco, CA: Jossey-Bass.

Cuban, L. (1991) History of teaching in social studies, in J.P. Shaver (ed.) *Handbook of Research on Social Studies Teaching and Learning*. New York: Macmillan.

Cushing, J.T. (1998) *Philosophical Concepts in Physics*. Cambridge: Cambridge University Press.

Davenport, T.H. and Prusak, L. (1998) *Working Knowledge*. Boston, MA: Harvard University Press.

Davidson, A., Teicher, M. and Bar-Yam, Y. (1997) The role of environmental complexity in the well-being of the elderly, *Chaos and Complexity in Nursing*, 3, 5–12.

Donnelly, J.F. (1999) Schooling Heidegger: on being in teaching, *Teaching and Teacher Education*, 15, 933-49.

Dweck, C. (1999) *Self-Theories: Their Role in Motivation, Personality and Development*. Philadelphia, PA: Psychology Press.

Easterby-Smith, M. (1997) Disciplines of organizational learning: contributions and critiques, *Human Relations*, 50(9), 1085–113.

Eden, C. and Huxham, C. (1996) Action research for the study of organizations, in S. Clegg, C. Hardy and W. Nord (eds) *Handbook of Organization Studies*. London: Sage, 526–42.

Edwards, A. and Talbot, R. (1994) *The Hard-Pressed Researcher*. London: Longman.

Eisner, E. (1991) *The Enlightened Eye*. Macmillan: New York.

Elliott, J. (1991) *Action Research for Educational Change*. Buckingham: Open University Press.

Entwistle, H. (1979) *Antonio Gramsci: Conservative Schooling for Radical Politics*. London: Routledge and Kegan Paul.

Eraut, M. (1995) Schön shock: a case for reframing reflection-in-action?, *Teachers and Teaching: Theory and Practice*, 1(1), 9–22.

Erlandson, D.A., Harris, E.L. Skipper, B.L. and Allen, S.D. (1993) *Doing Naturalistic Inquiry: a Guide to Methods*. Newbury Park, CA: Sage.

Evans, M. (1999) *Missing Persons: the Impossibility of Auto/Biography*. London: Routledge.

Feinstein, L. (2000) *The Relative Economic Importance of Academic, Psychological and Behavioural Attributes Developed in Childhood*. London: Centre for Economic Performance, London School of Economics.

Fielding, J. and Gilbert, N. (2000) *Understanding Social Statistics*. London: Sage.

Firestone, W.A. (1993) Alternative arguments for generalizing from data as applied to qualitative research, *Educational Researcher*, 22(4), 16–23.

Flood, R.L. (1999) *Rethinking the Fifth Discipline*. London: Routledge.

Foucault, M. (1975) *Discipline and Punish*. Harmondsworth: Penguin.

Frey, J.H. (1989) *Survey Research by Telephone*, 2nd edn (1st edn 1983). London: Sage.

Fullan, M. (1999) *Change Forces: The Sequel*. London: Falmer.

Gahan, C. and Hannibal, M. (1998) *Doing Qualitative Analysis with QSR NUD.IST 4*. Thousand Oaks, CA: Sage.

Galton, M., Simon, B. and Croll, P. (1980) *Inside the Primary Classroom*. London: Routledge and Kegan Paul.

Gelb, M. (1998) *Present Yourself*. Torrance, CA: Jaimar Press.

Giles, D. (1999) Retrospective accounts of drunken behaviour, *Discourse Studies*, 1(4), 387–403.

Gillham, B. (2000a) *Case Study Research Methods*. London: Continuum.

Gillham, B. (2000b) *The Research Interview*. London: Continuum.

Gillham, B. (2000c) *Developing a Questionnaire*. London: Continuum.

Goldstein, A.P. and Michaels, G.Y. (1985) *Empathy, Developmental Training and Consequences*. Hillsdale, NJ: Erlbaum.

Goleman, D. (1998) *Working with Emotional Intelligence*. New York: Bantam.

Gordon, A.F. (1997) *Ghostly Matters: Haunting and the Sociological Imagination*. Minneapolis, MN: University of Minnesota Press.

Gould, S.J. (1996a) *Dinosaur in a Haystack*. London: Jonathan Cape.

Gould, S.J. (1996b) *The Mismeasure of Man*, rev. edn. New York: Norton.

Gray, J., Hopkins, D., Reynolds, D., Wilcox, B., Farrell, S. and Jesson, D. (1999) *Improving Schools: Performance and Potential*. Buckingham: Open University Press.

Greenbaum, T.L. (1998) *Handbook for Focus Group Research*, 2nd edn (1st edn 1987). London: Sage.

Griffith, J., Steptoe, A. and Cropley, M. (1999) An investigation of coping strategies associated with job stress in teachers, *British Journal of Educational Psychology*, 69(4), 517–32.

Hacking, I. (1999) *The Social Construction of What?* Cambridge, MA: Harvard University Press.

Hammersley, M. (1993) On the teacher as researcher, in M. Hammersley (ed.) *Educational Research: Current Issues*. London: Paul Chapman, 211–31.

Hammersley, M. and Atkinson, P. (1995) *Ethnography: Principles in Practice*. 2nd edn (1st edn 1983). London: Routledge.

Happe, M., Gilmore, M., Valadez, D., Civic, D., Hartway, J. and Morrison, D. (2000) The relative costs and benefits of telephone interviews versus self-administered diaries for daily data collection, *Evaluation Review*, 24(1), 102–16.

Harré, R. (1998) *The Singular Self*. London: Sage.

Harvey, L. and MacDonald, M. (1993) *Doing Sociology*. London: Macmillan.

Haug, F. (ed.) (1987) *Female Sexualization*. London: Verso.

Hausman, C.R. (1993) *Charles S. Peirce's Evolutionary Philosophy*. Cambridge: Cambridge University Press.

Heard, K. and Vyse, S. (1999) Authoritarian and paranormal beliefs, *Imagination, Cognition and Personality*, 18(2), 121–6.

Henry, G.T. (1990) *Practical Sampling*. Newbury Park, CA: Sage.

Heron, J. (1996) *Co-operative Inquiry: Research into the Human Condition*, London: Sage.

Hesketh, A. and Knight, P.T. (1998) Secondary school prospectuses and educational markets, *Cambridge Journal of Education*, 28(1), 21–35.

Hickson, L., Worrall, L., Yin, E. and Barnett, H. (1999) Planning a communication education program for older people, *Educational Gerontology*, 22, 257–69.

Hillage, J., Pearson, R., Anderson, A. and Tamkin, P. (1998) *Excellence in Research on Schools*. London: HMSO.

Hookway, C. (1985) *Peirce*. London: Routledge and Kegan Paul.

Horvat, E.M. and Antonio, A.L. (1999) 'Hey, those shoes are not uniform': African American girls in an elite high school and the importance of habitus, *Anthropology and Education Quarterly*, 30(3), 317–42.

Huberman, A.M. and Miles, M.B. (1994) Data management and analysis methods, in N.K. Denzin and Y.S. Lincoln (eds), *Handbook of Qualitative Research*. London: Sage, 428–44.

Hughes, G. (1996) The politics of criminological research, in R. Sapsford (ed.) *Researching Crime and Criminal Justice*. Milton Keynes: Open University Press, 57–106.

Hunt, J.G. (1991) *Leadership: a New Synthesis*. Newbury Park, CA: Sage.

Jacobs, B.A. and Miller, J. (1998) Crack dealing, gender and arrest avoidance, *Social Problems*, 45(4), 550–69.

Jencks, C. et al. (1972) *Inequality: a Reassessment of the Effect of Family and Schooling in America*. Harmondsworth: Penguin.

Jenkins, C. (1999) Death by questionnaire: quality of life measurement could seriously damage your health, *Journal of Health Services Research and Policy*, 4(3), 129–30.

Keating, D. and Miller, F. (2000) The dynamics of emotional development: models, metaphors and methods, in M.D. Lewis and I. Granic (eds) *Emotion, Development and Self-Organization*. Cambridge: Cambridge University Press, 373–92.

Kelly, G.A. (1963) *A Theory of Personality*. New York: Norton.

King, D. and Wheeler, S. (1999) The responsibilities of counsellor supervisors: a qualitative study, *British Journal of Guidance and Counselling*, 27(2), 215–29.

Kinnear, P.R. and Gray, C.D. (1999) *SPSS for Windows Made Simple*, 3rd edn. Hove: Psychology Press.

Klein, R., Day, P. and Redmayne, S. (1996) *Managing Scarcity: Priority Setting and Rationing in the National Health Service*. Buckingham: Open University Press.

Knight, P.T. and Saunders, M. (1999) Understanding teachers' professional cultures through interview: a constructivist approach, *Evaluation and Research in Education*, 13(2), 61–72.

Knight, P.T. and Trowler, P.R. (2001) *Departmental Leadership in Higher Education*. Buckingham: Society for Research in Higher Education and Open University Press.

Krueger, R.A. and Morgan, D.L. (eds) (1998) *Focus Group Kit*, Vols 1–6. Thousand Oaks, CA: Sage.

Lather, P. (1991) *Getting Smart*. New York: Routledge.

Lavrakas, P.J. (1987) *Telephone Survey Methods: Sampling, Selection and Supervision*. Beverly Hills, CA: Sage.

Lee, R.M. (2000) *Unobtrusive Methods in Social Research*. Buckingham: Open University Press.

Levin, M. and Greenwood, D. (1998) *Introduction to Action Research: Social Research for Social Change*. Thousand Oaks, CA: Sage.

Lewin, R. and Regine, B. (1999) *The Soul at Work: Unleashing the Power of Complexity Science for Business Success*. London: Orion.

Light, R. and Pillemer, D. (1982) Numbers and narrative: combining their strengths in research reviews, *Harvard Educational Review*, 52(1), 1–26.

Lloyd, M. (2000) Analysis on the move: deconstructing troublesome health questions, *Qualitative Health Review*, 10(2), 149–63.

Locke, L.F., Silverman, S.J. and Spirduso, W.W. (1998) *Reading and Understanding Research*. Thousand Oaks, CA: Sage.

Ludema, J.D., Cooperrider, D.L. and Barrette, F.J. (2001) Appreciative inquiry: the power of the unconditional positive question, in P. Reason and H. Bradbury (eds) *Handbook of Action Research*. London: Sage, 189–99.

Machado, A., Lourenço, O. and Silva, F.J. (2000) Facts, concepts and theories: the shape of psychology's epistemic triangle, *Behaviour and Philosophy*, 28, 1–40.

Mader, C. (1999) Taking it back, passing it on: reverence for the ordinary in Bush Cree teacher education, *The Canadian Journal of Native Studies*, 19(1), 91–118.

Marsh, H.W. and Dunkin, M.J. (1997) Students' evaluation of university teaching, in R. Perry and J.C. Smart (eds) *Effective Teaching in Higher Education*. New York: Agathon 241–320.

Mason, J. (1996) *Qualitative Researching*. London: Sage.

McCulloch, G., Helsby, G. and Knight, P.T. (2000) *The Politics of Professionalism*. London: Cassell.

Mercier, C., Piat, M., Peladeau, N. and Dagenais, C. (2000) An application of theory-driven evaluation to a drop-in youth centre, *Evaluation Review*, 24(1), 73–91.

Michell, J. (1997) Quantitative science and the definition of measurement in psychology, *British Journal of Psychology*, 88, 355–83.

Miettinen, R. (1999) The riddle of things: activity theory and actor-network theory as approaches to studying innovations, *Mind, Culture and Activity*, 6(3), 170–95.

Moon, J. (1999) *Reflection in Learning and Professional Development*. London: Kogan Page.

Morgan, G. (1997) *Images of Organization*, 2nd edn. Thousand Oaks, CA: Sage.

Mostyn, B. (1985) The qualitative analysis of research data, in M. Brenner, J. Brown and D.V. Canter (eds), *The Research Interview: Uses and Approaches*. London: Academic Press, 114–45.

Nemeth, T. (1980) *Gramsci's Philosophy: a Critical Study*. Brighton: Harvester.

Nonaka, I. and Takauchi, H. (1995) *The Knowledge-Creating Company*. New York: Oxford.

Oakley, A. (1981) Interviewing women: a contradiction in terms, in H. Roberts (ed.), *Doing Feminist Research*. London: Routledge and Kegan Paul, 30–61.

Oppenheim, A.N. (1992) *Questionnaire Design, Interviewing and Attitude Measurement*. London: Pinter.

Orland, L. (2000) What's in a line? Exploration of a research reflection tool, *Teachers and Teaching*, 6(2), 197–213.

Ozga, J. (2000) *Policy Research in Educational Settings: Contested Terrain*. Buckingham: Open University Press.

Padgett, D. and Imani, N.D. (1999) Qualitative and quantitative assessment of land-use managers' attitudes toward environmental justice, *Environmental Management*, 24(4), 509–15.

Parker, S. (1997) *Reflective Thinking in the Postmodern World*. Buckingham: Open University Press.

Paterson, C. and Britten, N. (2000) In pursuit of patient-centred outcomes, *Journal of Health Services Research and Policy*, 5(1), 27–38.

Patton, M.Q. (1990) *Qualitative Evaluation and Research Methods*, 2nd edn. (1st edn. 1980). Newbury Park, CA: Sage.

Patton, M.Q. (1997) *Utilization-Focused Evaluation*, 3rd edn. Thousand Oaks, CA: Sage.

Peterson, R.S., Owens, P.D. and Martorana, P.V. (1999) The group dynamics of Q-sort in organizational research, *Organizational Research Methods*, 2(2), 107–39.

Petrosino, A. (2000) Mediators and moderators in the evaluation of programs for children, *Evaluation Review*, 24(1), 47–72.

Poland, B.D. (1995) Transcription quality as an aspect of rigour in qualitative research, *Qualitative Inquiry*, 1(3), 290–310.

Polkinghorne, D. (1988) *Narrative Knowing and the Human Sciences*. New York: State University of New York Press.

Potts, A. (2000) Coming, coming, gone: a feminist deconstruction of heterosexual orgasm, *Sexualities*, 3(1), 55–76.

Pratchett, T. (1992) *Witches Abroad*. London: Corgi.

Prigogine, I. (1997) *The End of Certainty*. New York: Free Press.

Putnam, H. (1995) *Pragmatism: an Open Question*, Oxford: Blackwell.

Resnick, L.B. (1999) From aptitude to effort: a new foundation for our schools, *American Educator*, 23(1), 14–17.

Rhodes, C. (2000) Reading and writing organizational lives, *Organization*, 7(1), 7–29.

Richards, Lyn. (1999) *Using NVivo in Qualitative Research*. London and Los Angeles: Sage.

Richardson, L. (1990) *Writing Strategies*, Newbury Park, CA: Sage.

Riessman, C.K. (1987) When gender is not enough: women interviewing women, *Gender and Society*, 1(2), 172–207.

Robinson, V. (1996) Critical theory and the social psychology of change, in K. Leithwood, J. Chapman, D. Corson, P. Hallinger and A. Hart (eds) *International Handbook of Educational Leadership and Administration*. Dordrecht: Kluwer, 1069–96.

Rosenthal, R. (1991) *Meta-Analytic Procedures for Social Research*. Newbury Park, CA: Sage.

Rubin H.J. and Rubin, I.S. (1995) *Qualitative Interviewing: the Art of Hearing Data*. London: Sage.

Sammons, P. Thomas, S. and Mortimore, P. (1997) *Forging Links: Effective Schools and Effective Departments*. London: Paul Chapman.

Sassatelli, R. (1999) Interaction order and beyond: a field analysis of body culture within fitness gyms, *Body and Society*, 5(2–3), 227–48.

Sayer, A. (1992) *Method in Social Science: a Realist Approach*, 2nd edn. London: Routledge.

Schön, D.A. (1983) *The Reflective Practitioner*. New York: Basic.

Schön, D.A. (1987) *Educating the Reflective Practitioner*. San Francisco, CA: Jossey-Bass.

Schratz, M. and Walker, R. (1995) *Research as Social Change*. London: Routledge.

Scott, D. and Usher, R. (2000) *Researching Education*. London: Cassell.

Scourfield, J.B. and Dobash, R.P. (1999) Programmes for violent men: recent developments in the UK, *The Howard Journal*, 38(2), 128–43.

Seale, C. (1999) *The Quality of Qualitative Research*. London: Sage.

Searle, J. (2000) *Mind, Language and Society*. London: Phoenix.

Sharples, M. (1999) *How We Write*. London: Routledge.

Shaw, M.E. and Wright, J.M. (1967) *Scales for the Measurement of Attitudes*. New York: McGraw-Hill.

Simco, N. and Warin, J. (1997) Validity in image-based research: an elaborated illustration of the issues, *British Educational Research Journal*, 23(5), 661–72.

Smith, M.J. (1998) *Social Science in Question*. London: Sage.

Smyth, J., Dow, A., Hattam, R., Reid, A. and Shattock, G. (2000) *Teachers' Work in a Globalizing Economy*. Falmer: London.

Spoto, A. (1995) *Jung's Typology in Perspective*. Wilmette, IL: Chiron.

Stacey, R.D. (1996) *Complexity and Creativity in Organizations*. San Francisco, CA: Bennett-Koehler.

Stake, R.E. (1995) *The Art of Case Study*. Thousand Oaks, CA: Sage.

Sternberg, R.J. (1993) *The Psychologist's Companion*, 3rd edn. Cambridge: Cambridge University Press.

Sternberg, R.J. (1997) *Successful Intelligence*. New York: Plume.

Strauss, A.L. and Corbin, J. (1990) *Basics of Qualitative Research: Grounded Theory Procedures and Techniques*. London: Sage.

Swann, R. and James, P. (1998) The effect of the prison environment on inmate drug taking behaviour, *The Howard Journal*, 37(3), 252–65.

Sweetman, P. (1999) Anchoring the (postmodern) self? Body modification, fashion and identity, *Body and Society*, 5(2–3), 51–76.

Taylor, B.J. (2000) *Reflective Practice: a Guide for Nurses and Midwives*. Buckingham: Open University Press.

Ten Eyck, T. (1999) Shaping a food safety debate, *Science Communication*, 20(4), 426–47.

Thrift, N. (1999) The place of complexity, *Theory, Culture and Society*, 16(3), 31–69.

Tomlinson, P. (1999) Conscious reflection and implicit learning in teacher preparation. Part I: recent light on an old issue, *Oxford Review of Education*, 25(3), 405–20.

Tooley, J. with Darby, D. (1998) *Educational Research: a Critique*. London: Ofsted.

Trochim, W. (1999) *The Research Methods Knowledge Base*, 2nd edn. <http://trochim.human.cornell.edu/kb/index.htm>.

Trowler, P.R. and Knight, P.T. (2000) Coming to know in higher education: theorising faculty entry to new work contexts, *Higher Education Research and Development*, 19(1), 27–42.

Upcraft, M.L. (1996) Teaching and today's college students, in R. J. Menges and M. Weimer (eds) *Teaching on Solid Ground*. San Francisco, CA: Jossey-Bass, 21–41.

van Buskirk, B. (1997) On publish or perish, pedagogy and getting a life – synergies and tensions, in R. André and P.J. Frost (eds) *Researchers Hooked on Teaching*. Thousand Oaks, CA: Sage, 64–75.

van Geert, P. (1994) *Dynamic Systems of Development: Change between Complexity and Chaos*. Hemel Hempstead: Harvester Wheatsheaf.

Weick, K. (1995) *Sensemaking in Organizations*. Thousand Oaks, CA: Sage.

Wenger, E. (1998) *Communities of Practice: Learning, Meaning and Identity*. Cambridge: Cambridge University Press.

White, J. (1997) Philosophical perspectives on school effectiveness, *Curriculum Journal*, 8(1), 29–44.

White, M. (1999) Representation of facial expression of emotion, *American Journal of Psychology*, 112(3), 371–81.

Wilczynski, A. and Sinclair, K. (1999) Moral tales: representations of child abuse in the quality and tabloid media, *The Australian and New Zealand Journal of Criminology*, 32(3), 262–83.

Wilkinson, L. and the Task Force on Statistical Inference (1999) Statistical methods in psychology journals, *American Psychologist*, 56(8), 594–604.

Witherell, C. and Noddings, N. (eds) (1991) *Stories Lives Tell: Narrative and Dialogue in Education*. New York: Teachers' College Press.

Wolpert, L. (1993) *The Unnatural Nature of Science*. London: Faber.

Woods, P.A., Bagley, C. and Glatter, R. (1998) *School Choice and Competition: Markets in the Public Interest?* London: Routledge.

Index